Our Selves,
Our Souls and Bodies

OUR SELVES, OUR SOULS AND BODIES

Sexuality and the Household of God

Charles Hefling, editor

 COWLEY PUBLICATIONS
Cambridge ✦ Boston
Massachusetts

Published in the United States of America by Cowley Publications, a division of the Society of St. John the Evangelist. No portion of this book may be reproduced, stored in or introduced into a retrieval system, or transmitted, in any form or by any means—including photocopying—without the prior written permission of Cowley Publications, except in the case of brief quotations embodied in critical articles and reviews.

Library of Congress Cataloging-in-Publication Data:
Our selves, our souls and bodies: sexuality and the household of God
  / Charles Hefling, editor.
       p.   cm.
Includes bibliographical references.
ISBN 1-56101-122-3 (alk. paper)
1. Sex—Religious aspects—Christianity. 2. Homosexuality—Religious aspects—Episcopal Church. 3. Sexual ethics. 4. Christian ethics—Anglican authors. 5. Episcopal Church—Doctrines. 6. Anglican Communion—United States—Doctrines. 7. Episcopal Church—Membership. 8. Anglican Communion—United States—Membership. I. Hefling, Charles C.
BT708.O87 1996
261.8'35—dc20   96-8069
                                                          CIP

Editor: Cynthia Shattuck
Copyeditor and Designer: Vicki Black
Cover Design: Vicki Black
Cover Art: Brian Willmer, SSJE
Study Guide: Charles Hefling and Vicki Black

This book is printed on recycled, acid-free paper and was produced in Canada.

Cowley Publications
28 Temple Place
Boston, Massachusetts 02111

To
Dr. David Hefling
and
Fr. Michael Dudley

And here we offer and present unto thee, O Lord,
our selves, our souls and bodies,
to be a reasonable, holy, and living
sacrifice unto thee....
(The Book of Common Prayer)

Table of Contents

The Christian Household (39)

Scripture and Tradition (47)

The Body of Christ (31

Contributors

∞ *The Reverend Marilyn McCord Adams* is professor of historical theology at the Yale Divinity School. She has published a two-volume work on *William Ockham* and for many years taught in the philosophy department of the University of California at Los Angeles and served in parishes in Hollywood and Santa Monica.

∞ *The Reverend Thomas E. Breidenthal* is associate professor of moral theology in the John Henry Hobart chair of Christian ethics and director of the Center for Jewish-Christian Studies and Relations at the General Theological Seminary in New York City.

∞ *The Reverend L. William Countryman* is professor of New Testament at the Church Divinity School of the Pacific in Berkeley, California. He is the author of several books, including *Good News of Jesus, Biblical Authority or Biblical Tyranny?, The Mystical Way in the Fourth Gospel,* and *Dirt, Greed, and Sex: Sexual Ethics in the New Testament and Their Implications for Today.*

∞ *The Most Reverend David Crawley* is archbishop of Kootenay and metropolitan of British Columbia and Yukon in the Anglican Church of Canada. He has been a parish priest, university chaplain, street worker, archdeacon, canon missioner, and television writer and interviewer for the Canadian Broadcasting Corporation.

∞ *Cynthia S. W. Crysdale* is associate professor in the department of religion and religious education at the Catholic University of America. Her areas of specialty include feminist ethics and faith development. She has served on the board of directors of the Society for Christian Ethics and edited a volume on *Lonergan and Feminism.*

∞ *B. Barbara Hall* is professor *emerita* of New Testament at Virginia Theological Seminary. She has taught at the General Theological Seminary and served as a missionary in Brazil.

∞ **The Reverend Canon Susan C. Harriss** is vicar of the Congregation of St. Saviour at the Cathedral Church of St. John the Divine in New York City, where she is canon residentiary. An associate of the Society of St. John the Evangelist, she is the author of *Jamie's Way: Stories for Worship and Family Devotion*.

∞ **Peter S. Hawkins** is professor of religion and literature at the Yale Divinity School, where he chairs a program in religion and the arts. He has published on American fiction, the literature of utopia, and Dante's *Divine Comedy*.

∞ **The Reverend Charles Hefling** is associate professor of systematic theology at Boston College and an associate of the Society of St. John the Evangelist. He has been president of the Conference of Anglican Theologians and is the author of *Why Doctrines?* and editor of *Charles Williams: Essential Writings in Spirituality and Theology*.

∞ **The Reverend Sheryl A. Kujawa** has been coordinator of youth ministries at the Episcopal Church Center since 1988. She serves as an assistant at the Church of the Incarnation in New York City, and with Lois Sibley has published *Resource Book for Ministries with Youth and Young Adults in the Episcopal Church*.

∞ **The Reverend David L. Norgard** is rector of the Church of St. John the Evangelist, San Francisco and secretary of Integrity. He was formerly missioner of The Oasis in the diocese of Newark.

∞ **James Robertson Price III** is director of the Shriver Peaceworker Program at the University of Maryland, Baltimore County. He has taught at the Catholic University of America in Washington, D.C., and the Institute for Conflict Analysis and Resolution, George Mason University, Fairfax, Virginia.

∞ **Timothy F. Sedgwick** is professor of Christian ethics and moral theology at Seabury-Western Theological Seminary in Evanston, Illinois. He is the author of *The Making of Ministry* and *Sacramental Ethics: Paschal Identity and the Christian Life*. He also edited with Philip Turner *The Crisis in Moral Teaching in the Episcopal Church*.

∞ **The Reverend Bonnie Shullenberger** is a religious journalist whose articles appear regularly in *The Living Church*. She is an assistant in Christian education at Trinity Church, Ossining, New York, and has been a lecturer in religious studies and literature at Makerere University in Kampala, Uganda.

∞ *The Reverend Martin L. Smith, SSJE* is Superior of the Society of St. John the Evangelist. He has an extensive ministry as a leader of retreats and conferences in the United States and Canada, and has written several books, including *Nativities and Passions, A Season for the Spirit, The Word is Very Near You,* and *Reconciliation.*

∞ *The Reverend Owen C. Thomas* is Frances Lathrop Fiske professor of theology *emeritus* at the Episcopal Divinity School in Cambridge, Massachusetts. He has served as president of the American Theological Society and is the author of several books, including *Theological Questions: Analysis and Argument.*

∞ *The Right Reverend Rowan Williams* is bishop of Monmouth, Wales. He was formerly the Lady Margaret professor of divinity in the University of Oxford. Among his many books are *Resurrection, Teresa of Avila, The Wound of Knowledge,* and *A Ray of Darkness.*

∽ *Charles Hefling*

Introduction

The turmoil in Christian churches over issues that have to do with sex and sexuality is hardly a blessing, but it need not be a wholly bad thing either. There has seldom been a time when Christians were not embroiled in one noisy dispute or another, and unedifying though the quarrels were, their result in the long run has been to refine and clarify what Christianity is and what it is for. If, as the adage says, the church is always getting reformed, its reformation seems to go hand in hand with controversy.

Whether the present controversies will likewise turn out to have been creative ferment depends in part on the spirit in which they are conducted. Sexuality is a sensitive topic—none more so—and the questions it raises for religious faith are anything but simple. Debating them is difficult and risky at best; emotion is apt to run high, and conversation easily gets cut off before it goes very far. In the Episcopal Church, which is no closer than any other to being of one mind on these issues, the House of Bishops has put out a pastoral study document that deliberately avoids making definitive pronouncements and urges instead what its title suggests: *Continuing the Dialogue.* In effect, the bishops are saying that even if they could call a halt to turmoil, it is better to let the conversation go forward, candidly and without sacrificing integrity, yet respectfully and without acrimony.

To such a conversation this book is meant to contribute.

In order to say what its contribution might be, it may be best to start with how these essays came to appear between the same covers—or rather, how they did not. A collection of short writings that address a complicated and contentious subject such as this one could be put together by deciding in advance what the contents are going to be. One way to do this would be to draw up a list of relevant topics, then look for the authors who could deal with them. Or the items on such a list might instead be specialized disciplines: exegesis, history, ethics, theology, spirituality, and so on. A third possibility, besides determining what should be written and how, would be to line up contributors at the outset, perhaps in such a way as to include the entire range of opinion and ensure that voices on each side of the debate would be heard. Any of these *a priori* methods might have produced a tidier and more comprehensive book than this one. As it is, not every topic that comes up in the discussion of sexuality is dealt with, not every method or approach is represented, and not every stand that Christians take is taken.

Nevertheless, these essays do cover a lot of ground. Since much, perhaps most of the current debate about sexuality centers on homosexuality, that is also a focus here; but the specific issues that have received the most attention—same-sex unions and the ordination of lesbians and gay men—cannot be separated from the wider question of what Christians, individually and as the church, are to make of sexuality in all its many-sided mysteriousness. The essays, in different ways, take that question seriously, and bring to it the learning, experience, and conviction of authors with diverse gifts and graces.

It has been said that the collection of essays is a characteristically Anglican genre—our unsystematic way of doing theology. All the authors are, in fact, Anglicans, and, except for the two bishops, members of the Episcopal Church. In-house matters understandably appear from time to time, more in some essays than in others. By and large, however, this is not an in-house book. All sorts and conditions of Christian readers will, we hope, find it worth reading for the light it may shed on their own situation. Prompted though it was by developments in one communion, it is offered to the church at large.

To take part as a Christian in dialogue about sexuality is all but impossible without taking a stand with which someone will disagree. This collection does not contain something for everyone; on the contrary. The authors are by no means all singing the same tune, as it were; they differ on many points, some of them major ones. As an ensemble, however, their voices are mostly in harmony. But while it does not purport to be representative of every party and shade of opinion, the book does attempt to reflect the fact that debate about sexuality in general, and especially about homosexuality, takes place at many levels. It is, as one of the contributors says, a passionate debate; at the same time, it is a debate that calls for all the critical intelligence Christians can muster. As sexuality itself is a matter of the whole person—of our selves, our souls and bodies—so too the questions it raises cannot but engage heart and mind alike. Some of the essays that follow are personal and experiential, some objective and scholarly. There are narratives, arguments, first-person accounts; there is theological reasoning and pastoral reflection. What there is none of is diatribe. Although as a whole it takes one side, the book is intended to further a conversation—to be less a manifesto than an eirenicon: this is how each of the authors sees the matter. Can you see it too?

॰

I have found that it takes nearly as much work to put together a volume with seventeen authors as to write the same number of pages alone. My job has been made easier, more stimulating, and more enjoyable by the people who are Cowley Publications, most especially by Dr. Cynthia Shattuck, without whose advice, cooperation, and encouragement this would have been a different collection. It is the fourth time we have worked together on a book, and my admiration for her editorial acumen increases with age. Two members of the Society of St. John the Evangelist should also be named, with special thanks on behalf of all the contributors: Paul Wessinger, who planted the seed of this project, and Martin Smith, who watered it with wisdom.

THE
PASSIONATE
DEBATE

∞ *L. William Countryman*

Finding a Way to Talk

Dealing with Difficult Topics in the Episcopal Church

Episcopalians have experienced a lot of conflict and controversy over the last few decades. We've had long-standing and often rancorous disagreements about a number of topics. Within my own adult lifetime, I remember in particular conflicts about desegregation and racism, ordination of divorced persons, the General Convention Special Program, the Vietnam War, the ordination of women to the priesthood and episcopate, revision of the *Book of Common Prayer,* the shape of American Indian/Native American Christianity, ordination of openly gay and lesbian people, and the blessing of same-sex unions. A few of those disputes have disappeared, thanks to changes in the world around us. In a few more cases, one side "won," though often without fully persuading the other side. None of them, I think, was ever truly resolved. We don't seem to have the means to resolve such questions; and this lies at the root of much of our present dissension.

Probably, we don't need anyone to underline for us the problems created by this ongoing pattern of unresolved conflicts. Most of us hanker for more coherence in our church, though we may disagree as to what we want that coherence to look like. Yet most of us probably would not accept a highly centralized kind of church authority that could hand down final decisions without regard to the will of the Christian people. We are Episcopalians, after all. If we wanted something absolutely decisive, we would probably be Roman Catholics or fundamentalists of some sort. Still, we would like to be able to move toward resolution of our conflicts. Instead, we find all too often that we are merely talking past one another, that we seem to begin from such different sets of presuppositions that we have trouble even taking one another's arguments seriously.

Part of the difficulty is that we tend to divide everybody up into two camps. We expect to identify a conservative and a liberal side to every question, and we expect people to line up consistently on one side or the other. We assume, half-consciously, that there are *only* these two sides to every question, that everyone must fit one or the other description. And the two sides seem never to have anything persuasive to say to each other. "Conservatives" usually feel that "liberals" are indifferent to the Bible and the church's tradition—that, for "liberals," basically anything goes. "Liberals" are prone to feel that "conservatives" are indifferent to human realities—that, for "conservatives," everything is based on inflexible rules. Ultimately, there's not much to talk about, no grounds for real conversation. All anyone can do is try to dominate the voting at the next diocesan or general convention.

Now, this picture is a little exaggerated, of course. But there's enough truth in it to make it uncomfortably lifelike. I confess to having a personal stake in seeing it change. My personal stake is that I can't ever seem to find a home for myself in either the liberal or the conservative camp. I'm always in some difficulty with both of them, struggling to make sense of a situation where I can't accept either of their interpretations. Let me explain by telling a little about myself. I'm not, I'm afraid, all that interesting, but that's just the point. I suspect that a good many Episcopalians are in a similar quandary and that the church at large is trying to deal with issues where the familiar liberal-conservative dichotomy just isn't helpful.

∞

I am, by temperament and training, a conservative. Sometimes I wish that I were a liberal instead. I incline to think that liberals are probably better people than I am—kinder and gentler people, in all likelihood. But there doesn't seem to be much I can do about it. There is a certain hard-edged quality in my thinking. I like to have things clear. I like to go back to the sources. I want to know how I got where I am. Some years back, when I published a little book called *Biblical Authority or Biblical Tyranny?*, I was described by one reviewer as a "spokesman for the critical right." That meant that I was defending the authority of the Bible, but with an awareness that the Bible was originally written to answer the questions of ancient people, not modern ones. I continue to have the same high regard for the Bible and its authority and for the Christian tradition.

On the other hand, people who have read some of my other books often think of me as a liberal—particularly people who have read only the last chapter of *Dirt, Greed, and Sex* and have ignored the argument that leads up to that chapter. They assume that I must be a liberal because some of my conclusions are ones they think of as liberal. Anybody who reads the whole book, however, probably realizes that only a conservative would bother arguing the matter in the way I did.

So I have the ill fortune to be a conservative whose conservative method sometimes leads him to radical conclusions. My liberal friends are perplexed that anybody would spend so much time with the Bible; my conservative friends are upset that anybody would find such radical conclusions there. I wind up feeling kind of lonely!

By way of illustration, let me say a little about how this worked out for me in the context of the ordination of women to the priesthood. I was originally quite opposed to that change in our church's discipline. It seemed to me that it represented a sharp and important break with our tradition, one that was likely to lead to a broader loss of connection with our past. I had become an Episcopalian as a teenager largely because the Episcopal Church had a connection with the larger Christian past that I had never encountered in the denomination I grew up in—a denomination whose history and membership are largely confined to the United States. I was very unwilling to lose the Anglican sense of catholicity, of being in continuity with our predecessors in the faith.

As the debate over ordination developed, I could respond to liberal arguments that stressed the importance of the equality of women and the changes that had taken place in our world. It seemed only right that women should have equal power in the church. I could also respond to conservative arguments that objected to any radical break with scripture and tradition, which seemed to know nothing of the idea of women as presbyters or bishops. At no point could I be entirely satisfied with the arguments from either side of the debate. Too many conservatives seemed to think that scripture and tradition justified misogyny and inequality; too many liberals seemed to think that current needs justified sweeping the past aside without even taking a close look at it.

Two things changed my mind about the ordination question. One of them happened to me in graduate school. I already knew the New Testament well enough to know that it offered no decisive evidence on the subject. Now, I was studying the North African church in the third century, an era of great saints like Perpetua and Felicity and Cyprian. I realized, to my surprise, that that church was heretical, by later standards. It taught the necessity of rebaptizing those who had been baptized outside the mainstream church, even if their baptism was clearly correct in form. In due course, that came to be regarded as a heretical position.

It was a surprise to me that the North African church could have been wrong on such an important subject; yet its error did not keep that church from making a major contribution to the church catholic through its martyrs and the writings of its confessors and theologians. I truly understood, for the first time, that the tradition is not eternally fixed. It has grown by a process of dialogue. It has responded to the world around it. And it has been all right for churches to make mistakes when they are grappling with new questions. It was all right for the North African church to make mistakes even in the matter of baptism—and if Cyprian's church was not catholic, nobody is catholic. Similarly, it was all right if the Episcopal Church took some risks or even made some mistakes in the process of dealing with new questions about the status of women. I was still not sure we were making the right decision; but I did not need to be overly anxious if it turned out to be the wrong one. Our catholicity, our faithfulness to the tradition, was not at stake.

The other thing that happened to change my mind was experience: getting to know a number of women who were priests, and observing the church as it assimilated this new phenomenon. Contrary to my fears, the ordination of women to the priesthood did not mean wholesale abandonment of our connection to the Christian past. In fact, the women priests I met were, on the average, as interested in maintaining that connection as anybody else. What was more, I could not question that the church was being blessed by the ministry of these new priests. I found us gaining a new breadth of awareness of the whole human experience and a new ability to minister to people of all sorts and conditions. In other words, I finally came round to the "liberal" position; but I did it in a decidedly "conservative" fashion. A better knowledge of the tradition itself taught me to be open to risk and to new possibilities and freed me to learn from our present experience. It still distresses me that that whole controversy had to be argued out on liberal *versus* conservative lines—in terms that pitted scripture and tradition against reason. For I am increasingly convinced that that had nothing to do with what was really going on. The terms of the discussion were themselves misleading.

∞

What can we do to make our modes of discussion serve us better? I think that one of our problems is that we have been following a legal model for discussing issues to which that model doesn't lend itself. The legal model is very useful for certain purposes; but it has some built-in assumptions that limit its usefulness in the kinds of conflicts we've been having. The legal model of discourse assumes that there are just two alternatives: one party to the dispute is right and one is wrong. In order to determine which is which, the legal model appeals to statute law, to precedent, and to general considerations of equity.

Within Anglicanism, we have easily fallen into the habit of identifying these three legal criteria with the legs of our proverbial theological "three-legged stool." *Scripture* is the constitution and statute law; we therefore invoke it as the decisive word, though we are not always in agreement about how we read and interpret it. *Tradition* is then equivalent to judicial precedent; if "it's always been done this way" (or, alternatively, if "it's never been done this way"), that constitutes a strong presupposition against change. And, finally, *reason* is comparable to equity; within the framework of constitution, law, and judicial precedent, it may be invoked to adapt the existing system or to modify it where changed circumstances have made it oppressive.

The "liberal" and the "conservative" use the same system. They simply begin from opposite ends of it. The conservative pleader will begin with the statute law, show how precedent supports it, and conclude by suggesting that, at least, equity doesn't compel us to make any adjustments. The liberal pleader begins with equity, in the hope of persuading us that, if elements of precedent and statute law conflict with it, we should discard them. Either way, one must argue on behalf of one position against the other. One of the positions has to be right and the other has to be wrong. There isn't much room for complexity. There can be only two parties.

The difficulty with this, of course, is that it doesn't represent what is actually going on. It assumes that we already have in hand all the criteria we need to decide our most difficult questions—and, more than that, that we understand those criteria fully. The only remaining question would be how we ought to weight them: is scripture more important than reason or vice versa? In actual experience, I think our truly difficult conflicts feel quite different—and much more chaotic. They are not just a matter of applying the familiar criteria to familiar problems. Instead, we find ourselves faced with genuinely new questions that our familiar norms may not deal with directly at all.

In the matter of ordination of women to the priesthood, for example, it was clear that scripture and tradition did not explicitly authorize the practice. Yet that fact was not really conclusive because we were aware, at some level, that the question had never been asked before in just this way. New factors had to be taken into account. Women themselves had become something different in our world as a result of changing social definitions of gender; they were not the same as they had been in the Victorian era, much less the first century. In the ancient Mediterranean world, women were private, not public beings, which made it difficult for most people to imagine their presiding at public assemblies. Today, such roles have long been commonplace. At the same time (and coming from the other direction of argument), the fact that equity demands the equal treatment of women did not, in and of itself, settle the matter. Was ordination a question of social power or of sacred law? Was equality even a relevant issue in the realm of the sacred? How would this new undertaking intersect with the rest of our religious belief and practice?

Much of our public discussion of the issue took the overt form of a debate between scripture and tradition, on one side, and reason on the other. Or alternatively, it took the form of a debate between a position that regarded the sacred forms of our religion as a primary value in their own right and a position that saw them as subject to the claims of a "higher" principle of equality. In a sense, we find that many of the real issues were never addressed because they did not fit neatly into this either/or pattern. For me, a personal resolution of the conflict finally came from a shift of focus. I discovered that the tradition itself is not only rich and full of grace, but also alive and changing and fallible, and I learned, from direct experience, that the Spirit was at work in the ministry of ordained women. Others, I know, had comparable experiences. Such learnings were conspicuously absent from the debate. The legal model made it difficult to talk in any terms but those of absolute right and wrong. One result of our poor mode of arguing the issue was that we are still left with two sides and an incomplete consensus in this matter. We made a majority decision but, as a church, we are not of one mind.

∞

I think we have another, better model available for these discussions—one that comes from within our agelong Christian tradition. It is the model of spiritual discernment. There has been a resurgence of interest in the Christian spiritual tradition. We often hear phrases like "spiritual direction" or "soul friends." (I still have a fondness for the antiquated Anglican terminology "ghostly counsel.") The spiritual tradition, from its earliest times, has grown out of a certain very important insight into our daily lives as Christians, the insight that each of us is living a life that is, in many respects, unique and without precedent. No one has ever stood quite where you or I stand in our lives today. There is no guaranteed blueprint for deciding all the conflicts that we each experience. We have some guidance from scripture and tradition, and we take that guidance seriously. But if we are presented with the necessity, say, of choosing between two evils—with the kind of choices, let us say, that faced prisoners in Nazi concentration camps—we will still have to make our own decision. And even on the level of daily existence, the tradition will seldom give us a perfect answer to our more complex questions. If at all possible, we will make our difficult and singular decisions with the counsel of other people—our ghostly counselors—but ultimately, it is up to us to discern our path in relationship with God.

The discourse of spiritual discernment is different from that of law. It does take accepted norms of right and wrong into account. But it does not merely measure us against the rules; nor does it absolutize or divinize the rules. It is focused, rather, on looking ahead and trying to see which decisions will contribute to spiritual health and which to spiritual sickness. The early Christians, after all, were people who rejected the norms of their own time and place in many important respects. They appeared disreputable to many of their contemporaries. They gave birth to a new tradition that focused primarily not on law, but on the good news of God's good will toward us and how we can live in response to it through faith, hope, and love. Above all, they were people who lived in and by hope. Rather than simply conforming to rules from the past, they sought to model their living on the life of the age to come—a model that we perceive only dimly, but which nonetheless draws us onward.

What, then, are some characteristics of spiritual health, as seen from the Christian perspective, that might help us in such spiritual discourse? I have asked a number of Episcopal audiences what characterizes those whom they regard as people of profound spirituality—their personal saints, if you will. Their answers, despite the fact that the groups were diverse, have been broadly consistent. Here are things they emphasized.

- *Centeredness* is a quality quite distinct from the polarity of "conservative" rigidity and "liberal" looseness that sometimes dominates our legal discourse. It is a quality of stability that is not mere fixity. It involves a sense of being genuinely present and attentive to the moment and the persons one is dealing with. It evinces balance and rootedness and the kind of tranquillity that comes from experience of God's presence even in difficult times.
- *Faith* is a confidence in God's grace that shines through and bestows authority on the faithful person. It is not just intellectual belief, but emerges from actual experience of God's unexpected (and sometimes difficult) goodness.
- *Generosity of spirit,* as opposed to mean-spiritedness or the desire to prove oneself in the right or the need to be always at center stage.
- *A sense of oneself* shows itself in respect for boundaries, in an honest and humble estimate of oneself, in what one person called an "engaged detachment."
- *Discipline* shows itself in commitment, reliability, persistence in prayer and in love.
- *Integrity and honesty,* as opposed to hypocrisy, self-deception, or a public façade unrelated to private realities. We expect of the spiritual person a kind of consistency and clarity of being, a certain transparency, grounded in the person's living relation with God, not simply in a set of learned principles.
- *Hospitality* is the quality that welcomes others into the good news of God's grace. It is opposed to the kind of defensiveness that sees the Christian religion primarily as something to be defended from unsuitable people or ideas.
- *Compassion,* as opposed to an attitude dismissive of others or an unwillingness to take the experience of others seriously.

- *Vulnerability and openness,* as distinct from the tendency to use religion as a kind of armor against whatever we fear. The truly spiritual person is still eminently human, fundamentally *like* the rest of us, not remote, legalistic, or cold.
- *Continuing growth in faith, hope, and love,* for the spiritual person assumes that our growth in the Spirit is never complete in this life.

The qualities of the holy person that my various respondents enumerated are, of course, gifts of the Spirit. But as with all gifts of the Spirit, much depends on how we appropriate and make use of them. We seek spiritual discernment in order to help us find the direction that will lead us to greater intimacy with God and therefore greater holiness. In this regard, what is true of the individual is true also of the Christian community. The community, too, can embody these qualities of holiness and can order its life by seeking to discern what paths will lead toward this goal.

How does this kind of discernment work itself out? Perhaps it is easiest to see this in historical terms, and I offer two examples, one individual and the other communal.

Dietrich Bonhoeffer

Bonhoeffer was a German pastor who could easily have remained outside Germany during World War II. (He was in America just before the war began and had had an earlier opportunity to go to India to spend time with Gandhi.) Instead, he returned to work for the Confessing Church, which was resisting the Nazification of the German churches. At first he was close to being a complete pacifist, but he finally came to the conclusion that it was right and even necessary for him to participate in a plot against Hitler's life. He was arrested in connection with the plot and hanged shortly before the end of the war.

We know some of his thinking about this matter from his writings, but much of what he wrote in his years of imprisonment had to be destroyed to protect others. Still, Bonhoeffer is a person who has received the respect and admiration of a very wide range of Christian people. There are many who would disagree with his decisions—those, on the one hand, who would say that he should not have departed from his pacifism and those, on the other, who would say that he ought to have accepted violent measures early on when they had a better chance of doing some good. But I know of no one who would criticize Bonhoeffer as having made his decisions lightly or carelessly or in a way that diminishes his stature.

We all know that, on this topic as on many others, the scriptures can be interpreted in a variety of ways. We can claim that the scriptures affirm pacifism or that they allow certain degrees of participation in violence under circumstances where violence may seem to be the only way to resist evil.

We know that the Christian tradition, too, has supported a variety of positions in regard to these issues. Yet people who would disagree about what is right and wrong in such situations can agree that Dietrich Bonhoeffer was a faithful Christian and made his decisions with appropriate care—in a way that was centered, generous, honest, and humble. Even if one does not agree with Bonhoeffer, one does not have to consign him merely to the realm of the wrong or mistaken. An English officer who was imprisoned with him shortly before his execution wrote:

> Bonhoeffer...was all humility and sweetness, he always seemed to me to diffuse an atmosphere of happiness, of joy in every smallest event of life, and of deep gratitude for the mere fact that he was alive....He was one of the very few men that I have ever met to whom his God was real and close to him.[1]

That kind of description would do honor to anyone and takes us far beyond the legal options of right or wrong. And this is how faithful people do in fact deal with difficult decisions in their own lives—respecting scripture and tradition, while meeting the needs of the time in the closest possible communion with their God.

A New Testament Instance

The same kind of process went on, communally, in earliest Christianity. Luke reports an occasion when leaders of the infant church gathered to decide the difficult question of the status of Gentile converts in the Christian community (Acts 15). Did the men have to be circumcised (and so become, in some sense, Jewish) in order to be part of the Christian community? It was a decision at least as difficult as the ones we have been faced with in our century. The early Christians did what we do, of course. They looked to scripture and to their own traditions for guidance in these matters. The guidance they received was not conclusive, but it was, without doubt, weighted on the side of excluding the uncircumcised.

Scripture made no allowance for the inclusion of uncircumcised Gentile men in the assembly of Israel—quite the opposite. At most, one might glean (as Paul does in Romans 15:9-12) a few texts that held out a vague hope of an inclusion of Gentiles in the remote future. The as-yet unwritten tradition of Jesus' teaching knew nothing of Gentiles being received into the community of disciples, either. Jesus had apparently never done anything of the sort. In Mark's gospel we find him explicitly refusing the request of one Gentile, the man from whom he had cast out the Legion of demons, to become a part of his entourage—though he did tell the man to go and tell his own people about the good things God had done for him (5:18-20). In other words, the Christian community was being asked to do something unprecedented. How did they go about making their decision?

First, according to Luke, they heard Peter tell about the time when the Spirit led him to visit a Gentile household, much against his own better judgment. Once he had arrived and preached the good news of Jesus, the Spirit fell upon these Gentiles in the same way the Spirit had fallen upon the Jewish Christians. Peter responded by saying, "Can anyone refuse water to baptize these people?" Not one of the Christians accompanying Peter was able to do so. It was a shocking break with scripture and tradition, but Peter had felt compelled to lay aside familiar norms of right and wrong—and Peter was a good conservative who *wanted* to maintain the existing norms—in order to become a part of what God was doing in the here and now.

After Peter had spoken, Paul and Barnabas were invited to tell about what God had been doing among the Gentiles through their ministry. Finally, James, the brother of the Lord and another conservative figure, introduced some scripture that said that the Gentiles *would* eventually become worshipers of Israel's God (but *didn't* say whether they had to become Jewish in the process!). And James summed up the discussion by saying that the Jewish Christians should not "cause any trouble to those from among the Gentiles who were turning to God" (Acts 15:19). In other words, the earliest Christian community listened carefully and then chose to set aside the apparent sense of scripture and tradition in the interest of respecting the work of the Spirit and of showing hospitality to people who wanted to be associated with the church. The decision finally turned not on simple, bipolar questions of right and wrong, liberal and conservative, but on questions of how the church community could grow in grace and respond in a healthy way to new opportunities that God had placed on its doorstep.

Neither Bonhoeffer nor the Council of Jerusalem was able to depend solely on prescriptions of scripture or tradition in making their decisions. Both found themselves having to make decisions in unexampled situations: Bonhoeffer in the context of the unparalleled viciousness of the Nazi regime, the early Christian community in the face of a stream of problematic, unanticipated, and perhaps unwanted converts. Bonhoeffer somehow made a decision in favor of the assassination that did not deprive him of intimacy with God; that it was a holy decision is manifest from the fact that he continued to grow in holiness. The Council of Jerusalem saw the Christian community as being in an ongoing relationship with God—a relationship that might even, under unforeseeable circumstances, justify deliberate departures from scripture and tradition. The church's continuing growth in holiness was at stake and pointed the way to the council's decision.

∞

How might we use such a model in our present circumstances in the Episcopal Church? I think what we do in our individual circumstances applies also in our communal ones. We seek counsel from one another as we try to discern our path. We try to determine how our various decisions might affect our relationship with God. We ask fundamental questions: Which decisions will be most likely to help us grow in faith, hope, and love? How do we remain grounded and centered in scripture and tradition without absolutizing them or being imprisoned by them? How do we listen to the voice of the Spirit here and now? What decisions will encourage integrity and honesty as opposed to hypocrisy? Which ones will encourage generosity of spirit? How do we remain centered in the love of God while also reaching out to the people around us?

What if we apply such discourse to our current conflicts? I take as an example the matter of ordaining openly gay and lesbian persons. This is a step which I favor; and I will not pretend to construct an uncommitted, completely neutral treatment of it. My hope here is simply to construct a kind of discourse that people with other perspectives can respond to in comparable terms.

In our present conflict, the church seems to have three basic options:

1. Determine that it is wrong to ordain such persons, and stop doing so.
2. Determine that it is wrong, and continue doing so.
3. Determine that the Spirit is drawing gay men and lesbians to the gospel, and accept them as full members of the church, including ordination, even if it contradicts existing norms.

Our discussion of these options needs to focus on their implications for the spiritual life of the church. Which decision is most likely to encourage growth in centeredness, in generosity of spirit, in integrity, in hospitality and the other values we have noted—above all, in faith, hope, and love? When I have asked groups of Episcopalians to discuss these three options in these terms, they have not all reached instant agreement. That was not the purpose of the exercise, in any case. There was a distinct gain, however, in the ability to find a common language for discussing the issues.

Option 2, for example, probably has the best claim to represent the Episcopal Church's "tradition" in this matter. Before the conflict over the matter reached its present level of rancor, the church routinely asserted that same-sex sexual acts were wrong and, just as routinely, ordained homosexual men—provided they were not perceived as likely to cause public scandal. In the context of spirituality, however, it was easy to agree that this "traditional" option is no longer acceptable. As long as the issue of lesbian/gay ordination had not taken center stage, the whole process went on in a rather offhand fashion. Yes, there was a public stance about sexual ethics. Yes, this homosexual person or that looked, otherwise, like excellent material for the ordained ministry. And bishops sometimes decided simply to overlook the conflict. Under present circumstances, however, Option 2 would involve the church in a kind of overt and deliberate hypocrisy that cannot but undermine our growth in the Spirit.

It is apparent, then, that we are in a previously unexampled situation. Even Option 2, "traditional" though it is, would represent a change in the tradition, since it would make deliberate what was previously more or less unreflective behavior. In such a situation, prefabricated solutions are seldom of much use. The central need is to discern what the Spirit is doing among us in continuity with the gospel, and we move toward that discernment by asking how the possible decisions are likely to affect our holiness, the intimacy of our relationship with God. As Christians, we do not change traditional norms casually; but we do not have an absolute commitment to them, either. Our absolute commitment is to the gospel and to the God of grace who has become one of us in Jesus.

What, then, would be the spiritual consequences of Option 1? Any effort really to halt further ordination of lesbians and gay men will involve the church in ever closer and potentially more hostile inspection of the lives of ordinands. This will discourage (but not totally dissuade) homosexual candidates; but it will also discourage many other good candidates because such inspection goes so much against the grain for Americans. In addition, it will tend to infantilize ordinands and to screen out those with enough sense of self that they are unwilling to have their personal lives invaded in this way. Rejection of gay or lesbian candidates will also tend to call every discernment of vocation to ordination into question, in much the way that refusal to ordain women did. In the latter case, we held that the spiritual experience and community roles that would indicate a vocation to ordination in a man must have some radically different meaning in a woman. In the case of sexual minorities, are we to hold that such experience, even if apparently the same, must have some meaning radically different from the case of heterosexual candidates? The apparent arbitrariness of this prejudgment militates against the kind of consistency, clarity, and attentiveness to the person and moment that we regard as hallmarks of the holy person.

A process designed principally to weed out lesbians and gay men will only produce a clergy made up of highly submissive persons—or, worse yet, of unscrupulous persons who are willing to practice hypocrisy in order to look good to commissions on ministry. This can already be a problem in our existing system, but it will certainly become worse. And even if we succeed in screening openly gay men and lesbians out of the ordination process, it will not, of course, mean that there are no homosexual persons in the ordained ministry. Some will practice deliberate concealment. Others, like myself, who were genuinely self-identified as heterosexual at the time of their ordination, will later realize that they are homosexual and have been hiding from their true sexual orientation. This will perpetuate our collective sense of confusion.

The effort to identify and remove homosexual candidates from the ordination process will thus exact a substantial spiritual toll from clergy and would-be clergy. Add to this that the effort will make the Episcopal Church less hospitable to homosexual lay persons than it was in the past, before the conflict sharpened. There are many such people in our church. Before we decide to drive them away, we should at least reflect on why so many gay and lesbian converts have been coming to our doors. We do not dare turn them away without being truly convinced that they represent a temptation to be rejected rather than a gift of the Spirit. Those who advocate Option 1 will need to show that it promises spiritual gain that is at least comparable to the spiritual loss with which it threatens us.

The third option—that of opening full membership in the church (including the possibility of ordination) to lesbians and gay men—certainly raises significant questions. As Christians, we are no more eager now than in the first century to depart from established norms. Yet, we do need to discern what the Spirit is doing in drawing gay or lesbian people to the church in the first place. The Gentile Christians of the first century were clear, by and large, that they were being called to the gospel—and equally clear that they were not being called to become Jews. The situation of homosexual people in our time seems to be similar; they are called to the gospel, but not to heterosexuality. Scripture and tradition appear, at least at first glance, to weigh in against the inclusion of such persons. As in the matter of Gentiles, however, closer inspection reveals that scripture and tradition do not speak with a single voice about sexuality and that, in any case, they were not dealing with the question exactly as it is raised in our own time. Like the Christians of the first century, we will have to make a decision based not on perfect proof from scripture or tradition but on our understanding of the Spirit's work here and now.

What will be the probable spiritual consequences of opening ordination to homosexual persons? I think there is a long list of benefits to be expected. For one thing, it will encourage integrity and honesty, since we already have a great many gay men and lesbians among our clergy who feel they cannot afford to be open. (This would work to the advantage of heterosexual people, too, since public heterosexuality would no longer be required as a screen for persons who would otherwise be deemed unacceptable.) The church would be exhibiting hospitality to people previously held at arm's length, and practicing a generosity of spirit that overcomes fear. By dealing more honestly with homosexuality, the church might grow in its ability to deal constructively with issues of heterosexuality as well—something that has been very difficult for us hitherto. We can then hope to move in the direction of a clearer and more convincing sexual ethic for everyone, one that has the real consent of the Christian people. Gay people will contribute to the church at large their particular experience of faith in God, refined by the trials and spiritual growth of the coming-out process. The church at large can move toward a more centered and outward-looking stance in its life, as opposed to a position characterized by defensiveness and anxiety about its own purity. It is very hard, after all, to carry on evangelism from behind fortress walls. We might become truly a people of good news again.

The third option, then, seems to be most consistent with the criteria of holiness suggested above—criteria derived from our living tradition of spirituality. It recognizes that, both as individuals and as communities, we are living out a unique experience of God's grace. Scripture and tradition help to ground and center us, but they cannot provide detailed answers to all our questions. Those must come about as we practice living, with discernment, in intimate relationship with God. The spiritual benefits to the community of ordaining openly gay or lesbian persons are clear. Opponents of Option 3—the ordination of gay and lesbian people—would need to show that there are dangers to the church's spirituality that outweigh these potential gains.

The objective of the discussion I propose is not that we will all agree at once in our answers. My expectations are not that utopian. Luke makes it clear that even the Council of Jerusalem did not instantly resolve the struggle over the inclusion of uncircumcised Gentiles. The difficulties we experience today in coming to agreement are not radically different from what our first-century forebears went through, and they will not vanish overnight. I only wish to suggest that, by shifting the model of our discussion, we might be able to talk the same language and might begin to understand why different persons among us weigh the considerations differently and come out with different results. Perhaps we could come to a broad, if not universal, consensus about the way forward. Perhaps we might come to respect those whose answers differ from our own, in the way that we can respect Dietrich Bonhoeffer whether we agree or disagree with his particular decisions. That would be a major step forward, from my perspective, for the life of the Episcopal Church.

NOTES

1. Payne Best, *The Venlo Incident,* 180; quoted in Eberhard Bethge's foreword to Dietrich Bonhoeffer, *Letters and Papers from Prison*, ed. Eberhard Bethge, trans. Reginald Fuller (New York: The Macmillan Company, 1962), 13-14.

∞ *Bonnie Shullenberger*

What Are the Bishops Really Telling Us?

A few years ago, during the coffee hour at church, some people were engaged in a passionate debate about—you guessed it—sex. One of the debaters was quoting the Bible, and another replied, "But we know so much more about sexuality than they did in those days!" Later, my daughter's godmother, a no-nonsense lady in her seventies, asked me with a frown, "Is that true? Do we really know anything more about sex now than they did back then?"

I wasn't sure. True, we have discredited the homunculus theory of reproduction, and Masters and Johnson have made some interesting measures of the physiology of orgasm. Heaven knows we talk about sex enough: during a recent hospitalization, I had my first exposure to American talk television, and I had heard more about incest by the end of the day than I had expected to hear in my whole lifetime. But for all the talk, all the publicity, do we really have a deeper, more serious, more Christian appreciation of sexuality, sexual attraction, the relationship between love and sex, than St. Paul did? Can anyone give me empirical data as to why my heart turned over the first time I looked—almost a quarter of a century ago—at the man who is now my husband? Or why it still does?

It is my view that we have little more information about sexuality than our ancestors did, but that we have a great deal of something else, which is ideology. Ideology in its original sense was simply the science of ideas; it has come to connote visionary theorizing without benefit of reasoned support. As Holmes told Watson, it is a capital mistake to theorize in advance of your evidence, but just that mistake is the characteristic practice of contemporary ideology. As Louis Kern has written, ideology

> can, and often does, express the parochial viewpoint of a particular country, ethnic group, class, or even sex. But from a broader sociological perspective, an ideology is assumed to be a universal cultural phenomenon which implies a conscious ideational construct that is not only a re-

sponse to, but also a tool for coming to grips with, social reality and historical change.[1]

I doubt if I am the first to notice that America has become a culture in which ideological absolutism has infected almost every form of discourse and conversation across ideological positions has grown increasingly troubled, whether the topic is gun control, nursery school, or military intervention abroad. And in this regard, at least, the church certainly mirrors the culture. One particularly public place where I was able to examine the variants and conflicts in sexual ideology currently operating in the Episcopal Church is the two statements, signed by various bishops, in response to *Continuing the Dialogue,* the House of Bishops' pastoral study document presented at General Convention in 1994. Since I was out of the country through most of that convention, I never saw the pastoral study document and had no idea what it might or might not say. But soon after my return from East Africa I was given a copy of *The Living Church* that contained these two "response" statements. I was not surprised that the signatories of one of these made a powerfully embracing statement on behalf of the experiences and ministries of homosexual persons, and that the other group reiterated the traditional position of the church, which is that homosexual practice is inconsistent with Christian moral teaching. What did surprise me was that neither of the statements contained a reasoned theological position. They were assertions of opinion—full stop.

Now this struck me as odd. It seemed to me that it would be the intent of both groups to try to speak to the troubled or the uncertain (of whom there are far more, I have come to realize, than firm adherents on either side) through careful theological reasoning. I tried to find the possibility of common ground; I tried to find the logical center of disagreement. Finally a comment in the "Statement of Koinonia" suggested to me the crux of the difference between the two groups. "We believe," the statement reads, "that some of us are created heterosexual and some of us are created homosexual." Now those who signed the "Statement of Koinonia" believe that sexual orientation is a given of creation; that is their prerogative. "Believe" is their term, so the question I asked was, what kind of belief is this?

I am laboring this point about my own effort to sort out these documents because, as someone absent from this debate for over two years, I am a kind of stand-in, not only for those I have met who are troubled or uncertain about how to assess the place of sexuality in the church today, but also for our partners elsewhere in the Anglican communion. In East Africa, at least, the American church's obsession with sexuality is observed with various mixtures of amusement, embarrassment, and horror. It worries me that there is no effort by the American church to convey the theological and ethical *reasoning* that informs our debates on sexuality, and it infuriates me when I am told that Africans in general are too backward to understand what we're about.[2]

So, when I examine what I'm calling the "crux" remark from what I imagine to be my informed outsider's stance, what do I think of it? I cannot accept it as a belief based on compelling scientific evidence. The existing examples of twin studies and brain anatomy that may hint at some biological basis for sexual orientation are far too slender to bear the weight of the kind of no-going-back inevitability implicit in the word "created." I am aware of studies of the genetic marker Xq28, but like the twin studies these are limited to males, and their sex-exclusiveness alone ought to give us pause.[3] And if someone did discover a biological component in sexual orientation, what would it mean? Myron Hofer, writing in *The New York Times* in regard to the book *The Bell Curve*, said, "Geneticists have known for years that the estimates of the genetic contribution to a trait cannot be assumed to extend to a sample of the population reared in a different environment."[4] In responding to the debate over *The Bell Curve*'s argument on behalf of a genetic, racially-linked factor in intelligence, Hofer reminds us that there is an interplay between environment and inheritance—nurture and nature—that can affect how genetic material exhibits itself. Biology alone simply is not the last word.

An argument for biological determinism not only raises scientific objections; it ought to raise moral ones as well. Genetic screening, which began as an effort to alleviate the suffering of families whose children would be afflicted by irreversible, fatal conditions such as Tay-Sachs Disease, is now used routinely to screen for a variety of conditions, including some which are neither fatal nor disfiguring, such as, in certain communities, being female. Stanley Hauerwas, in his essay "Killing Compassion," notes that contemporary approaches to disability and pain frequently assume death is the "compassionate" response. Compassion, he argues, "fuels [an] extraordinary desire to eliminate the retarded in the name of caring for them."[5] It is chilling, then, to consider that one of the strongest appeals to the consciences of Christians in respect of their homosexual sisters and brothers has been an appeal to "compassion." How unlikely is it that "compassion" in respect of gays could become the same as "compassion" exercised in respect of those with Downs Syndrome?[6]

But if the "crux" statement must be repudiated as a scientific belief, neither is it a theological belief, although it tries to sound like one. If some of our bishops were to state that they believe some people (who just happened to be male) were "created" extraordinarily skilled at mathematics, all kinds of objections would be raised. Women might reply that girl students are poorly served in the teaching of math. To place girls' lesser achievements in math as a "given" of creation (thus ordained by God) would be to use theological-sounding language in service of a human situation that, in fact, we do not understand. Theological-sounding language is no substitute for theology—or intelligent investigations of troublesome issues.

The "crux" statement cannot express an experiential belief, either. For, if anything, the lesson of the past fifty years in North America is that human love and sexual desire, far from being so firmly fixed in one direction—either heterosexual or homosexual with little or no middle ground—as to be exclusive and unchanging, is actually remarkably elastic. Fluidity, not determinism, seems to be characteristic of sexual behavior in North America.[7] Living all my adult life in academia has made me skeptical about statements like the ones I am examining, for in the academy one tends to see a full range of human proclivity, probably because once one has tenure one can't be fired. For nearly thirty years I have known openly gay people; I have worked with transsexuals and militant feminist celibates; in one college where I taught, three men in my department made no secret of their interest in young men and boys, and yet two of these men were married and had children. I have friends who lived openly as homosexuals for years and then found themselves drawn to a person of the opposite sex whom they married; I know people who have ended marriages of as long as twenty-five years in duration to turn to a lover of the same sex. Efforts to reduce such fluidity to either biology or oppression sound remarkably hollow.

Since the belief that the Koinonia bishops express cannot be credited as either scientific or theological or experiential, what is it? It is an ideological belief. In the early 1970s, when America's primary sexual ideology began to be brought out of the male-oriented *Playboy* mode into a feminist mode, those of us who worked in the women's movement were under enormous pressure to adopt lesbianism. Women like theologian Mary Daly and poet Adrienne Rich argued that heterosexuality was a betrayal of women, and growing numbers of lesbian activists refused to work with straight women at all. Theorist Charlotte Wolff wrote in 1971 that "the lesbian was and is unquestionably in the avant-garde of the fight for equality of the sexes, and for the psychical liberation of women."[8] If you were serious about feminism, it was better to be a lesbian. Additionally, men who were sympathetic to feminism were urged to involve themselves homosexually, as a way of opting out of the "heterosexist" oppression of women. If people during those years expressed a sense that they had "always been this way," it was expressed politically. From early childhood we were supposed to have intuited the oppressiveness of sex roles and rebelled against them via homosexuality. Political consciousness, not biology, not grace, was assumed to be the prime mover of our sexual selves.

More to the point for the situation in which we now find ourselves was the attack on faithful paired bonding—the ghost of *Playboy* still lurking in our supposed liberation. How well I remember young lesbians sneering at long-time committed women partners as "hopeless monogs." How deeply I regret the night when, after much talk and wine, I bitterly chastised a gay Christian couple with an earnest desire to live in something like marriage for buying into patriarchal oppression. In those days I was, like so many other angry young idealists, a believer in sexual communism—no one should claim to own anyone else's body. As I come to the end of my forties and watch people I love struggling with AIDS and with the ongoing nightmare of sexual abuse and harassment, I see all too clearly the fruit of an ideology that tried to account for sex without love, for love without sin.

The collapse of the part of this ideology that promoted fluidity and choice in sexual desire, and its replacement with determinism, seems to be part of a growing tendency to bestow a pseudo-scientific benediction upon all kinds of conditions and behaviors, under the rubric of genetic causality. Progressives and conservatives have been equally willing to fall back on (yet undiscovered) genes to explain persistent and contentious moral and political issues, as the debates over the book *The Bell Curve* demonstrate. Historian Carl Degler has shown how since Darwin the intellectual response to human suffering and inequality has swung from nature to nurture—from assertions of unalterable innate characteristics in humans to assertions of innate human plasticity shaped primarily by external forces—and back again.[9] Today we are in the confused position of refusing to acknowledge that nature might have something to do with, say, girls' math performance, while claiming on the other hand that it exercises inexorable power on the object of love and desire. The secular sexual ideology of the last quarter of the twentieth century, with its increasing demands that the pleasure of the sexual act can and must be separated from other elements of sexuality, such as emotional intimacy and reproduction, informs our debate about the place of sexuality in the church as much as the secular craving for determinism.

∞

Thus it has come about that in our discussions of sexuality theology has become captive to ideology. And while the biological explanations of the basis of sexual preference that I have been examining are clearly, even when professed by serious Christians, influenced by secular ideologies, that does not mean that the traditionalist view is not. Turning from the "Koinonia" document to the second one, "An Affirmation," which expresses the traditional position, I find a response that is no less ideological. The bishops who wrote and signed this statement expect that moral agency rather than biological determinism or political expedience is at the center of human identity—and yes, even that expectation is in a sense ideological. They too assume a kind of determinism, that divine determinism which must always give us pause. Although they do not describe their reasoning (one of the failures of "An Affirmation," as I see it), I am familiar enough with the underpinnings of the argument to discern the shape of their assumptions.

The order of creation implies a preference ("God's plan") for heterosexuality, an ecology of sexuality in which male and female of nearly every vertebrate species pair and reproduce. Created beings thereby enter into the ongoing work of continuing the creation. Whether anyone is inherently "determined" to be heterosexual or homosexual is left open; the preference for heterosexual expression of desire is a consequence rather than a cause. Heterosexual practice is not valued in and of itself, even though the rhetoric may suggest that at times; rather, it fulfills certain conditions within creation, most specifically reproduction but also the development of social structures in which the new generations that result from reproduction are nurtured. If one is to honor the structure of creation and participate in its ongoing life, then the embrace of heterosexuality is the embrace of the "givenness" of the created order. In sum, the traditionalist decision on behalf of heterosexuality must be seen as a consequence of other, prior decisions about creation itself.

Those who find they cannot participate in this ecology of sexuality are nevertheless called upon to honor it both in principle and in practice; no alternative structures are offered. Celibacy may not be a structure, exactly, but it is more than a "lifestyle." It is at least a vocation which has been followed by Christians as unlike as male Italian hermits and Shaker eldresses. While celibacy may be the best alternative that the traditional position on sexuality has offered, and while such an alternative is valuable in many ways, it can't be treated casually. The emotional intimacy that committed sexual love particularly provides is, I would argue, as much a part of the created order as reproduction: it is part of who we are as human beings. In being required to relinquish such intimacy, persons who understand their affectional-sexual orientation to be homosexual are asked to be not schizophrenic but schizogenic—formed by splitting, by cleavage in themselves.

To abandon both the hope of offspring and the possibility of physical intimacy splits or cleaves persons in a particularly poignant fashion. Their situation is, as the lives of many celibates have shown, not intolerable, but that kind of life requires much, not least a studied indifference to the sexual pressures of contemporary culture. In monasticism the ongoing spiritual care needed by people committed to celibacy was understood, if not always wisely handled; but today organized support for celibates is rare. I have heard again and again how agonizingly lonely that life can be. It is not surprising that many people find the expectation of celibacy to be a hard saying.

More overtly, the bishops who signed "An Affirmation" confront the reigning secular sexual ideology, arguing that responsibility and self-control, not pleasure and self-fulfillment, are the "conscious ideational constructs" by which sexuality is best understood and guided. Their ideology of sexuality thus refuses the consumerist bent of the postmodern West; they want no truck with a culture that Harold Fickett once described as a place where anything is deemed moral if you can pay for it with a credit card. Again, a studied indifference to the assumptions and enticements of contemporary culture is necessary. The traditionalist bishops thus wind up insisting on an approach to sexuality that, as another bishop put it, "will not fly."

Why will it not fly? Because most of us in the West—even those who might be called cultural conservatives like me—have become inured to the fluidity of sexual desire and practice that is a hallmark of our culture; if we are not participants in it, we are at least spectators. The amount of patience, love, and persistence required to direct our culture into a revision of sexual monism for the twenty-first century is certainly present in our church. But those are the very energies in the church that are now typically, and perhaps not incorrectly, addressing the daily human lot of massacre, disease, and despair. What genuinely consenting adults do in private seems less urgent somehow.

Moral agency is a very good thing. I applaud its being emphasized. But how it is understood in relation to love and desire in practice is a problem. We must ask if there is a definitive tie between the kind of natural-law observations that a defense of exclusive heterosexuality employs, and moral agency. Can the expectation of heterosexual practice be understood as a clear and binding correlative of the strict moral expectations of responsibility and self-control? I would say that in fact the opposite is true: moral agency is the result of discipline and struggle, empowered, a Christian must add, by grace. It most assuredly is not something any of us are born with. Reproductive fecundity, which is a given of creation, is one of the very things that human beings have developed moral codes and practices to control and regulate. There is no intrinsic reason why moral effort and responsibility and self-control cannot equally apply to those whose affectional inclinations are not within the bounds of reproductive ecology. My earlier caveat applies again: biology alone is not the last word. Which brings me to the problem that I believe the church ought to be addressing.

∞

What is worth noticing about the two response statements—and the place where they may be able to conquer ideology and speak theologically—is what they agree on, which is the faithful and permanent character they expect of sexual love relationships. This agreement is remarkable because if there is one thing that we cannot honestly expect of couples any more, homosexual or heterosexual, it is faithfulness and permanence. That we ought to expect Christians to cultivate these virtues is not the point; that they are no longer modeled or taught is. Christopher Webber's recent book *Re-Inventing Marriage*, with its wise and helpful plan for a premarital program modelled on a monastic novitiate, not only discusses, but demonstrates by its very existence, how the church lost its way in presenting the meaning and requirements of Christian marriage.[10] While there may be some notions about love and sex that we are well rid of, there are others that we desperately need to know again.[11]

A theologian friend remarked to me recently, "The problem in the church is not homosexuality. It's promiscuity." Exactly. Promiscuity is the real disease that the secular culture has sold us, and it is killing us. The decline of faithfulness cuts a broad swath across male and female, gay and straight, as does sexual harassment. I do not need here to rehearse the dismal stories from church after church, of all denominations and styles of churchmanship, where promiscuity has destroyed lives, ripped congregations apart, and made a scandal of the gospel. We know these events: some of us have lived through them. I know I am not alone when I say that I would be grateful if all concerned would join together to speak—publicly, fervently, and above all hopefully—about faithfulness and permanence in sexual love relationships as an eschatological sign of God's faithfulness to us. We can't just tell people to be monogamous because they'll go to hell if they don't; that's about 180 degrees away from the gospel as I understand it. We are not faithful in our lifetime pairings because we're prudes or because we're scared: we are faithful because God is like that. That's the meaning of Ezekiel 16 and Ephesians 5, and that, I think, is an example of what Jesus meant when he told us to be holy as God is holy.

That old devil Screwtape may have a cautionary word for us here. Remember when Screwtape advises his nephew Wormwood how to sabotage his patient's conversion to Christianity?

> If the patient knows that the woman with the absurd hat is a fanatical bridgeplayer or the man with the squeaky boots is a miser and an extortionist—then your task is so much the easier. All you then have to do is keep out of [the patient's] mind the question, "If I, being what I am, can consider that I am in some sense a Christian, why should the different vices of those in the next pew prove that their religion is mere hypocrisy and convention?"[12]

No matter how one defines the vices of one's neighbor in the pew, Screwtape's counsel remains in force: the surest way to destroy faith is to devote as much time as possible to contemplating the wrong done by everyone else. I do not mean, God forbid, that we should be "nonjudgmental." It is most assuredly the proper role of the church and her individual members to seek to discern the will of God in every element of our public and private life, and to enunciate the same. But if it seems "good to the Holy Spirit and to us" (note: "to *us*," not "to me") that we call another Christian to account, it must be done in a spirit of graciousness, generosity, and humility. Otherwise our concern with the real or supposed sins of others becomes a screen by which we obscure our own desperate need for a Savior.

Meanwhile, academic theorists of sexuality have a new idea: "All gender is performance." Sexuality, and all its expressions, are enactions and manifestations of one's relationship to the world and one's body. So perhaps in my monogamous marriage I am enacting and manifesting to the world my conviction that there is joy in faithfulness, my hope for the reconciliation of opposites, and my acceptance of the eschatological hope that child-bearing announces and embodies. How gay Christians may be able to use this idea to enhance their own spirituality is their work, and God go with them as they try. But if we really are "one body and one Spirit" then we can't, any of us, go it alone. I hope that "old" monogamous couples are going to be willing to advise and encourage those, straight or gay, who are new to the discipline of faithful commitment. I hope that gay Christians, new Christians, and burned-out Christians will not look at the scandals of sexual misbehavior in the church and assume that fidelity and truthfulness are virtues to which they need not strive to conform. And I hope that we—all of us, without sex or sexual preference or race or churchmanship dividing us—will stand together and challenge this society to know that God in Jesus Christ has sent us a high calling to live out. The hope, faithfulness, and self-surrender that his cross and resurrection uniquely embody are the marks by which we must be known. For ultimately how we live and who we are refer not to ourselves, but to Christ, who died for us while we were yet sinners. If we say that all sexuality is about performance, we who are named as the followers of Christ must acknowledge another "performance," that of our God who became human for our sakes.

Time alone will tell whether this tantalizing concept of gender as performance will lead us to a new theology of sexuality that will free us to be the moral agents that I believe we as Christians are called to be, or whether it will prove to be another ideological straightjacket from which we the church will have to struggle free in years to come.

NOTES

The author is most grateful to Charling Chang Fagan and Barbara Hickey of the Sarah Lawrence College Library for research assistance.

1. Louis J. Kern, *An Ordered Love: Sex Roles and Sexuality in Victorian Utopias* (Chapel Hill: University of North Carolina Press, 1981), 6.

2. In 1993 I was invited to address the Ecumenical Association of Third World Theologians (EATWOT) at Bishop Tucker Theological College, Mukono, Uganda. My talk compared North American and Ugandan ecumenism. The questions following nearly all referred to sexuality, especially abortion and homosexuality. The majority of those present had studied in either North America or the United Kingdom, and they generally felt the American church was on the verge of apostasy. I report this; my own views may be inferred from this essay.

3. See Jonathan Weiner, review of *The Science of Desire: The Search for the Gay Gene* in *The New Republic* (2 January 1995); David Fernbach, "Xq28 Marks the Spot," *New Statesman and Society* (30 July 1993); and the critique of this research by Neil Risch *et al.*, "Male Sexual Orientation and Genetic Evidence," with a reply by Dean Hamer *et al.*, *Science* (24 December 1993).

4. Myron Hofer, "Behind the Curve," *The New York Times* (26 December 1994): 39. Hofer gives an example of Siamese cats: if raised in a warm room as young kittens, they do not develop the characteristic dark points on their paws and ears. The dark-point trait is genetic, but only comes into play in a specific environment.

5. Stanley Hauerwas, "Killing Compassion," in *Dispatches from the Front* (Durham, N.C.: Duke University Press, 1994), 164.

6. According to John Cornwell, head of the Science and Human Dimension project at Cambridge, England, "The prospect of a supermarket for designer genes—both for the sick and the healthy—is not far off, and along with it a new set of social and ethical questions....Should we be allowed to choose the intelligence level, the height, the hair color, the sexual orientation of our children? Is a new dark age of eugenics looming?" Quoted in "While We're At It," *First Things* (October 1995): 89.

7. See Barbara Ehrenreich, "The Gap Between Gay and Straight," *Time* (10 May 1992): 76.

8. Charlotte Wolff, *Love Between Women* (London: Duckworth Press, 1971), 66.

9. Carl Degler, *In Search of Human Nature: The Decline and Revival of Darwinism in American Social Thought* (New York: Oxford University Press, 1991).

10. Christopher Webber, *Re-Inventing Marriage* (Harrisburg, Penn.: Morehouse Publishing, 1994). Webber is, unfortunately, strangely silent on marriage as an embodiment of eschatological hope.

11. Stanley Hauerwas, for instance: "Marriage for Christians, after all, is not a necessity, since we believe our lives as Christians do not require marriage for the simple reason that the true family is the Church" ("Killing Compassion," 167). Also: "Marriage provides the set of practices and expectations that allow us over a lifetime to name our lives together as love" ("Killing Compassion," 168).

12. C. S. Lewis, *The Screwtape Letters* (New York: Macmillan, 1943), 18.

∞ Timothy F. Sedgwick

The Transformation of Sexuality and the Challenge of Conscience

D ialogue on sexuality poses two sorts of moral questions for the church. First, what gives wholeness to sexual relationships? Specifically, what are the purposes of sexual relationships, and how should we form our relationships in order to realize these purposes? The second sort of question is rather different. What are the obligations or responsibilities of the church and its members toward honoring and supporting relationships? What range of relationships should be accepted? And why do members of the church—or why should they—care about what others do sexually? Questions of this kind are ecclesial. They are often ignored in the attempt to make sense of sexuality itself, yet they are essential to the church's understanding not only of Christian faith but of human sexuality as well.

These two questions—what is normative for human sexual relationships and how should the church deal with differences of judgment—are not theoretical questions. They are posed most poignantly and practically by gay and lesbian couples who have asked their communities of faith to celebrate and bless their vows to form a life together. For these couples, their vows should be celebrated because they see that their sexual identities are given and good, that their identities in Christ have been given in the church, and that they have honored and deepened both of these identities in their sexual relationship with another person of the same sex.[1]

In order to honor the consciences of gay and lesbian Christians and those who share their convictions, the church and its members must hear first-hand accounts of the integrity of these relationships. In hearing the testimony of the consciences of others, the second set of questions needs to be addressed. What does it mean for the church when persons in good conscience remain in conflict over the support that should be given to same-sex relationships? How then is the church to govern such a conflict of conscience? How are norms for action established? And what happens when norms are transgressed?

In the first part of this essay I want raise the question of what is normative in sexual relations, how sexual relationships may bear witness to and deepen the Christian relationship to God. Such an account will make sense of the claims of the consciences of gay and lesbian couples that the church should celebrate and bless their vows to form a life together. But precisely because this account of human sexuality makes plausible—even if it does not prove—the morality of same-sex relations, it needs to be placed in the larger context of what the church should do when its members are in conflict as to what actions are in accord with Christian faith. In the second part of the essay, therefore, I will focus on questions of conscience and community and how these should be addressed by the church.

Christian Transformation of Human Sexuality

Understandings of a historical tradition and a historical faith can only be developed retrospectively, if you will, through the rear-view mirror. For example, coming to see Jewish and Christian understandings of religious faith as radically monotheistic is only possible by looking back and seeing where the community of faith has come from in order to see the central direction in which its faith was directed. Likewise, Hebraic and Christian understandings of human sexuality require looking back, beginning with a description of what has been normative for Christian understandings and practices and then seeing within these what is essential in how sexuality and God are related. It is theologically and ethically as well as historically naive to claim that tradition speaks with a singular voice. Just as there is no golden age, there are no golden tablets.

Differences in the understanding and practice of human sexuality in both Judaism and Christianity can be seen in the strands of tradition that are present in scripture. Taking these different and at times conflicting understandings and practices into account, what is normative is what is central or required so that sexual relationships reflect and deepen holiness, which is to say, so that sexual relationships are sanctified and we are made whole and connected.

In the ancient Near East in general and in the beginnings of the Hebrew people in particular, sexuality was experienced as part of the great rhythm of life. Sexual symbols of desire and procreation, birthing, intercourse, and death interpreted and connected the world in "an unending interplay of mutual correspondences."[2] As depicted in the creation account that opens the book of Genesis, all the world is created in complementary opposites, opposites that depend upon each other and together yield life. Darkness and light, sky and water, water and land together produce the seasons and the conditions for seeds to grow and bear fruit. Fish, birds, and animals inhabit this world with the blessing "be fruitful and multiply" (1:22). And so humans are an extension of this world. Created male and female, they too are to "be fruitful and multiply, and fill the earth and subdue it" (1:28).

This picture reflects a natural, organic world infused, permeated, with desire. Human identity—the experience of and participation in what is enduring for the human person—is given in the participation in these cosmic processes. Emil Durkheim in *The Elementary Forms of the Religious Life* observed this sense of the sacred in the totemism and orgiastic rites of the aboriginal peoples of Australia.[3] The same sense of sexuality was alive in the world of late antiquity into which Christianity came. Humans, as Peter Brown describes,

> felt pulsing in their own bodies the same fiery spirit that covered the hills every year with newborn lambs and that ripened the crops, in seasonal love-play, as the spring winds embraced the fertile ears. Above them, the same fire glowed in the twinkling stars. Their bodies, and their sexual drives, shared directly in the unshakable perpetuity of an immense universe, through which the gods played exuberantly.[4]

Paul Ricoeur calls this archaic sense of sexuality "infra-personal," literally below or beneath the personal. Instead of being personalized, sexuality tied people to what they experienced as "the cosmic liturgy of vegetative sacredness and to the invitation it extends to individuals to lose themselves in the flux of generations and regenerations." In its most fundamental expression, procreation "remains fundamentally irresponsible, hazardous, animal."[5] More specifically, sexual desire is open-ended, experienced as a matter of insatiable hunger. This is a hunger for transcendence, for what would give the experience of participation in the powers of creation, powers that were before and will continue after the death of individual persons. From a later perspective, sexual desire appears disordered. Desire in itself lacks order and will move the human person to action that will in itself makes impossible a unity of meaning and purpose. This has led many, most influentially Augustine, to identify desire itself with sin; at the least, desire is the occasion for sin. But whichever perspective is taken, sexual desire and pleasure are never entirely lost from consciousness. Sexuality, says Ricoeur, is after all a matter of *eros* and not *logos*. It marks the body of desire and not the prescribed order of reason.[6] Such is the deep mystery of sexuality, of its restless longing and of its ecstatic character.

Human sexuality, however, is more than a cosmic-vital force. Looking back through the practices of marriage, sexuality is also "a language without words," a language of "mutual recognition" which acknowledges man and woman as persons. This is the dimension of sexuality Ricoeur calls tenderness.[7] Sexuality expresses love, love as recognition of and care for the other. We may speak of these two dimensions of sexuality as that of desire and of tenderness.

As in all transformations of human life, the transformation of sexuality from the infra-personal to the personal is not the substitution of something new for something old, something personal for something archaic. Changes in sexuality take up the old into the new, never all at once but in mutations and permutations that all but imitate the biological processes of reproduction itself.[8] Sometimes desire is forbidden, addressed as a matter of the unruly will, as in the ascetic tradition for example. Or, alternatively, in reaction to the unruly experience of sexual desire, desire is sublimated in an idealized love so that what is desired is not flesh and blood, the lover for the beloved, but a world together, in harmony, above and beyond bodily desire. Desire and tenderness are then complements, as in the courtly love tradition or in the romantic vision of lover and beloved. Perhaps the play between desire and tenderness is always some combination of denial and idealization. Never, though, is desire lost, eliminated, or removed. Always sexuality is the experience of bodily desire as it is formed by specific practices and understandings of human life.

The personalization of human sexuality develops as sexual desire is tied to human purposes that transcend the immediacy of bodily desire. Because these purposes express what it means to be a person, they personalize sexuality. Moreover, these purposes themselves undergo critique and transformation as what was enduring proves finite and fleeting. In this transformation, desire is enlarged so that what is desired is not simply the body but the body that embodies purposes that draw the person beyond him or herself. In this sense, sexuality reflects religious faith, what ultimately provides a transcendence that is enduring or, in more theological language, the purposes of God and so what persons can entrust themselves to. From the point of view of the faithful, the transformation of human sexuality is a matter of the revelation of God.

The integral connection of human sexuality and forming a people is reflected in the very beginnings of Genesis with its account of creation that concludes with the mandate to humans to "be fruitful and multiply, and fill the earth and subdue it"(1:28).[9] For some archaic peoples procreation was not understood as arising from sexual intercourse, but here through intercourse humans are responsible for procreation. Human sexuality is personalized, joined to human purposes and values. In ancient Israel, though, sexuality was joined not just with procreation but with the formation of a people. This connection is reflected in the laws of Deuteronomy and in the Law of Purity and the Holiness Code in Leviticus (11-16 and 17-26). These laws circumscribe sexual behavior in such a way that sexuality was experienced as inseparable from the social relationships that constituted and sustained Israel's being a people. At one level sexuality was a matter of property and purity.[10] Divorce, as regulated by the laws in Deuteronomy, was a male prerogative or right exercised when acts of sexual wrongdoing or "impropriety" (Deut. 24:1) had been committed—acts, that is, in violation of the laws of purity and property. In terms of property, adultery was wrong because it was a matter of theft. Incest was wrong because it was a violation of the family hierarchy. Prostitution was wrong because a woman had violated her family's and her future husband's rightful claims on her. All such actions directly or indirectly threatened social identity and were therefore forbidden. In this way sexuality was personalized in the sense that it subserved the value of forming and being a people. In turn, sexual desire for another was experienced as inseparable from these social goods, as tied to the good or as a violation of the good, as permissible or forbidden.

This joining of sexuality to procreation and progeny increased in post-rabbinic Judaism. In the face of assimilation upon return from exile in Babylonia, Judaism put more and more emphasis on procreation, on bearing children, to such an extent that infertility itself became grounds for divorce:

> Jewish teachers agreed that the purpose of marriage is to "increase and multiply"; that one must accept whatever facilitates procreation, including divorce and polygamy; and that one must reject whatever hinders procreation—even a marriage itself, in the case of an infertile wife.[11]

Such proscriptions sought to guarantee the survival and identity of the people by making sure that things did not get "out of place."[12] Human sexuality was subordinated to the family and its place in the divine economy.

The Hebraic traditions I have been referring to, reflecting what may be called a clan ethic, were edited and written by a writer or writers in the sixth century B.C. This "author" has been called the Priestly writer because "he" reflects the priestly interest in the temple and in regulations that would ensure the identity of the Hebrew people. Personalizing sexuality in terms of procreation and progeny, however, was not the only way of shaping and understanding sexuality. Immediately following the Priestly account of creation (Gen. 1:1–2:4a), a further account of creation (Gen. 2:4b–3:24) tells the story of creation in terms of man and woman as the first human couple and of their loss of paradise as the beginning of human history in the world. This narrative, called the Jahwist account because in it God is named Jahweh, was given its edited form some three hundred years earlier than the Priestly account[13] and reflects something of a vision of human life apart from the "salvation history" in which salvation is tied to the nation and becoming a people.

In the Jahwist account of creation, the human one (*'adam*) is formed from the dust of the ground (*'adamah*). God then declares, "It is not good that *'adam* should be alone" (Gen. 2:18). So the human one is cast into a deep sleep. Woman is taken from the human's rib, and in this creation man ('*is*) and woman ('*issa*) are formed, only now distinguished as male and female. From one flesh they are called to unity. Here, instead of being tied either to nature or to forming a people, human sexuality is tied to companionship. As the image of the rib taken from the side of the human one suggests, woman and man are made for each other. "This at last is bone of my bones and flesh of my flesh" (Gen. 2:23). In light of this account of the creation of man and woman, marriage is understood to be created for the sake of companionship. In the relationship of husband and wife, male and female become one flesh. The Jahwist concludes with the avowal of this fundamental purpose as the good of sexuality: "Now they were both naked, the man and his wife, but they had no feeling of shame towards one another" (Gen. 2:25, *NEB*). Here sexuality is personalized in terms of the other person. Sexuality is tied to the acknowledgment and embrace of the other. Sexual desire is not narrowly a matter of having the other: it is the desire to be loved and to love.

These two traditions, Priestly and Jahwist, reflect two central ways in which sexuality has been related to human persons, first in Judaism and then in Christianity. One tradition emphasizes the procreative end or purpose of human sexuality; the other, older tradition emphasizes companionship. Each tradition may be developed in various ways.[14] Procreation, for example, may be broadened so that the meaning of sexual intercourse is not narrowly a matter of biological reproduction but expresses a broader purpose, what has been called generativity.[15] The meaning of companionship may be likewise deepened, for example, from being the enjoyment of another to being an unconditional care for that person, from being a matter of self-fulfillment to being a love that is fulfilled in the other.

Procreation, companionship, and sexual desire need not be and were not always opposed, though in the tradition desire was in fact largely distinguished from procreation and companionship as itself sinful or the occasion for sin. The exception in the canon of Hebrew scripture is the Song of Songs, where desire is exalted as good and at least an end in itself.[16] The dominant tradition in Judaism, moreover, subordinated companionship to procreation and progeny. Sexual relationships were, for example, a matter of companionship, of enjoyment and care, only when they were placed in the context of forming a family and, more broadly, a people who as heirs may prosper. Companionship was in this sense included within a larger contract of mutual expectations and conditions that had to be fulfilled and that are appropriately called patriarchal. Desire was shaped by these ends, being joined with what was permitted and what was forbidden. Practices and proscriptions thus consecrated sexual desire with meanings and expectations such that pleasure could never be a simple good or an end in itself. The danger of unformed desire was then replaced by the danger of idolatry, of identifying some set of purposes, practices, and proscriptions as God-given ends in themselves so that these alone were desired.

For Christians the further transformation of sexuality is given in Jesus' challenge to Jewish understandings of human sexuality. In the gospel of Mark, Jesus responds to the question of whether it is lawful for a man to divorce his wife by quoting the Jahwist account of creation:

> From the beginning of creation, "God made them male and female." "For this reason a man shall leave his father and mother and be joined to his wife, and the two shall become one flesh." So they are no longer two, but one flesh. Therefore what God has joined together, let no one separate. (Mark 10:6-8)

In this and parallel sayings[17] Jesus claims a fundamental equality between men and women and sets forth the primacy of companionship over procreation and progeny. The radicalness of his teaching in this regard may be understood as lying in the difference between contract and covenant.

Jesus' call to love one another as it was in the beginning of creation is to overthrow the most fundamental contract upon which society is based: as man and woman, husband and wife perform their respective parts children will be born and, in turn, bear the identity of the parents into the future. But Jesus claims that men and women, instead of gaining identity and fulfillment in the future through children, share in eternity now, in their love for one another. It finally makes no difference what the future brings. Sexuality is to be tied not to pleasure, not even to procreation, but only to the embrace and care of the other. *Agape* as a love that serves the other, embraces and cares for the other for the other's own sake, becomes then the chief image of this relationship.[18] The other is to be loved without conditions. Therein is grace given; therein is the kingdom of God.

In sum, this transformation or conversion of human sexuality replaces *contract* with *covenant*. This is reflected in a transformation of marriage. No longer is marriage grounded first of all on an agreement in which something is done in order to achieve or realize something else. Instead, marriage is a matter of mutual commitment to love one another, for better or for worse, regardless of any consequences. The relationship is unconditional, without conditions, and hence a matter of steadfast love and fidelity marked by acceptance and trust. In marriage this is expressed in the commitment to abide with the other, to love until death.[19] Love then is founded in the relationship between husband and wife but is not turned in upon themselves and their future, together or through their children. Instead, such love turns outward to embrace and care for others. This is exemplified in the change in the relationship between parents and children. Children are not the fulfillment of sexuality and marriage, the means of securing identity in the future. They are uniquely other, different, with their own gifts and skills, their own distinctive sense of the world, their own humor and beauty. Like Abraham, called by God to sacrifice Isaac, husband and wife give up children as the basis of their hope in the future only to have children given back, but now not as their hope but as gifts from God. Like the beloved, they are not extensions to the self but call members of the family beyond themselves. They call others to acknowledge them, to care for them, and in love to be drawn out with them into a future marked by such love.

This vision of marriage as covenant is at best what Christians have called an eschatological reality.[20] The reality may be realized here and now, but only in part and never fully. Sometimes sexual desire may be only controlled and frustrated or repressed and sublimated. Ideally, however, desire is integrated into the broader purposes of life, providing both the energy and verve that animate these purposes. We live into covenants. We come to know another person only over time. We are able to acknowledge another in his or her uniqueness, as different, ever more fully only as we abide with him or her over time. In turn, we come to support and care, enjoy and delight in the other only over time. Only over time do we discover that the mystery of the other person is far greater than we had imagined.

There is no straight-line progress in such matters of love. Where relationships deepen as covenants they do so through the crises that form a life together. The danger is always that such a love will fail to enlarge, to draw us beyond our immediate concerns and goods. Instead of integrated in a covenanted love of another person as person, desire is narrowly focused on some extrinsic good such as children, success, or self-sufficiency. Alternatively, desire runs amok so that the human person is left scattered, as in the Don Juan syndrome for which immediate pleasure is everything.

Marriage itself does not ensure the integration of love and desire. So, while Jesus calls us to the original intent of marriage, he also challenges the institution of marriage itself and commends celibacy. In the gospel of Matthew, after he has rejected any grounds for divorce, the disciples observe, "If such is the case of a man with his wife, it is better not to marry." Knowing the difficulties of not falling back into the narrowing of the marriage relationship to some implicit contract to secure identity in the future, Jesus says:

> Not everyone can accept this teaching, but only those to whom it is given. For there are eunuchs who have been so from birth, and there are eunuchs who have been made eunuchs by others, and there are eunuchs who have made themselves eunuchs for the sake of the kingdom of heaven. Let anyone accept this who can. (Matt. 19:10-12)

Jesus challenges marriage and all human institutions because they all may be obstacles to responding to God. As told in the gospel of Luke, he says, "Blessed are the barren, and the wombs that never bore, and the breasts that never nursed" (Luke 23:29). Jesus even goes so far as to identify celibacy with eternal life and marriage with the opposite: "Those who belong to this age marry and are given in marriage, but those are considered worthy of a place in that age and in the resurrection from the dead neither marry nor are given in marriage" (Luke 20:34-35). Elaine Pagels writes:

> By subordinating the obligation to procreate, rejecting divorce, and implicitly sanctioning monogamous relationships, Jesus reverses traditional priorities declaring, in effect, that other obligations, including marital ones, are now more important than procreation. Even more startling, Jesus endorses—and exemplifies—a new possibility and one he says is even better: rejecting both marriage and procreation in favor of voluntary celibacy, for the sake of following him into the new age.[21]

Jesus' call to celibacy is among the most radical expressions of the gospel, a call to give up everything for the sake of the kingdom of God, to take up the cross in renunciation of maintaining the world in order to be raised into God. What matters is the unreserved giving up of oneself in the care and embrace of the world about us. This response is a radical expression of faith in that such a way of life gives a singularly full expression to the deepest intention of faith: not denying the world but making the human self available to God. For ascetics, then, the traditional vows lead to hospitality, the giving up of oneself in the embrace of the other.[22] For others, this vivid sense and taste of God's presence is to be lived within the social order as people find themselves members of families, heads of households, neighbors, laborers, soldiers, and citizens.

The challenge of faith is to make faith incarnate in daily life, to deepen the experience of God's presence among us. Where sexual relationships are concerned, this has meant marriage. Not that marriage has been one thing, or that marriage has been uniformly pure and holy; rather, marriage in its development as a practice and as an institution has borne the vision and reality of faith incarnate even as it was consecrating the social order with its sinful ends and hierarchies. What has been normative is not the institution of marriage itself, any more than procreation and progeny. Instead, as Jesus makes clear, marriage is holy as a covenant in which the love between two persons is manifest as it draws each beyond the self in welcome, care, and joy in each other and in the world beyond. Rejecting traditional proscriptions against sexual relationships between homosexual persons is, in this light, no more radical than Jesus' challenge to what were the traditional, sacred practices of marriage in Israel.

The foregoing account of Christian faith and human sexuality is, like all such arguments, an attempt to make sense of the variety of particular practices and understandings that constitute the Hebraic-Christian tradition.

Central to this account is the integral relationship between understandings and practices. Practices shape our experience and form our understandings as much as understandings shape experience and lead to the critique and revision of practices. Sexuality is not one thing, then, but has a history formed at its core by the institution of marriage as that institution has undergone change and transformation. Judgment as to what is normative is thus a matter of judging what the purposes of human life are and what practices are essential to these purposes.

It may be argued, as some Roman Catholic moral theologians have done, that marriage open to procreation and the raising of children is essential to the sanctification of sexuality.[23] This argument rests on a judgment to the effect that, apart from these particular practices and prescriptions, human love turns inward upon itself. In contrast, others have argued that the human person is sanctified and grows in love in sexual relationships outside of marriage where there is equality and the intent to respect and care for the other.[24] Specific judgments like these reflect broader judgments on the relationship of purposes and practices. The account given here is not the only account that may be given. However, to the extent that this account makes sense of human sexuality, as formed in the Hebraic-Christian tradition, it offers one way in which to make sense of the claims of gay and lesbian couples who are convinced that the church should celebrate and bless their vows to form a life together. The argument is that, given the judgment that sexual orientation is for some given and not a matter of choice, *if what is normative in sexual relationships lies in covenants of love formed by a life together and not necessarily the ends of procreation and progeny, same-sex relationships may be blessed and celebrated.*

Issues of Conscience and Community

What I have said about sexual relations for the church is not unassailable—there are no doubt reasons for disagreement, whether based on scripture, tradition, or human understanding. What is significant about this account is that it provides an understanding of human sexuality that makes plausible the claims of conscience of those who seek to bless and celebrate gay and lesbian couples who have committed themselves to each other in a life together. Beyond making sense of human sexuality and so informing the conscience of individuals, the account given here raises for members of the church the further, different question of what to do when there are conflicts of conscience within the community of faith. To be in communion requires the respect and support of the consciences of others. Thus we are led from the first to the second set of questions posed earlier.

Individuals must reach some conclusion about their own convictions, about what they believe is right and wrong and what they believe is the basis of their membership in the community, but the community must also decide what to do. Questions about respect and support of conscience arise not for isolated individuals, but for communities of faith. And for communities the question is not a restricted one, a question of whether an action is right or wrong. It is a question of how far particular congregations, and the church at large, can and should respect and support differences in the consciences of their members.

Persons who fail to honor their consciences act against themselves. Their self-understanding and life are thus separated. Alienation and loss of identity are the result. For this reason, moral theology ranks the honoring of conscience among the most fundamental of obligations, both for individuals and for the community.[25] Yet the further question remains: how much acceptance and support can the community provide and remain a community? In this sense, the conflict of conscience poses the larger question of the nature of Christian faith that binds the church together as a communion of individuals and as a communion of particular communities. As Wayne Meeks has asked, restating the question of the early church, "How much unity is achievable? How much diversity is tolerable?"[26]

Differences between Christians and between Christian churches regarding the use of force may provide a helpful example. There is nearly universal agreement among Christians that individuals and communities are called to honor the absolute worth and dignity of human life. For those who embrace some form of just-war theory, this obligation has meant the use of force in order to defend the innocent against unjust attack. For those who stand in the pacifist tradition, the only way to honor the worth and dignity of human life is to renounce the use of force entirely.[27] These two very different ways of working out in practice the call to honor human life have not, however, necessarily led to two separate communities of faith. Instead, in what have been called churches or church denominations (as distinct from sects or sectarian denominations) both the pacifist and the just-war stance have been claimed as Christian responses. These two sides differ in their judgments regarding what Christians should do, while sharing the more fundamental conviction regarding the worth and dignity of human life. They see their differences not as a matter of faithfulness but as a matter of judgment regarding what faithfulness demands. Those who differ have thus been able to respect and support the consciences of others, and have remained in communion.

Gay and lesbian relationships raise for the church much the same question as the one about the use of force: to what extent can differences in understanding and practice be accepted and supported? If a church is to be a communion of communities, it must move toward resolution when matters of conscience deeply divide the community; otherwise, the church becomes simply a collection of separate communities, each going its own way, bound together only by toleration. Respect for the consciences of its members requires something more. The church as a communion of communities must move toward a decision whether they will be a communion on the basis of affirming a diversity on a matter of conflict or, alternatively, a communion bound by particular judgments.

A first task in addressing conflict is educational. Its aim is to promote understanding and to ensure that members of the church understand each other. Education, of course, is not neutral. There is no value-free pedagogy. How something is taught will itself convey an understanding of Christian identity, of what is at the heart of Christian faith and how this is related to more specific matters of ethics such as sexual relationships. How questions of gay and lesbian relationships are studied and explored already reflects a set of assumptions about what stands at the center of Christian faith. Should I begin with what scripture says about homosexuality, with what gay men and lesbians confess about their own self-understanding, with understandings from the natural and social sciences, or with some combination of these sources or some other sources? How this question is answered will reflect an answer to the larger question of what is centrally Christian.

In the education of conscience the church may hope that it will come to a common understanding of its life in faith, even in the midst of differences. Such a final unity, however, is not ours to enjoy in this world. The church must therefore address the difficult question of how to address and resolve conflict—the question of governance. Regardless of the outcome, some individuals and communities will very likely find that as a matter of conscience they will have to separate themselves from the larger church. Failure to enable such separation—failure to give definition to the church in addressing issues of conflict—is failure to respect the integrity of conscience and communities.

Specific questions of governance focus on decision-making and discipline. How can we come to decisions, not about our individual convictions, but about what we should do as a community, as a particular congregation, and as a larger church? How then do we proceed to ensure that individuals and congregations are bound by such decisions? How do we exercise discipline that is pastorally sensitive to the consciences of others but maintains integrity, wholeness, in our relationships with each other so that individuals and congregations support each other?

Such questions are especially difficult in Anglicanism, which throughout its history has given broad scope to the rule of conscience in the interpretation of doctrine and in the exercise of personal life. Anglican churches reflect the English tradition of common law. In this tradition the rule of law is not, as in Roman law, a matter of principles that are understood to be based on the nature of things and are applied to individual cases. Instead, law arises from individual cases themselves and as such represents the accumulation of a people's practical wisdom. New cases are addressed in light of past cases which, having some similarity, may cast light on what would be a fitting response now.[28] Authority—the legitimate voice to speak and decide upon an issue—is in this sense borne by the community and dispersed through its life. Anglicans thus look to the common consent of the faithful, the *sensus fidelium*, rather than to the authoritarian teachings of the church.

As Roman Catholics see so clearly, Anglican churches have no formal magisterium, no teaching office in which matters of conscience are formally addressed and resolved, even for the time being. The ideal of consensus places almost all the burden in addressing differences at the informal level of relationships as they may be aided by educational materials and more general discussion. In the past, consensus on a range of issues has been sustained because of the cultural homogeneity of the churches of the Anglican communion, combined with a general assent to what were at least the *pro forma* hierarchical lines of authority. Such consensus has always been unstable but has become more so because of the increasing diversity of the churches and within churches. This has been inevitable with the movement of the Anglican church beyond its English borders, the indigenization of the Anglican church in very different cultures throughout the world, the diversity of peoples within congregations and dioceses, and the breakdown of traditional authority.

In the United States, the Episcopal Church has taken further the characteristically Anglican dispersal of authority.[29] Bishops have increasingly become presiding officers of a democratic body of clergy and lay representatives. Differences are addressed by majority rule. In response to majority rule, the minority can appeal to conscience and act on the basis of its own convictions. As congregations act independently of each other, communion between particular communities is weakened. Conscience becomes further individualized. As this cycle continues, faith itself becomes individualistic. Neither education nor majority rule provides adequate means to address the conflicts of conscience that threaten to divide the community of faith. Among recent examples are the ordination of eleven women as priests in Philadelphia in 1974, the refusal of some congregations to use the 1979 *Book of Common Prayer*, the deliberate ordination of homosexual persons living in sexually active relationships, and the refusal of certain dioceses to consider women for ordination to the priesthood or to allow women priests to exercise their priestly ministries. In each of these cases, the actions of some of the members of the church—actions of conscience—conflict with the consciences of others. As the level and extent of such conflicts increases, the sense and connection of a faith shared in common is threatened.

The structure of authority in the Episcopal Church provides little guidance on how to proceed. According to the ordinal of the *Book of Common Prayer*, a priest is "called to work as a pastor, priest, and teacher, together with [the] bishop and fellow presbyters, and to take [his or her] share in the councils of the Church; similarly, the bishop is to work to "sustain [his or her] fellow presbyters and take counsel with them" (BCP 517, 531). Together bishops and priests assume pastoral oversight over the life of the community. Such is the ideal: together the clergy work to form a common mind and body. They act together as a body formed by common trust and respect, a *collegium*, the college of presbyters over which the bishop presides. In similar manner, bishops as representatives of dioceses form a *collegium*, the House of Bishops.

As presiding officers in their respective communities, priests and bishops have formal authority for administering discipline and the larger responsibility for presiding over the community.[30] In this sense, the burden of addressing conflicts and administering discipline is with clergy—with priests in congregations and with bishops in dioceses, in the national church, and in the Anglican communion. This happens usually in the midst of a crisis in which in a particular case—where the conflict of consciences appears irreconcilable—they are forced to act. Such a formal, judicial context provides a limited opportunity to address the conflict more broadly in terms of the whole church.

As to the celebration and blessing of covenants between gay or lesbian couples, some bishops have left the decision to the priests who have pastoral oversight in the life of a congregation. Such a decision, though, addresses the conflict of conscience only as the broader decision has been made and communicated that the diocese accepts a diversity of judgments on the blessing of such relationships. In other dioceses bishops have made it clear that these blessings are unacceptable—a judgment that clergy and congregations who celebrate and bless such covenants will be disciplined and, if they continue to fail to support the diocesan norms, inhibited or removed from office. What is often not clear is whether such a policy is meant to be for the time being, while the conflict of conscience is being addressed, or whether instead the policy expresses for the foreseeable future the judgment of the diocese and hence a necessary condition for membership. Only clarity on these issues will allow individuals and congregations to decide on the basis of their consciences whether they will remain within the church or separate themselves. In turn, only resolution of such issues will allow the church to move beyond the conflict of conscience in order to focus energy and resources on common tasks of building up the community of faith in its life and mission.

NOTES

1. Few works present the questions confronting the church within this, context from which they arise. As an exception see Patricia Beattie Jung and Ralph F. Smith, *Heterosexism: An Ethical Challenge* (Albany, N.Y.: SUNY, 1993). For a broader discussion of the questions and challenges before the church, see Joseph Monti, *Arguing About Sex: The Rhetoric of Christian Sexual Morality* (Albany, N.Y.: SUNY, 1995).

2. Paul Ricoeur, "Wonder, Eroticism, and Enigma," *Cross Currents* 14 (1964)/21: 134.

3. Emil Durkheim, *The Elementary Forms of the Religious Life* (New York: Free Press, 1965; first published 1915), book 2, esp. 183-93, 235-255.

4. Peter Brown, *The Body and Society: Men, Women and Sexual Renunciation in Early Christianity* (New York: Columbia University Press, 1988), 27, 28.

5. Ricoeur, "Wonder, Eroticism, and Enigma," 135.

6. *Ibid.*, 141.

7. *Ibid.*, 135. For a contemporary account of Christian understandings of love as a matter of desire and tenderness, see Edward C. Vacek, *Love, Divine and Human* (Washington, D.C.: Georgetown University Press, 1994).

8. For a historical account of the changing understandings of love and sexuality, see Irving Singer, *The Nature of Love*, 3 vols. (Chicago: University of Chicago Press, 1984-87).

9. See Lisa Sowle Cahill, *Between the Sexes* (Philadelphia: Fortress, 1985), 45-53; Phyllis A. Bird, "'Male and Female He Created Them': Gen. 1:27b in the Context of the Priestly Account of Creation," *Harvard Theological Review* 74 (1981)/2: 129-159; Phyllis A. Bird, "Genesis I-III as a Source for a Contemporary Theology of Sexuality," *Ex Auditu* (Annual Princeton Theological Seminary) 3 (1987): 31-36.

10. See L. William Countryman, *Dirt, Greed, and Sex* (Philadelphia: Fortress, 1988), especially 20-44 for a description of sexual proscriptions in ancient Israel. See also Roland de Vaux, *Ancient Israel*, vol. 1: *Social Institutions* (New York: McGraw-Hill, 1965), 34-37.

11. Elaine Pagels, *Adam, Eve, and the Serpent* (New York: Random House, 1988), 13 and 13-16 on the challenges described below.

12. Countryman, *Dirt, Greed, and Sex*, 12.

13. See Cahill, *Between the Sexes*, 53-56; Bird, "Genesis I-III as a Source," 36-39.

14. On the goods or ends of sexuality three reference articles provide a summary of the tradition. See Margaret Farley, "Sexual Ethics," *The Encyclopedia of Bioethics*, ed. Warren T. Reich (New York: Macmillan, 1995) 5: 2363-2375; Lisa Sowle Cahill, "Sexual Ethics," *The Westminster Dictionary of Christian Ethics*, ed. James F. Childress and John Macquarrie (Philadelphia: Westminster, 1986), 579-583; Helen Oppenheimer, "Marriage," *The Westminster Dictionary of Christian Ethics*, 366-368.

15. Bernard Häring was among the first Roman Catholic moral theologians to understand the end of procreation as a particular expression of the larger end of fecundity or what may be called "generativity." See Häring, *Free and Faithful in Christ*, vol. 2 (New York: Seabury, 1979), 492-530. For a fuller development of this understanding see André Guindon, *The Sexual Creators: An Ethical Proposal for Concerned Christians* (Washington, D.C.: University Press of America, 1986), 63-68. On generativity see Erik Erikson, *Childhood and Society* (New York: W. W. Norton, 1963), 266-268, and *Insight and Responsibility* (New York: W. W. Norton, 1964), 130-132.

16. For an exploration of erotic desire and the love of God, including a study of the Song of Songs, see Julia Kristeva, *Tales of Love*, trans. Leon S. Roudiez (New York: Columbia University Press, 1987), esp. 83-100, 139-187. For a broader discussion see Irving Singer, *The Nature of Love*, vol. 1: *Plato to Luther*, 162-311.

17. See parallels in Matt. 19:3-6, Luke 16:18, and 1 Cor. 7:10-11.

18. This is not to make the self-sacrificial characteristic of such love the singular feature of true love as has been the case in much of Christian tradition. See Vacek, *Love, Divine and Human*, esp. 157-197.

19. For the development of these vows in terms of the service for the celebration and blessing of a marriage in the *Book of Common Prayer*, see James M. Gustafson, "Marriage and Family," *Ethics from a Theocentric Perspective*, vol. 2 (Chicago: University of Chicago Press, 1984), 177-184. For a study of the nature of vows themselves see Margaret Farley, *Personal Commitments* (New York: Harper & Row, 1986).

20. See Nigel Biggar, *The Hastening that Waits: Karl Barth's Ethics* (Oxford: Clarendon, 1993), 122; Karl Barth, *Church Dogmatics* III.4, ed. G. W. Bromiley and T. F. Torrance (Edinburgh: T. & T. Clark, 1951), 400.

21. Pagels, *Adam, Eve, and the Serpent*, 16.

22. Brown, *The Body and Society*, 213-338.

23. See, for example, Walter Kasper, *The Theology of Christian Marriage* (New York: Crossroad, 1980).

24. See, for example, Beverly Wildung Harrison, "Human Sexuality and Mutuality," in Judith L. Weidman, ed., *Christian Feminism* (New York: Harper & Row, 1984), 141-157.

25. See Ronald Preston, "Conscience," *The Westminster Dictionary of Christian Ethics*, 116-118. For an extended discussion see Bernard Häring, "Conscience: The Sanctuary of Creative Fidelity and Liberty," in *Introduction to Christian Ethics: A Reader*, ed. Ronald P. Hamel and Kenneth R. Himes (Mahwah, N.J.: Paulist, 1989), 252-280.

26. Wayne Meeks, *The Origins of Christian Morality* (New Haven, Conn.: Yale University Press, 1993), 216. On the question of the unity and integrity of the church, see Timothy Sedgwick and Philip Turner, eds., *The Crisis in Moral Teaching in the Episcopal Church* (Harrisburg, Penn.: Morehouse, 1992), especially the two concluding essays: Ellen K. Wondra, "The Dispersal of Moral Authority," 119-136, and Philip Turner, "How the Church Might Teach," 137-159. On human sexuality see also Harmon L. Smith, "Decorum as Doctrine: Teachings on Human Sexuality," 15-40.

27. On the pacifist and just war traditions see the National Conference of Catholic Bishops' pastoral letter, *The Challenge of Peace* (Washington, D.C.: U.S. Catholic Conference, 1983), section I, paras. 5-121. For a more recent discussion see Lisa Sowle Cahill, *Love Your Enemies: Discipleship, Pacifism, and Just War Theory* (Minneapolis: Fortress, 1994).

28. On the nature of casuistry see Stephen Toulmin and Albert R. Jonsen, *The Abuses of Casuistry* (Berkeley, Calif.: University of California Press, 1988).

29. For a broad discussion of these issues see Stephen W. Sykes, ed., *Authority in the Anglican Communion: Essays Presented to Bishop John Howe* (Toronto: Anglican Book Centre, 1987).

30. See *Constitution and Canons for the Episcopal Church* 1994, Title IV on ecclesiastical discipline, especially canons 3-5.

SEXUALITY
AND
THE SOUL

∞ *Thomas E. Breidenthal*

Sanctifying Nearness

In *Continuing the Dialogue: A Pastoral Study Document of the House of Bishops to the Church as the Church Considers Issues of Human Sexuality,*[1] the bishops have set out to define several broad areas of consensus in the Episcopal Church, as a basis for further discussion. The document succeeds admirably in this task. We as a church do agree that our sexuality is a part of God's creative intention for us and is therefore good; we agree that all forms of sexual abuse, harassment, and sexualized violence are bad; and we all agree (I hope) that no individual should be denied respect or civil rights on the basis of sexual orientation. Unfortunately, none of this agreeing has brought us a step closer to the resolution of the issues that divide us, namely, whether the church should bless covenanted same-sex unions and whether the church should ordain practicing gays and lesbians.

The reason for this stalemate is, in my view, that we have not yet begun to grapple with the question that really lies at the heart of this debate: Why is our sexuality a spiritual concern? What has our use of it to do with our salvation? I do not mean to suggest that no one is asking this question. Nor do I mean to suggest that the bishops have not raised it in their *Pastoral Study*. But they, and we, have not raised the religious question radically enough.

"Traditionalist" voices urge us (rightly) to take the will of God as the starting-point for our moral deliberation about issues like the blessing of same-sex unions. "Progressive" voices point out (also rightly) that the non-traditional lifestyles of many committed Christians may have something to teach us. Yet both choruses may leave us uneasy. Certainly, we must do more than invoke the will of God if we wish to recover a viable Christian sexual morality. It is not simply that the will of God has proven notoriously difficult to determine in this matter. Even if God's will is obvious, it cannot provide a rationale for any moral code until we are able to say, clearly and simply, how God's command speaks to us, how and why it addresses us not only as a demand but as good news. But we can learn from each other's Christian witness only if we have some notion of what we need to hear.

Before we can have a fruitful conversation about our Christian lives as sexual beings, we need to back up and consider first, how our sexuality encounters us as a spiritual problem, and second, how this problem is addressed by the Christian faith. I think the problem is *radical availability*.

To say that I am radically available is to say that anyone can become my neighbor: anyone can get under my skin. The word *neighbor*, after all, simply means someone who is *nigh* to me, close to me. This is also the literal meaning of the Hebrew and Greek words in the Bible that we translate as "neighbor." Nearness is experience of the other as neighbor, that is, as one to whom I am radically available. One might say that nearness "precipitates" or is the precipitation of radical availability. Nearness can be good news or bad. (The arrival of the good Samaritan could have been bad news instead of good news for the Israelite lying by the roadside.) At any moment and at any time the tactful and protective reserve that we maintain in our dealings with most human beings can be torn asunder, and we can find ourselves, for good or ill, at the disposal of a stranger, who is aware of us, sees us, and judges us.

We tend to view such chance encounters as exceptions to the distance which ordinarily separates us from one another. But what if the occurrence of nearness indicates our true condition—that is, our radical availability to one another? Then the distance that so often seems to divide us is mere pretense—a pretense which denies the close connection every human being shares with every other human being. Sometimes the occurrence of nearness seems to create distance rather than diminish it. This is particularly the case when we are suddenly confronted with the otherness of someone whom we have "annexed" to ourselves, or viewed as an extension of ourselves. But the abyss that opens between me and such a one is not a distance that protects or isolates me from the other. On the contrary, it is a distance through which and in which the other looms before me and I before the other. It is the distance that, like the space between an audience and an actor, makes for more visibility, not less.

The neighbor is neither reducible to being an extension of myself nor able to be dismissed because he or she is different from me. It is true that we can refuse to hear the cry or the invitation of the neighbor, just as we can deny the experience of availability into which the neighbor plunges us. It is also true that we can collude with one another to "paper over" these experiences—we can support one another in the illusion of self-sufficiency. But however much we may prefer to think of ourselves as essentially separate from and independent of one another, in charge of the relationships we make and the degrees of exposure we permit, the truth is that we are always already available to every other human being, and cannot prevent even a momentary encounter with a stranger from touching us to our very core.

Sexual desire can be an especially intense and unsettling reminder of our radical availability to the other. Like parental affection or simple compassion, sexual desire can cause our heart to "belong" to another, even if we do not want it to, even if we wish our desire were otherwise, and quite apart from the fact that we may refuse to allow our actions to be governed by our heart. That is to say, sexual desire, once roused, places us in a relation of connection to the object of our desire—a relation which we have not chosen and which, although we can resist acting upon it, we cannot wish away. Thus, this desire shatters any illusions we may have regarding our ability to choose when and if we shall be connected to others; indeed, it is itself a warrant for the claim that our fundamental relation to one another is one of connection. The experience of sexual desire is also intensely physical, and involves desire for physical contact with its object. Thus, by its very nature, sexual desire gives the lie to the conventional assumption that our bodies "hide" us and stand, as it were, as a barrier of defense between our inmost selves and the world with its other selves. Far from protecting us from the world, our bodies reveal the fact that we belong unqualifiedly to the world—and to one another.

Such a shift in how we regard our bodies is, I think, reflected in our ever-increasing concern with the danger of physical and sexual abuse. Our very reasonable fear of such abuse goes far beyond avoiding bodily harm. The real fear is that disrespect for our bodies or physical and sexual violence committed on our bodies constitutes an attack on our souls as well as our bodies, and it is this aspect of abuse that is the most horrifying to us. But we have come to recognize or admit the soul-destroying potential of sexual and physical abuse (and I include here sexual and physical stereotyping) only because we have acknowledged the extent to which our bodies, far from being a first line of defense against the world, are in fact the very field upon which the self is called daily to meet the world.

Given our propensity to harm one another, our radical availability to one another can be very frightening. We may dream of retreating from human community, from the world, even from our bodies. But we cannot escape from our availability to one another: it is a condition of our existence as human beings. Nor, it appears, can we stop hurting one another. This is why the question of nearness is fundamentally a religious question—because we cannot do anything about our radical availability to one another, and we cannot do anything to make our radical availability to one another safe. We are driven to look beyond ourselves for help. Depending on where we find that help, or how we frame that help theologically, salvation from the dangers of radical availability will be understood as an ultimate escape from nearness or as its ultimate redemption.

The dialogue about sexuality seldom gets down to the issue of nearness because at crucial points it falls prey to three ways of talking about the human condition that do not so much reject radical availability as pretend it isn't there. These may be summarized as follows:

1. Talking about the self as if it were essentially *cut off* from other selves;
2. Talking about the self as if it were *inviolable;* and
3. Talking about spiritual and moral values as if they were products of the *will.*

Such talk reflects an understanding of who and what we are that has dominated Western thinking for some centuries now. According to this view—which, for want of a better name, I shall call *radical individualism*—nearness is not inevitable, because we are not radically available to one another. We start out disconnected, and whatever connection we have is something we have chosen and *made.* On this view, sexuality does not so much reveal connection as facilitate it. Cast in this role, sexuality inevitably presents itself as something external to a self that remains isolated and untouchable. However much we may think of our sexuality as part of us, a dimension of who we are, it becomes very difficult not to speak of it as if it were something we "have"—a tool or resource, a kind of software program for networking between isolated selves.

Radical individualism as I have just characterized it is not compatible with the gospel, for two reasons. First, it denies the biblical insistence that we are all "one flesh," that the human race is a body that is being redeemed, a lump of dough that is being leavened. Were we really not available to one another, it would make no sense to say that the Word initiated the transformation of the human race by becoming a member of it. That transformation requires that each of us be at once the recipient and the conductor of the grace of God in Christ. But Jesus cannot get through to me unless (whether I like it or not) I am radically available to him as a fellow human being, and I cannot minister Jesus to others unless every person I engage with is radically available to me (and *vice versa*).

Second, radical individualism denies the fundamental biblical understanding of our relationship with God. It presupposes that the self is self-grounding, autonomous, the sole author of its own actions, the final arbiter of its own values. In its extreme form, radical individualism sets the self up in God's place. In its less extreme and seemingly more religious form, it imagines the self invited into a kind of reciprocal relationship with God. But there is no reciprocity between God and us. We cannot even, in the strict sense, reciprocate God's love. God's love is the act whereby we are created and preserved. This love is always ahead of ours, because God is pure act, the only true beginner. ("I chose you before you chose me.") It is true that I can respond to God's love by loving God back, but the response is not a new initiative. In this sense, as Bonhoeffer says in his *Ethics,* we are passive before God.[2]

To respond to God in thanksgiving is to acknowledge that we have no center in ourselves and no existence apart from God's power and will. This is not to say that we have no freedom, or that we are incapable of real action. But our action is always an answer to God: either we are praising God or denying God. Moreover, only when we respond to God in praise (rather than turning from God in pride) do we discover what we were made for, and the freedom that comes in the doing of it. True human action is always eucharistic in character.

The notion that our freedom is grounded in passivity with respect to God finds concise expression in the claim that we are made in the image of God. This "image" is none other than our capacity to love, that is, to affirm the existence of another, and this capacity is Godlike. But this capacity is God's imprint upon us, God's inscription upon our hearts, the divine impress with which we have been stamped. We have not chosen to be the bearers of the divine image, and we will always be just that—*bearers* of God's imprint, not little gods in our own right. There is no common ground between us and God. We praise God because God is *worthy* of praise, and God's worth is not (like the worth of the other in Aristotle's theory of friendship) a correlative or mirror of our worth. God is not "another self."

Even though loving God constitutes our highest happiness, we cannot speak properly of any "interest" we may have in a relationship with God. And this is so because the encounter with God is the undoing of all "interest" grounded in self-control or autonomy. God's love for us calls for a response that we cannot give if we seek to maintain the pretense of any agency that is not grounded in God's agency. If we cling to this pretense, God's love confronts us as a demand, perhaps even as an assault. If we do not cling to it, that love wells up within us as the ground of our own true freedom, which is the freedom to offer service and glory to God.

∞

We late twentieth-century Christians—conservatives and liberals alike—are perhaps more attracted to the radical individualist ideology than we might care to admit. At any rate, our moral vocabulary very often plays two notional ends against the middle, leaning now on the notion of the self as disconnected and autonomous, and now on the notion of the self as available and passive. This is no less true of the moral vocabulary we use to discuss human sexuality. Three words come particularly to mind: *gift, intimacy,* and *mutuality.* I would like to reflect briefly on each of these words.

First, *gift.* The claim is frequently made in church circles that sexuality is a divine gift to be celebrated and used. This claim is intended (quite rightly) to affirm the goodness of sexuality as part of our created nature. But the likening of sexuality to a gift is problematic because, without quite intending to, it can suggest that our sexuality is something external to us, a resource that we can use or leave to one side, like the talents in the parable.

The difficulty here lies in the ambiguity of the word *gift.* On the one hand, I can claim that sexuality is a part of my nature: since my nature is the handiwork of a good God, my sexuality, along with everything else about me, is the good gift of God. Here *gift* retains its absolute sense as something *given;* it is my own existence and nature, including my sexuality, that is given. On the other hand, *gift* can refer to something outside myself, something given to me for my use. In this sense, the thing given is not a part of me; I exist quite apart from the gift, although I may benefit from it. It is very easy to slip unreflectively from the first meaning of sexuality-as-gift to the second, especially when one tends, as we all do, to forget that the word *sexuality* does not designate a thing but a dimension of our existence.

After all, what is sexuality but the fact of sexual desire (ranging from mild interest to passion) as it is experienced by human beings? *Sexuality* refers not to a thing but an experience, and to give thanks to God for this experience is to thank God for making us precisely what we are. But when we begin to talk about sexuality as if it were a thing, abstractable from the rest of us, something we can "use" or "get a handle on," then we are in danger of glossing over the relation of sexuality to connection, and an assertion intended to anchor our discussion firmly in the doctrine of creation becomes an ensign under which the conversation, having lost its moorings in radical availability, drifts inexorably toward radical individualism.

A similar drift is occasioned by the notions of mutuality and intimacy, respectively. By *intimacy* I mean a certain understanding of closeness which has its roots in the ideology of disconnection, even if the word *intimacy* is not always intended in that sense. Intimacy means the kind of connection that is possible on radical individualist grounds. Literally, the word means the sharing of what is most inward (from the Latin *intimus,* "innermost"). From the radical individualist perspective, there is a certain deliciously oxymoronic quality to the idea of what is innermost being shared, that is, being held in common. From that perspective the inward is, after all, the domain of the unavailable self.

Not surprisingly, this notion of intimacy first gained currency in connection with the bourgeois myth of the family as a safe haven from the challenges and tumults of the public world. The frictionless togetherness of this family depended, of course, on mother, children, and servants all functioning as extensions of the father's own self; the intimacy or sacralized inwardness of the domestic scene coincided perfectly with his projected inwardness. Today, intimacy denotes the coming together of two impenetrable domains of inwardness—an almost ineffable transgression of the boundaries between two radically individual selves. This idea plays itself out in one of two ways. On the one hand, intimacy comes to mean the absorption of one self into another, or the mutual absorption of many selves to create a collective self. On the other hand, intimacy can name a brief and titillating exercise in gamesmanship in which two selves "play" at availability with one another. In neither case does intimacy overthrow the ideological assumption that connection and difference cannot go together. Intimacy stands for a connection which is either totalitarian or artificial—the collaborative project of two wills that remain essentially unconnected.

The term *mutuality* is no less problematic. Increasingly, this word designates a necessary (and sometimes sufficient) condition for the moral worth of a sexual act. But what is mutuality? Mutuality has always connoted reciprocity in the sense of a return in kind. That is, it refers to equals who can pay each other back. For this reason, mutuality has something to do with respect—the respect we have for an equal. Again, mutuality has tended to suggest something that is had in common—a "third term" which relates two otherwise disparate terms to each other. Thirdly (and this is, I believe, a new meaning, forged in the smithy of the church's dialogue about sexuality), mutuality has come to suggest tenderness as well as respect.

What does this mean when it comes to the consideration of what constitutes a morally worthy sexual act? In connection with the notion of intimacy, mutuality seems first to point to the agreement whereby two equal (that is, two equally autonomous and equally self-grounding) individuals exchange the gift of sexuality; it also seems to refer to the relation into which these two individuals are brought by virtue of sexuality, the "third term" which unites them. If we understand this relation as one of vulnerability, then we can see why mutuality, *as a moral principle*, has become practically synonymous with tenderness. It is because, on this view, we have a moral duty to treat tenderly those who have freely chosen to make themselves vulnerable to us in the sexual act, and we are owed the same tenderness in return. Obviously, I think there is more than a hint of radical individualism in the idea that we could *choose* to be vulnerable. Taken literally, vulnerability means something very like radical availability. Yet vulnerability often suggests a stance voluntarily taken rather than an unavoidable condition.[3]

Taken together, the notions of mutuality, intimacy, and sexuality-as-gift comprise the key features of an emerging sexual morality which sounds biblical but is in fact deeply rooted in radical individualism. According to this scheme, sex (or the vulnerability into which sex leads us) is a gift (that is, an instrument), possessed equally by all (mutuality), by which two or more individuals can achieve intimacy (that is, an achieved connection between otherwise disconnected souls) if and only if they agree not to take advantage of the vulnerability each has voluntarily entered into (mutuality again). Sex is then a moral practice whose object is intimacy and whose cardinal virtue is mutuality. This scheme seems to fit in with a vaguely Christian moral vision, since intimacy looks so much like communion or *koinonia,* and *koinonia* is surely the Christian goal. But in fact mutuality and intimacy have little to do with true communion. The reign of God is precisely *not* about the tender exchange of what is most private and inward. It is about something boundless, public, noisy, and unashamedly urban—our enjoyment of each others' uniqueness as praisers of God.

Mutuality and intimacy have very little to do with sex, either. The cult of intimacy and mutuality distracts us time and again from what is most obvious about sex, namely, its revelation of our connection to one another, its being, simply and familiarly, a register (not a cause or a condition) of our nearness to the other as neighbors who are always already radically available to each other. In so doing, the cult of intimacy and mutuality also distracts us from the spiritual question that our sexuality poses: "Are we happy with our radical availability, or not?" I imagine that many of us, to begin with, are not. Connection seems like a good thing if we can have it when we want it, on our own terms (if we are interested in power) or at least on equal terms (if we are interested in sharing). But to prefer connection as an option is precisely to recognize the ways in which the neighbor is *dangerous*—which is why a sexual morality rooted in radical individualism never involves an unqualified embrace of nearness, no matter how "permissive" it may be.

The difficulty comes when we consider embracing nearness (and therefore radical availability) not as an option, but as a given—still more, when we consider whether or not to include radical availability in our idea of salvation. Are we willing, first of all, to recognize nearness not as a product of our own will but as something that comes upon us, the manifestation of an already existing availability in the unsought-for event of connection? Can we, in the second place, rejoice that we are so available to one another, even when we abuse each other's availability more often than not?

The Bible's answer to the question about nearness is, I believe, unambiguously affirmative. The Bible is no stranger to the theme of the dangerous neighbor. Yet the New Testament, echoing the Hebrew scriptures, places before us a twofold command: Love God, and love your neighbor as yourself. This command engages us directly with the neighbor, maximizes our nearness to the neighbor, and acknowledges the neighbor's permanent involvement in our life. This is because the command to love the neighbor is also a command to love nearness itself. Love of neighbor is not the same thing as benevolence at a distance, but a "going out" of the heart to the neighbor which assumes our embracing of our radical availability to the neighbor.

This sounds like Buber's I-Thou relation. Yet the I-Thou relation allows for a kind of reciprocity which I do not mean to suggest is present here. I have in mind something more like Levinas's insistence (as against Buber) that the neighbor meets me not as my equal, in relation with whom I truly become an "I," but as one who undoes me, stripping me of my false "I" but not providing me with the counterpoise for a new "I."[4] There is no counterpoise here; there is only claim and vertigo. Love of the neighbor, like love of God, is a kind of death to self, the death of any pretense to disconnection-on-demand. Such love is direct and involving—it demands that I myself draw near to the one who has drawn near to me—and it concerns the neighbor as one who is not "another self," to whom I am nevertheless radically available and into whose hands I am, as it were, to deliver myself. Worse yet, unlike God, the neighbor whose claim on me I recognize and to whom I surrender myself is perhaps very far from loving *me*.

Yet if we consider almost any passage in the New Testament we see that this kind of surrender is what is enjoined, often with explicit reference to the neighbor who may be dangerous or unsympathetic. (Think of going the extra mile, giving the second tunic, loving the enemy, the patience of the slave in affliction, forgiving seventy times seven, turning the other cheek, blessing not cursing.) To be sure, the Christian gospel commends love as redemptive, not only for the lover, but for all whom it touches. Our Christian response to the neighbor must therefore be guided by the conviction that our love not only transcends but undoes the sin that vitiates every human relationship. Love of neighbor looks toward the overcoming of everything that makes radical availability a cause for fear, toward the restoration of everything that makes radical availability a cause for joy. The Bible witnesses in numerous ways to the dangers posed by our radical availability to one another under the condition of sin, but it also affirms the essential goodness of this availability as part of God's intention for us. Indeed, the Bible teaches us repeatedly to look forward to more nearness in the reign of God, not less. More specifically, Christian faith, when it insists on the full and irrevocable humanity of the incarnate Word, offers no escape from nearness and acknowledges no path to Jesus that does not begin and end in nearness. The whole point of the Incarnation is that the Word of God has become our neighbor, and has done so not in order to rescue us from nearness (that was the Gnostic error), but to set our nearness right.

I do not think it is an exaggeration to say that this "take" on nearness, in both its negative and positive aspects, provides Christian moral theology with one of its fundamental principles. Moral theology (or Christian ethics) is about holiness. We have already been justified by faith in Christ. Now how shall we be sanctified? How shall we grow into the full stature of Christ? One way is to live out our availability to one another in such a way that, encounter by encounter, relationship by relationship, Christ's redemption of the whole body of humanity finds its concrete fulfillment.

This brings us back to the beginning of the discussion. Why is our sexuality a spiritual concern? What has our use of it to do with our salvation? Indirectly, sexuality is a spiritual concern because it casts a spotlight on radical availability, which is the distinguishing feature of the human spirit as the image of God. Directly, sexuality is a spiritual concern because it names a domain of human experience in which I always find myself face-to-face with another who is near to me, delivered over to me (even if I am his or her victim), called to praise God in company with me. In my sexual dealings, as in all my dealings (all our dealings may involve sexual feelings, but sexual feelings are not the only way in which we find ourselves thrown into nearness), I must, as a Christian, both affirm the nearness of the neighbor and, acknowledging my own sinfulness, refer that nearness to Christ for sanctification. As Christians we seek to live lives that honor the connection which all human beings share, while recognizing that in a fallen world this connection is as likely to facilitate violence as to enable communion. Surely, lives so led are not ordered solely to our own individual sanctification. They embody disciplines by which our availability to one another, and the corporate nature of our common humanity which that availability presupposes, begin to be transformed and sanctified.

All Christian moral practices, including sexual practices, involve such rules and boundaries. Yet—and it is crucial that we remember this—the purpose of the rules is not to keep human beings apart from each other. Rather, it involves recognizing that when we draw close to one another in Christ we are still sinners. Our ability to avoid abusing those who are close to us is limited, as is our capacity to suffer inevitable abuse without buying into it ourselves.

Nowhere, perhaps, is this more the case than in our sexual dealings with one another. For centuries the church has tended to treat our sexuality with contempt. This contempt reflected an underlying refusal to affirm radical availability. We must be careful lest our new zeal to affirm sexuality leave the older and deeper sin undisturbed. I have no doubt that in heaven we will enjoy a measure of delight and fulfillment in every other praiser of

God which we should not shrink from calling sexual delight and sexual ful-fillment. But the wholehearted affirmation of our sexuality—an affirmation which, as I have argued, depends on the acknowledgment and affirmation of our radical availability—goes hand-in-hand with the acceptance of a cer-tain *askesis,* a certain discipline, for the sake of the neighbor. As Christians we undertake to bring every part of our lives under the rule of Jesus, who is neighbor to each of us.

What should such an *askesis* look like? Here there is ample scope for dis-agreement among us—although I would not be surprised if renewed atten-tion to the risk as well as the surpassing goodness of nearness yielded some new configurations of moral conviction. It is not so unusual these days to run across church people who are, for instance, at one and the same time increasingly open to the blessing of same-sex unions and increasingly dis-approving of premarital sex. I confess to being one such person. At any rate, I offer three broad areas (beyond those already defined by the bish-ops' *Pastoral Study*) where consensus ought to be within reach.

First, *promiscuity is not consonant with a life devoted to the sanctifica-tion of nearness.* At its worst it exhibits, if not contempt for one's sexual partners (or for oneself), then contempt for nearness itself as the revelation of a real and lasting connection with the other. At its best, it exhibits a na-ive or prideful desire to jump the gun on the eschaton, an attempt to live out under the condition of sin the realization of a universal communion that is reserved for the saints in light.

Second, *infidelity is not consonant with the Christian way.* Infidelity clearly does exhibit contempt for neighbor and for nearness alike. This is so not primarily because infidelity involves a breach of contract (that really would be radical individualism talking), but because it demonstrates a fail-ure to take responsibility for someone who has simply placed himself or herself in one's hands. It hardly makes a difference if one is released or per-mitted by some prior agreement to have sex with someone else, since (if we reject the individualist line) it is not in anyone's power to decide whether and how much one will "give" or "open oneself" to another. Sex is not a mere mode of communication or self-expression that leaves the inner self untouched. The Christian should know this, and should be faithful to the other for the other's sake, no matter what the other claims to permit.

Third, *sexual relations should not be entered into unless a lifetime to-gether of spiritual work—that is, a lifelong and exclusive union—is in-tended.* Sex precipitates nearness, and nearness cannot be sanctified unless our actions and, in the end, our disposition toward one another are purged of every pretense to autonomy, every tendency toward collusion, annexa-tion, or domination. I am not saying that Christians should not get out of violent and oppressive marriages; I am merely saying that marriages with built-in escape hatches are not likely to be engaged in the work of sanctification.

To Summarize

1. Before we can locate sexuality as a moral challenge for Christians, we must understand how and why sexuality encounters us as a spiritual problem. I have suggested that the problem lies with a radical availability that has been vitiated by sin. Sexuality is a particularly insistent reminder of this radical availability.

2. Christian faith involves an affirmation of radical availability, and of the connection which it presupposes, and looks forward to the sanctification and perfection in Christ of all the bonds that already unite us one to another.

3. Christian faith is therefore a call to lifelong participation in this sanctification and perfection.

4. Christian faith also recognizes the ongoing dangers that we pose to one another in our sinfulness, and therefore relies on the preservation and development of a wide range of moral practices (for example, Christian marriage) which help to ensure that our relations with one another (sexual and otherwise) are, indeed, ordered to holiness.

5. This ordering to holiness, which is also an ordering to happiness, is what supplies any Christian moral practice with its "point," regardless of whether the practice happens to be viewed as something enjoined by the revealed command of God or as something arrived at in the painful crucible of Christian spiritual experience.

6. Christians can in good faith disagree about the value and necessity of various moral practices. We must, however, agree that all moral practices worthy to be called Christian will be grounded in the sanctification of our nearness to each other.

NOTES

1. Cincinnati, Ohio: Forward Movement Publications, 1995.
2. "There is no love which is free or independent of the love of God. In this the love of [human beings] remains purely passive. Loving God is simply the other aspect of being loved by God." See Dietrich Bonhoeffer, *Ethics,* ed. Eberhard Bethge (New York: Macmillan, 1955), 53.

3. I do not, of course, mean to suggest that the words *mutuality* and *intimacy* are always or even usually intended to carry the freight I have assigned to them in this essay. I merely argue that these words, which we all use frequently, signal a shift in the center of gravity of current Christian discourse about sexuality—a shift in the direction of what I have been calling radical individualism.

4. See Emmanuel Levinas, [extracts from] "Time and the Other" and "Martin Buber and the Theory of Knowledge" in *The Levinas Reader*, ed. Sean Hand (Oxford: Basil Blackwell, 1989), 54 and 72-74 respectively.

∾ *Rowan Williams*

The Body's Grace

Why does sex matter? Most people know that sexual intimacy is in some ways frightening for them, that it is quite simply the place where they began to be taught whatever maturity they have. Most of us know that the whole business is irredeemably comic, surrounded by so many odd chances and so many opportunities for making a fool of yourself. Plenty know that it is the place where they are liable to be most profoundly damaged or helpless. Culture in general and religion in particular have devoted enormous energy to the doomed task of getting it right. In this essay, I want to try and understand a little better why the task is doomed, and why the fact that it's doomed is a key to seeing more fully why and how it matters—and even seeing more fully what this mattering has to do with God.

Best to start from a particular thing, a particular story. Paul Scott's *Raj Quartet* is full of poignant and very deep analyses of the tragedies of sexuality: the theme which drives through all four novels and unites their immense rambling plots is Ronald Merrick's destruction and corruption of his own humanity and that of all who fall into his hands. That corruption effectively begins at the moment he discovers how he is aroused, how his privacy is invaded, by the desirable body of a man, and he is appalled and terrified by this. His first attempt to punish and obliterate the object of his desire is what unleashes the forces of death and defilement that follow him everywhere thereafter. Sexual refusal is dramatized by him in enactments of master-slave relations: he humiliates what he longs for, so that his dominion is not challenged and so that the sexual disaster becomes a kind of political tragedy. Merrick is an icon of the "body politic": his terror, his refusal, and his corruption stand as a metaphor of the Raj itself, of power willfully turning away from the recognition of those wants and needs that only vulnerability to the despised and humiliated stranger can open up and satisfy.

Interwoven with Merrick's tragedy is the story of Sarah Layton, a figure constantly aware of her powerlessness before events, her inability to undo the injuries and terrors of the past, but no less constantly trying to see and respond truthfully and generously. At the end of the second novel in the sequence, Sarah is seduced, lovelessly but not casually: her yielding is prompted perhaps more than anything by her seducer's mercilessly clear perception of her. She does not belong, he tells her, however much she tries to give herself to the conventions of the Raj. Within her real generosity is a lost and empty place: "You don't know anything about joy at all, do you?"[1]

Absent from the life of the family she desperately tries to prop up, absent from the life of European society in India, Sarah is present fully to no one and nothing. Her innate truthfulness and lack of egotistical self-defense mean that she is able to recognize this once the remark is made: there is no joy for her, because she is not able to be anywhere. When she is at last coaxed into bed, as they "enact" a tenderness that is not really that of lovers, Sarah comes to herself: hours later, on the train journey back to her family, she looks in the mirror and sees that "she had entered her body's grace."[2]

What does this mean? The phrase recurs more than once in the pages of the novel that follow, but it is starkly clear that there is no lasting joy for Sarah. There is a pregnancy and an abortion; a continuing loneliness. Yet nothing in this drainingly painful novel suggests that the moment of the "body's grace" for Sarah was a deceit. Somehow she has been aware of what it was and was not: a frontier has been passed, and that has been and remains grace; a being present, even though this can mean knowing that the graced body is now more than ever a source of vulnerability. But it is still grace, a filling of the void, an entry into some different kind of identity. There may have been little love, even little generosity, in Sarah's lovemaking, but she has discovered that her body can be the cause of happiness to her and to another. It is this discovery which most clearly shows why we might want to talk about grace here. Grace, for the Christian believer, is a transformation that depends in large part on knowing yourself to be seen in a certain way: as significant, as wanted.

The whole story of creation, incarnation, and our incorporation into the fellowship of Christ's body tells us that God desires us, *as if we were God,* as if we were that unconditional response to God's giving that God's self makes in the life of the Trinity. We are created so that we may be caught up in this, so that we may grow into the wholehearted love of God by learning that God loves us as God loves God.

∞

The life of the Christian community has as its rationale—if not invariably its practical reality—the task of teaching us to so order our relations that human beings may see themselves as desired, as the occasion of joy. It is not surprising that sexual imagery is freely used, in and out of the Bible, for this newness of perception. What is less clear is why the fact of sexual desire, the concrete stories of human sexuality rather than the generalizing metaphors it produces, are so grudgingly seen as matters of grace, or only admitted as matters of grace when fenced with conditions. Understanding this involves us in stepping back to look rather harder at the nature of sexual desire; and this is where abstractness and overambitious theory threaten.

In one of the few sensible and imaginative accounts of sexual desire by a philosopher, Thomas Nagel writes:

> Sexual desire involves a kind of perception, but not merely a single perception of its object, for in the paradigm case of mutual desire there is a complex system of superimposed mutual perceptions—not only perceptions of the sexual object, but perceptions of oneself. Moreover, sexual awareness of another involves considerable self-awareness to begin with—more than is involved in ordinary sensory perception.[3]

Initially I may be aroused by someone unaware of being perceived by me, and that arousal is significant in "identifying me with my body" in a new way, but is not yet sufficient for speaking about the full range of sexuality. I am aroused as a cultural, not just a biological being; I need, that is, to bring my body into the shared world of language and (in the widest sense!) "intercourse." My arousal is not only my business: I need its cause to know about it, to recognize it, for it to be anything more than a passing chance. So my desire, if it is going to be sustained and developed, must itself be perceived; and, if it is to develop as it naturally tends to, it must be perceived as desirable by the other—that is, my arousal and desire must become the cause of someone else's desire.

For my desire to persist and have some hope of fulfillment, it must be exposed to the risks of being seen by its object. Nagel sees the whole complex process as a special case of what's going on in any attempt to share, in language, what something means. Part of my making sense to you depends on my knowing that you can "see" that I want to make sense. And my telling you or showing you that this is what I want implies that I "see" you as wanting to understand. "Sex has a related structure: it involves a desire that one's partner be aroused by the recognition of one's desire that he or she be aroused."[4]

All this means that in sexual relation I am no longer in charge of what I am. *Any* genuine experience of desire leaves me in this position: I cannot of myself satisfy my wants without distorting or trivializing them. But in *this* experience we have a particularly intense case of the helplessness of the ego alone. For my body to be the cause of joy, the end of homecoming, for me, it must be there for someone else, must be perceived, accepted, nurtured. And that means being given over to the creation of joy in that other, because only as directed to the enjoyment, the happiness, of the other does it become unreservedly lovable. To desire my joy is to desire the joy of the one I desire: my search for enjoyment through the bodily presence of another is a longing to be enjoyed in my body. As Blake put it, sexual partners "admire" in each other "the lineaments of gratified desire." We are pleased because we are pleasing.

It is in this perspective, Nagel says, that we can understand the need for a language of sexual failure, immaturity, even "perversion." Solitary sexual activity works at the level of release of tension and a particular localized physical pleasure; but insofar as it has nothing much to do with being perceived from beyond myself in a way that changes my self-awareness, it isn't of much interest for a discussion of sexuality as process and relation, and says little about grace. In passing, Nagel makes a number of interesting observations on sexual encounters that either allow no exposed spontaneity because they are bound to specific methods of sexual arousal—like sado-masochism—or that permit only a limited awareness of the embodiment of the other because there is an unbalance in the relation such that the desire of the other for me is irrelevant or minimal—rape, pedophilia, bestiality.[5] These "asymmetrical" sexual practices have some claim to be called perverse in that they leave one agent in effective control of the situation—one agent, that is, who doesn't have to wait upon the desire of the other. (Incidentally, if this suggests that, in a great many cultural settings, the socially licensed norm of heterosexual intercourse is a "perversion"— well, that is a perfectly serious suggestion.)

If we bracket, for the moment, the terminology of what is normative or ideal, it seems that at least we have here a picture of what sexuality might mean at its most *comprehensive.* And the moral question, I suspect, ought to be: How much do we want our sexual activity to communicate? How much do we want it to display a breadth of human possibility and a sense of the body's capacity to heal and enlarge the life of others? Nagel's reflections suggest that some kinds of sexual activity distort or confine the human resourcefulness, the depth or breadth of meaning such activity may carry: they involve assuming that sexual activity has less to do with the business of human growth and human integrity than we know it can have. Decisions about sexual lifestyle, the ability to identify certain patterns as sterile, undeveloped, or even corrupt, are, in this light, decisions about what we want our bodily life to say, how our bodies are to be brought into the whole project of "making human sense" for ourselves and each other.

To be able to make such decisions is important. A purely conventional (heterosexual) morality simply absolves us from the difficulties we might meet in doing so. The question of human meaning is not raised, nor are we helped to see what part sexuality plays in our learning to be human with one another—to enter the body's grace—because all we need to know is that sexual activity is licensed in one context and in no other. Not surprising, then, if the reaction is often either, "It doesn't matter what I do (say) with my body, because it's my inner life and emotions that matter" or, "The only criterion is what gives pleasure and does no damage." Both of those responses are really to give up on the human seriousness of all this.

They are also, like conventional ethics, attempts to get rid of risk. Nagel comes close to saying what I believe needs saying here, that sexual "perversion" is sexual activity without risk, without the dangerous acknowledgment that my joy depends on someone else's, as theirs does on mine. Distorted sexuality is the effort to bring my happiness back under my control and to refuse to let my body be recreated by another person's perception. And this is, in effect, to withdraw my body from the enterprise of human beings making sense in collaboration, in community, withdrawing my body from language, culture, and politics. Most people who have bothered to think about it have noticed a certain tendency for odd sorts of sexual activity to go together with political distortion and corruption (the *Raj Quartet*'s Merrick again—indeed, the whole pathology of the torturer). What women writers like Susan Griffin have taught us about the politics of pornography has sharpened this observation.

But how do we manage this risk, the entry into a collaborative way of making sense of our whole material selves? It is this, of course, that makes the project of "getting it right" doomed, as I suggested earlier. Nothing will stop sex being tragic and comic. It is above all the area of our lives where we can be rejected in our bodily entirety, where we can venture into the "exposed spontaneity" that Nagel talks about and find ourselves looking foolish or even repellent, so that the perception of ourselves we are offered is negating and damaging (homosexuals, I think, know rather a lot about this). And it is also where the awful incongruity of our situation can break through as comedy, even farce. I'm tempted, by the way, to say that only cultures and people that have a certain degree of moral awareness about how sex forms persons, and an awareness therefore of moral and personal risk in it all, can actually find it funny: the pornographer and the scientific investigator of how to maximize climaxes don't as a rule seem to see much of the dangerous absurdity of the whole thing.

The misfire or mismatch of sexual perception is, like any dialogue at cross-purposes, potentially farcical—no less so for being on the edge of pain. Shakespeare (as usual) knows how to tread such a difficult edge: do we or don't we laugh at Malvolio? For he is transformed by the delusion that he is desired—and if such transformations, such conversions, were not part of our sexual experience, we should not see any joke.

And it's because this is ultimately serious that the joke breaks down. Malvolio is funny, and what makes him funny is also what makes the whole episode appallingly and irreconcilably hurtful. The man has, after all, ventured a tiny step into vulnerability, into the shared world of sexually perceived bodies, and he has been ruthlessly mocked and denied. In a play which is almost overloaded with sexual ambivalence and misfiring desires,

Malvolio demonstrates brutally just why all the "serious" characters are in one or another sort of mess about sex, all holding back from sharing and exposure, in love with private fantasies of generalized love.

The discovery of sexual joy and of a pattern of living in which that joy is accessible must involve the insecurities of "exposed spontaneity"—the experience of misunderstanding or of the discovery (rapid or slow) that this relationship is not about joy. These discoveries are bearable, if at all, because at least they have changed the possibilities of our lives in a way which may still point to what joy might be. But it should be clear that the discovery of joy means something rather more than the bare facts of sexual intimacy. I can only fully discover the body's grace in taking time, the time needed for a mutual recognition that my partner and I are not simply passive instruments to each other. Such things are learned in the fabric of a whole relation of converse and cooperation; yet of course the more time taken the longer a kind of risk endures. There is more to expose, and a sustaining of the will to let oneself be formed by the perceptions of another. Properly understood, sexual faithfulness is not an avoidance of risk, but the creation of a context in which grace can abound because there is a commitment not to run away from the perception of another.

When we bless sexual unions, we give them a life, a reality not dependent on the contingent thoughts and feelings of the people involved; but we do this so that they may have a certain freedom to "take time" to mature and become as profoundly nurturing as they can. We should not do it in order to create a wholly impersonal and enforceable "bond"; if we do, we risk turning blessing into curse, grace into law, art into rule-keeping.

In other words, I believe that the promise of faithfulness, the giving of unlimited time to each other, remains central for understanding the full "resourcefulness" and grace of sexual union. I simply don't think we would grasp all that was involved in the mutual transformation of sexually linked persons without the reality of unconditional public commitments: more perilous, more demanding, more promising.

Yet the realities of our experience in looking for such possibilities suggest pretty clearly that an absolute declaration that every sexual partnership must conform to the pattern of commitment or else have the nature of sin *and nothing else* is unreal and silly. People do discover—as does Sarah Layton—a grace in encounters fraught with transitoriness and without much "promising" (in any sense): it may be just this that prompts them to want the fuller, longer exploration of the body's grace that faithfulness offers. Recognizing this—which is no more than recognizing the facts of a lot of people's histories, heterosexual or homosexual, in our society—ought to be something we can do without generating anxieties about weakening or compromising the focal significance of commitment and promise in our Christian understanding and "moral imagining" of what sexual bonding can be.

Much more damage is done here by the insistence on a fantasy version of heterosexual marriage as the solitary ideal, when the facts of the situation are that an enormous number of "sanctioned" unions are a framework for violence and human destructiveness on a disturbing scale; sexual union is not delivered from moral danger and ambiguity by satisfying a formal socioreligious criterion. Decisions about sexual lifestyle, to repeat, are about how much we want our bodily selves to mean, rather than what emotional needs we're meeting or what laws we're satisfying. "Does this mean that we are using faith to undermine law? By no means: we are placing law itself on a firmer footing" (Rom. 3:31, *NEB*). Happily there is more to Paul than the (much quoted in this context) first chapter of Romans!

$$\infty$$

I have suggested that the presence or absence of the body's grace has a good deal to do with matters other than the personal. It has often been said, especially by feminist writers, that the making of my body into a distant and dangerous object that can be either subdued or placated with quick gratification is the root of sexual oppression. If my body isn't me, then the desiring perception of my body is bound up with an area of danger and foreignness, and I act toward whatever involves me in desiring and being desired with fear and hostility. Man fears and subdues woman; and—the argument continues—this licenses and grounds a whole range of processes that are about the control of the strange: "nature," the foreigner, the unknowable future. This is not to assert uncritically that sexual disorder is the cause of every human pathology, but to grant, first, that it is pervasively present in all sorts of different disorders, and second, that it constitutes a kind of paradigm case of wrongness and distortion, something that shows us what it is like to refuse the otherness of the material world and to try to keep it other and distant and controlled. It is a paradigm of how not to make sense in its retreat from the uncomfortable knowledge that I cannot make sense of myself without others, cannot speak until I've listened, cannot love myself without being the object of love or enjoy myself without being the cause of joy.

Thinking about sexuality in its fullest implications involves thinking about entering into a sense of oneself *beyond* the customary imagined barrier between the "inner" and the "outer," the private and the shared. We are led into the knowledge that our identity is being made in the relations of bodies, not by the private exercise of will or fantasy: we belong with and to each other, not to our "private" selves—as Paul said of mutual sexual commitment (1 Cor. 7:4)—and yet are not instruments for each other's gratification.

All this, moreover, is not only potentially but actually a *political* knowledge, a knowledge of what ordered human community might be. Without a basic political myth of how my welfare depends on yours and yours on mine, a myth of personal needs in common that can only be met by mutuality, we condemn ourselves to a politics of injustice and confrontation. Granted that a lot of nonsense has been talked about the politics of eroticism recently, we should still acknowledge that an understanding of our sexual needs and possibilities is a task of real political importance. Sexuality-related "issues" cannot be isolated from the broader project of social recreation and justice.

As I hinted earlier, the body's grace itself only makes human sense if we have a language of grace in the first place; this in turn depends on having a language of creation and redemption. To be formed in our humanity by the loving delight of another is an experience whose contours we can identify most clearly and hopefully if we have also learned, or are learning, about being the object of the causeless, loving delight of God, being the object of God's love for God through incorporation into the community of God's Spirit and the taking-on of the identity of God's Child. It is because of our need to keep that perspective clear before us that the community needs some who are called beyond or aside from the ordinary patterns of sexual relation to put their identities directly into the hands of God in the single life. This is not an alternative to the discovery of the body's grace. All those taking up the single vocation must know something about desiring and being desired if their single vocation is not to be sterile and evasive. Their decision (which is as risky as the commitment to sexual fidelity) is to see if they can find themselves, their bodily selves, in a life dependent simply upon trust in the generous delight of God—that Other who, by definition, cannot want us to supply deficiencies in the bliss of a divine ego, but whose whole life is a "being-for," a movement of gift.

Sebastian Moore remarks that "True celibates are rare—not in the sense of superior but in the sense that watchmakers are rare."[6] Finding a bodily/sexual identity through trying to expose yourself first and foremost to the desirous perception of God is difficult and precarious in a way not many of us realize, and it creates problems in dealing with the fact that sexual desiring and being desired do not simply go away in the single life. Turning such experience constantly toward the context of God's desire is a heavy task—time is to be given to God rather than to one human focus for sexual commitment. But this extraordinary experiment does seem to be "justified in its children," in two obvious ways. There is the great freedom of the celibate mystic in deploying the rhetoric of erotic love in speaking of God; and, even more important, there is that easy acceptance of the body, its needs and limitations, which we find in mature celibates like Teresa of Avila in her last years. Whatever the cost, this vocation stands as an essential part of the background to understanding the body's grace: paradoxical as it sounds, the celibate calling has, as one aspect of its role in the Christian community, the nourishing and enlarging of Christian sexuality.

It is worth wondering why so little of the agitation about sexual morality and the status of homosexual men and women in the church in recent years has come from members of our religious orders. I strongly suspect that a lot of celibates indeed have a keener sensitivity about these matters than some of their married fellow Christians. And anyone who knows the complexities of the true celibate vocation would be the last to have any sympathy with the extraordinary idea that homosexual orientation is an automatic pointer to the celibate life—almost as if celibacy before God is less costly, even less risky, for the homosexual than the heterosexual.

∞

It is impossible, when we're trying to reflect on sexuality, not to ask just where the massive cultural and religious anxiety about same-sex relationships that is so prevalent at the moment comes from. In this final section I want to offer some thoughts about this problem. I wonder whether it is to do with the fact that same-sex relations oblige us to think directly about bodiliness and sexuality in a way that socially and religiously sanctioned heterosexual unions do not. When we're thinking about the latter, there are other issues involved, notably what one neo-Marxist sociologist called the ownership of the means of production of human beings. Married sex has, in principle, an openness to the more tangible goals of producing children; its "justification" is more concrete than what I've been suggesting as the inner logic and process of the sexual relation itself. If we can set the movement of sexual desire within this larger purpose, we can perhaps more easily accommodate the embarrassment and insecurity of desire: it's all for a good cause, and a good cause that can be visibly and plainly evaluated in its usefulness and success.

Same-sex love annoyingly poses the question of what the meaning of desire is—in itself, not considered as instrumental to some other process, such as the peopling of the world. We are brought up against the possibility not only of pain and humiliation without any clear payoff, but, just as worryingly, of nonfunctional joy—of joy, to put it less starkly, whose material "production" is an embodied person aware of grace. The question is the same as the one raised for some kinds of moralists by the existence of the clitoris in women: something whose function is joy. If the Creator were quite so instrumentalist in "his" attitude to sexuality, these hints of prodigality and redundancy in the way the whole thing works might cause us to worry about whether "he" was, after all, in full rational control of it. But if God made us for joy...?

The odd thing is that this sense of meaning for sexuality beyond biological reproduction is the one foremost in the biblical use of sexual metaphors for God's relation to humanity. God as the husband of the land is a familiar enough trope, but Hosea's projection of the husband-and-wife story onto the history of Israel deliberately subverts the God-and-the-land clichés of Near Eastern cults: God is not the potent male sower of seed but the tormented lover, and the gift of the land's fertility is conditional upon the hurts of unfaithfulness and rejection being healed.

The imagery remains strongly patriarchal, not surprisingly, but its content and direction are surprising. Hosea is commanded to love his wife "as I, the LORD, love the Israelites" (Hos. 3:1, *NEB*)—persistently, without immediate return, exposing himself to humiliation. What seems to be the prophet's own discovery of a kind of sexual tragedy enables a startling and poignant reimagining of what it means for God to be united, not with a land alone, but with a people, themselves vulnerable and changeable. God is at the mercy of the perceptions of an uncontrolled partner.

John Boswell, in his Michael Harding Address, made a closely related observation: "Love in the Old Testament is too idealised in terms of sexual attraction (rather than procreation). Samuel's father says to his wife—who is sterile and heartbroken because she does not produce children—'Am I not more to you than ten children?'" And he goes on to note that the same holds for the New Testament, which "is notably nonbiological in its emphasis."[7] Jesus and Paul equally discuss marriage without using procreation as a rational or functional justification. Paul's strong words in 1 Corinthians 7:4 about partners in marriage surrendering the individual "ownership" of their bodies carry a more remarkable revaluation of sexuality than anything else in the Christian scriptures. And the use of marital imagery for Christ and the church in Ephesians 5, for all its blatant assumption of male authority, still insists on the relational and personally creative element in the metaphor: "In loving his wife a man loves himself. For no one ever hated his own body" (5:28-29, *NEB*).

In other words, if we are looking for a sexual ethic that can be seriously informed by our Bible, there is a good deal to steer us away from assuming that reproductive sex is a solitary norm, however important and theologically significant it may be. When looking for a language that will be resourceful enough to speak of the complex and costly faithfulness between God and God's people, what several of the biblical writers turn to is sexuality understood very much in terms of the process of "entering the body's grace." If we are afraid of facing the reality of same-sex love because it compels us to think through the processes of bodily desire and delight in their own right, perhaps we ought to be more cautious about appealing to scripture as legitimating only procreative heterosexuality.

In a church that accepts the legitimacy of contraception, the absolute condemnation of same-sex relations of intimacy must rely either on an abstract fundamentalist deployment of a number of very ambiguous biblical texts, or on a problematic and nonscriptural theory about natural complementarity, applied narrowly and crudely to physical differentiation without regard to psychological structures. I suspect that a fuller exploration of the sexual metaphors of the Bible will have more to teach us about a theology and ethics of sexual desire than will the flat citation of isolated texts; and I hope other theologians will find this worth following up more fully than I can do here.

A theology of the body's grace which can do justice to the experience of concrete sexual discovery, in all its pain and variety, is not, I believe, a marginal eccentricity in the doctrinal spectrum. It depends heavily on believing in a certain sort of God—the trinitarian Creator and Savior of the world—and it draws in a great many themes in the Christian understanding of humanity, helping us to a better critical grasp of the nature and the dangers of corporate human living.

It is surely time to give time to this, especially when so much public Christian comment on these matters is not only nontheological but positively antitheological. But for now let me close with some words from a non-Christian writer who has managed to say more about true theology than most so-called professionals like myself.

> It is perception above all which will free us from tragedy. Not the perception of illusion, or of a fantasy that would deny the power of fate and nature. But perception wedded to matter itself, a knowledge that comes to us from the sense of the body, a wisdom born of wholeness of mind and body come together in the heart. The heart dies in us. This is the self we have lost, the self we daily sacrifice.[8]

I know no better account of the body's grace, and of its precariousness.

NOTES

*A slightly different form of this essay was delivered on 2 July 1989
as the tenth Michael Harding Memorial Address.*

1. Paul Scott, *The Day of the Scorpion* (London: Heinemann, 1968), 450.
2. *Ibid.*, 454.
3. Thomas Nagel, *Mortal Questions* (Cambridge: Cambridge University Press, 1979), 44-45.
4. *Ibid.*, 47.
5. *Ibid.*, 49-50.
6. Sebastian Moore, *The Inner Loneliness* (New York: Crossroad, 1982), 62.
7. John Boswell, "Rediscovering Gay History" (London: Gay Christian Movement, 1982), 13.
8. Susan Griffin, *Pornography and Silence: Culture's Revenge against Nature* (New York: Harper and Row, 1981), 154.

∞ Martin L. Smith, SSJE

Intimate Listening

Paying Attention to the Religious Experience of Gay and Lesbian People

Twenty years ago spiritual direction was virtually invisible, a specialized ministry available to a small, serious minority of the devout. Now it is at the center of a flourishing ecumenical culture of spirituality. A vast literature and many training resources are available. To a degree unheard of in the past and quite unpredicted a few decades ago, large numbers of people are claiming the privilege of a relationship with a spiritual guide or companion who will help them understand and own their religious experience. I would like to examine how this development might bear on the current struggle to hear what the Spirit is saying to the churches about and through the quest and claims of lesbian and gay people.

The burgeoning culture of spiritual direction is one of many movements exemplifying a shift in values toward religious experience. The ambivalence about the worth of this culture often evident among academics and leaders of religious institutions is not surprising. Increasing concern with lived experience of the divine goes hand-in-hand with a loss of interest in the claims and priorities of ecclesiastical institutions and authorities, and with a recoil from religion as both its traditional dogmatic form and its modern critical versions have intellectualized it. Those who have a detailed knowledge of Christian history, and indeed the history of other religions, will recognize a tension here that has been played out many times before. Guardians of religious institutions have repeatedly been made nervous by movements of lay people who vest authority less in official teachers than in their own religious experience as tested, validated, and encouraged by spiritual guides. The practice of spiritual direction is by nature subversive. It fosters freedom, a shift out from under the weight of precedents and the control of institutions.

One result of the rapid rise in the number of women and men qualified to offer spiritual direction has been that lesbian and gay seekers have a better chance of finding someone within the church who will listen to them intently and dispassionately. This in itself is a very significant development.

Some church leaders and pastors are able to give wise counseling and courageous support, but they are in a minority. Gay men and lesbians still have to be prepared to encounter hostility, ignorance, or superficial affirmation in their dealings with the clergy. In any case, few priests or ministers, except those who have chosen to specialize in counseling, have the skills or the time to listen at length over a long period of time to any one individual who is struggling to understand and deepen a relationship with God. But there are now a substantial number of population centers where gay and lesbian people can reasonably expect to find a spiritual companion who is equipped to listen to them, who will take them with the utmost seriousness as men and women of God, and who will help them to appropriate over time their own experience of the divine. As time goes on, the likelihood will grow that they will actually find spiritual directors who themselves are self-affirming gay men and lesbians.

∞

Now while it is a great gain to have access to ministry of this kind, we need to explore further exactly *what* kind of ministry it is in order to appreciate the significance of this development. First, then, spiritual direction is not primarily concerned with problems and crises. We need not be having trouble with anything in order to seek out spiritual companionship. In the past the main kind of ministry to which lesbians and gay men had access was based on the assumption that being primarily attracted to the members of one's own sex is *the* problem, a chronic kind of disability to be corrected or coped with. Spiritual direction, however, is based on the assumption that God is intimately involved already in the life of every human being. Its purpose is to foster, primarily through experiments in prayer, reflection, and action, an understanding of and a deep responsiveness to that intimacy. Far from being a problem, being gay or lesbian is a distinctive "given" for the spiritual director, one to be respected in its particularity and honored by empathetic attention. The only real problem is the persistent one common to everyone—that it is very exacting and frightening, as well as attractive, to let go and deal with being loved and indwelt by God. Being undead is not the same as being alive, and it takes conversion to know the difference.

Second, spiritual direction is not primarily concerned with issues of sin and guilt. Gay and lesbian Christians in the past often had access to ministry on condition that the issue of their sexuality remained squarely in the zone of confession and absolution, or of remorse and resolution to amend their lives. Attention to their experience was often narrowly focused by the lenses of official teaching that dictated which tendencies were morally dangerous and which behaviors sinful. The focus of spiritual direction is quite different—it is on allowing oneself to experience life as shot through with the grace of God. This does not make it a permissive exercise that ignores the demands of the new life in Christ; instead, it is a training in trust, the trust of experience rather than secondhand authorities. The further one goes in realizing and responding to the gift of God's self to one's self, the more certain it is that one will be made painfully aware of what it is, in actual reality, that gets in the way of that intimacy and disconnects one from what God desires. Issues of sin and reconciliation will inevitably occur in spiritual direction—not, however, on the prior basis of official prohibitions, but on the basis of what is actually discovered through growing intimacy with God about one's own pattern of resistance to love and truth.

There is another feature of the spirituality which informs this ministry in its ancient and contemporary forms that is especially relevant to the concerns of gay men and lesbians. Spiritual direction is the practice of acute attention to the spiritual experience of a particular man or woman, by which I mean her or his *whole* experience, understood in terms of God's participation in it. Women and men show that they have the gift to be spiritual guides by their exceptional awareness and valuation of particularity and personal uniqueness. The best spiritual directors are those who have become attuned to recognizing just how unique human beings are, and how resistant their intricate patterns of identity are to categorization. Just how much this gift demands is shown by the popularity of systems like the enneagram that seem to promise relief from the sheer infinity of human variation by providing clear outlines of human identities. Certainly traditions of spiritual guidance have always made use of schemes and typologies of temperament to assist in understanding religious experience, but the most authentic forms of direction are skeptical of every facile scheme and base themselves instead on a deep conviction of the uniqueness of each person's identity.

It was in an account of a retreat based on the *Spiritual Exercises* of St. Ignatius Loyola that the celebrated poet and Jesuit priest Gerard Manley Hopkins wrote some of his most strangely eloquent words about the utter uniqueness of personal identities:

> my selfbeing, my consciousness and feeling of myself, that taste of myself, of *I* and *me* above and in all things, which is more distinctive than the taste of ale or alum, more distinctive than the smell of walnut leaf or camphor, and is incommunicable by any means to another man (as when I was a child I used to ask myself: What must it be to be someone else?). Nothing else in nature comes near this unspeakable stress of pitch, distinctiveness, and selving, this selfbeing of my own.[1]

It is not surprising that these forceful words should emerge from an exposition of the theme of human beings as God's creation in the foundation of the *Spiritual Exercises*, the greatest text about the art of spiritual guidance in the Western spiritual tradition.

Now that Hopkins's homosexuality has been amply documented, we see further implications of his words. The experience of being different, and of having to conceal that difference from almost everyone on pain of intolerable sanctions, has tended to make gay and lesbian people especially sensitive to the mystery of identity, the inevitability of masks, the oppressive nature of conventions and stereotypes. The message of gay experience is that there is much more sheer diversity among us than most people can stand to know. As lesbians and gay men emerge more and more into the open and begin to require church and society to reckon with this diversity, the milieu of spiritual direction is one where they are likely to experience support. A large part of the process of religious maturation that spiritual direction is intended to foster through prayer and reflection concerns the growing freedom to shed the layers of false identity that have been imposed upon us, or adopted as defenses against external pressures to conform. This process is about the discovery of our inmost identity as indwelt by God, and about the freedom to accept our own particularity. Such a conversion is one that all are called to undergo, but its urgency and seriousness are especially evident to religious lesbians and gay men. They know that their well-being depends on the ability to undergo this liberation from inauthenticity, an inauthenticity that is continually reinforced not only by powerful elements in society at large, but also from within the gay world itself, fraught as it is with its own deadening conventions and specious stereotypes.

Those circles and communities in the church that are experienced in plumbing the resources of the great spiritual traditions are likely to be ones where gay and lesbian seekers will find allies in the arduous challenge of exploring their vocation. These traditions map out paths of exploration and integration that are radically different from the ones taken for granted as normal in the world. They tend to subvert many of those conventions—for example, conventions about what constitutes the masculine and feminine in human identity—that have been most oppressive for lesbians and gay men. They lead away from the constraints of the patriarchal family. While it is true that the ascetical traditions are marked with a bias against sexuality that limits their relevance, the great traditions nevertheless hold up extraordinary examples of men and women of God who have found the secret of radical freedom. One fascinating example is the recent reemergence of the great Sufi mystic of the thirteenth century, Jallaludin Rumi. His vast cycles of poetry celebrate not only the mystery of being totally in love with God, but also his deep love for women and the pivotal and passionate love he had for his spiritual master, Shams. With saints like Rumi modern labels such as homosexual and heterosexual appear grotesquely crude.

Gay and lesbian spiritual seekers are growing in their ability to articulate their own religious experience and create an authentic narrative of their "exploration into God." This growing ability to appropriate religious experience always involves being listened to. We are "listened into speech," to use an expression coined by feminism. The milieu in the church most committed to intense and intimate listening is the one that cultivates the ministry of spiritual direction.

∞

Now if the churches are to hear what the Spirit is saying about the lives and the callings of gay and lesbian people, and about God's will for them, they will need to pay prolonged and patient attention to the gradually accumulating evidence arising from the religious experience of lesbians and gay men themselves. The scriptures give no warrant for the notion that God communicates exclusively through the judgments of the hierarchy or the assertions of theological experts. If we believe that God genuinely communicates with us in the life of prayer and that through the many promptings of grace we can learn to discern the unfolding of our lives, then we can hear God by paying attention to narratives of religious experience from the people of God themselves. This claim has serious implications for theology, ethics, and Christian practice. A great deal of the energy now being spent on controversies about the morality of same-sex relationships concerns inherited prohibitions and the authority that is or is not to be attributed to them. Further energy is consumed in a political and ideological debate about liberation that hardly acknowledges the issue of God at all. But theology and ethics arise from reflection on actual experience. Concrete experience provides the data, which must then be organized and grasped through reflection.

If we are still at an extremely early stage in the process of attending to this primary level of experience, then where homosexuality is concerned our existing theology and ethics can only be provisional. To what degree do most Christians, or most of those who bear responsibility for the church's official teaching, have any direct access to the actual religious experience of gay men and lesbians? The answer is, hardly at all. First-person narratives about how gay and lesbian people experience the grace of God in their lives of prayer, their work, and their relationships are only just beginning to emerge.

There is no question, however, but that these narratives are now breaking the surface. Recently I shared an outline of this essay with friends. Later, to my surprise, one of them put into my hands a remarkable work of autobiography with the subtitle *Gay Catholic Reflections from Age Fourteen to Forty-two*. The strength of the narrative account derives from the way in which the story of an intimate relationship with Christ in prayer is intertwined with the quest and attainment of human love and partnership. Its authenticity is evident from its unflinching reckoning with loss and struggle as well as joy. That spiritual direction has been a constant element through the writer's whole adult life is no coincidence.

Spiritual direction has a significant role to play in encouraging these narratives. It remains to be seen how the church will react and whether it will take seriously these essential data for discerning what God desires for gay and lesbian people. In spiritual direction there are rules for the "discernment of spirits" inherited from the past that have been fine-tuned and revalidated in contemporary experience. For Christians these rules are based on the fundamental proclamation of Jesus that a good tree cannot bear bad fruit, nor a bad tree good fruit. In the life of the believer deep and prolonged resistance to what God desires prevents the burgeoning of the fruits of joy, ardor for the kingdom, and that mysterious kind of inner acceptance and spiritual tranquillity which comes with the ability to bear the truth and live with its paradoxes.

What, then, if gay men and lesbians who live in intimate sexual partnerships should manifest the fruits of the Spirit, showing over long years the same interior signs of harmony with God in their lives of prayer and communion that tradition has always confirmed as signs of God's good pleasure and blessing? What if it is discovered there are thousands of gay and lesbian believers of deep prayer who show no signs of bad faith, conflicted consciences, split selves, or cheap self-exoneration based on denial? What if thousands of gay and lesbian Christians should make available to the church at large something of the complexity and richness of their sexuality, and expose the brittle thinness of the stereotypes that at present are taken for granted by the majority of believers? What if the church is enabled to read in this body of narrative the signs of the Holy Spirit's struggling and creative presence, and the companionship of the Man of Sorrows who has shared the lot of those who suffer so much contempt and discrimination? The emergence into the light of day of gay and lesbian religious experience may well precipitate a fateful crisis in the church. What if its prevailing response should be a denial of the evidence of God's blessing, even though the classic principles of discernment of spirits would confirm it? What was it that Jesus said about blasphemy against the Holy Spirit...?

Even now it is not too early for some spiritual directors and for some gay and lesbian people in spiritual direction to begin to issue their testimony. There are hundreds of gay and lesbian people of God who have deep lives of prayer and committed lives of gospel service, who live in dedicated sexual partnerships, and who (in the light of the classic criteria of the discernment of spirits) show the same signs of God's blessing as is typically shown by the faithfully married and the faithfully celibate.

Of course the numbers of "those who have ears to hear" this reporting in the church may be limited at present. It is sobering to accept what the famous physicist Max Planck said about what we have come to call paradigm shifts in consciousness: "A new scientific truth does not triumph by convincing its opponents and making them see the light, but rather because its opponents eventually die."[2] Those who can already hear today what the Spirit appears to be saying to the churches through the religious experience of gay men and lesbians are likely to belong to a new generation who urgently feel the need for the healing of the chasm between sexuality and spirituality that is one of the most tragic flaws in the Christianity we have inherited. The disconnection between *eros* and worship; the separation of body from spirit; the exaltation of the mental over what is earthy, grounded, embodied; the taming and moralizing of the sexual realm and the equation of faithfulness with safety, normality, and propriety—these are all aspects of a sickness in Christianity that is painfully evident to large numbers of searching believers. Healing is underway in a vast corporate experiment, in which spiritual directors are deeply involved by definition, by their vocation.

No single group of human beings has been made to suffer more acutely from this chasm and refusal of integration than gay and lesbian people, who have been made to suffer the sickness in its most chronic form by the religious ban imposed on their erotic selves and their lives. Consequently, when lesbians and gay men experience healing, when they discover singleness of heart that unifies the joys and struggles of erotic and sexual living, and the joys and struggles of intimacy with God in Christ, it is good news not only for them but for the spiritual community at large. If gay and lesbian people can experience integration in the Spirit, in spite of the terrors of the past and the painful obstacles still present, then there is hope for us all. Any reports of this integration that we can hear now, if we tune out the noisy repetitive static of controversy, could be good news for the wider community, promising a renewed and passionate way of being Christian.

NOTES

1. *The Sermons and Devotional Writings of Gerard Manley Hopkins,* ed. Christopher Devlin, SJ (London: Oxford University Press, 1959), 123.
2. Max Planck, *Scientific Autobiography and Other Papers,* trans. F. Gaynor (New York: Philosophical Library, 1949), 33-34.

∽ *Peter S. Hawkins*

"Counter, Original, Spare, Strange"

Cradle Episcopalian. The familiar phrase suggests the smug good fortune of being born into a family older than the Mayflower, with silver to inherit and privileges to assume. I have never liked it. And yet, if the notion of "cradle" describes an identity that seems to have been there long before it was ever confirmed, I can find no better way to identify myself in the context of this book than as a "cradle homosexual." "Cradle" dispenses with the still unanswered question of nature or nurture by placing the whole matter of origins at a point very early in a person's life. By then, the genetic die has been cast and the complicated effects of parents and environment already begun their work.

Does this mean that the child I recognize from family photographs—the infant swallowed up by a christening gown, the little boy proud to be learning to walk between the hands of mother and grandmother—was gay? I do not know. But from the beginning of sexual memory, long before puberty, I recall the deep emotional and physical draw of men. At the time there was no way to voice this. Our home was not particularly straightlaced, but sexuality was simply not the subject of conversation or, as far as I could tell, of action. There was the expectation of courtship and marriage and children; the slight disapproval of brides who were already pregnant; concern over a cousin's husband who had become "impotent." The rest was silence.

Formally, therefore, homosexuality did not exist. And yet I remember savoring the tiny crumbs that fell from the parental table. A girlfriend of my mother's, a painter who had produced the portrait of my father that hung above the television set, was said to be "funny that way." A man in the office much beloved by my father had never married, "if you know what I mean." My older brother was equally unforthcoming. Only once, when I was a young teenager, did the topic get broached, and I recall his incredulity that any man could find another man physically attractive when, after all, women were so beautiful. I said nothing at the time because what I felt had as yet no words. But there was absolutely no mistaking the objects of my own longing, different from those that compelled my brother, to be sure, but beautiful to me.

The overwhelming desire to be a good boy (motivated almost entirely by the fear of social disapproval rather than by any higher conviction) provided me with a convenient way out of any kind of sexual experimentation or discovery; indeed, it kept me a virgin until my early twenties, long after the sixties had initiated most of my peers. When at long last I stumbled into bed with a woman graduate student during my first year at Yale, it was with a sense of relief and gratitude. But it was not, alas, filled with joy. I did not feel "natural"; it was as if I were doing something I should do but that otherwise went against the grain. Surely a partner deserved more enthusiasm than what I seemed able to offer, much as I wanted to please. Was it because I was incapable of passion?

By my mid-twenties that fear was lifted. For the first time I listened to my heart and allowed my body to follow after. He was beautiful and warm, predisposed to sunshine rather than to my emotional stormy weather, a fellow Christian, and the unwitting victim of my pent-up need to adore. All of my world changed. Or, as Andrew Sullivan describes his own version of this transformation, "It was like being in a black-and-white movie that suddenly converted to color."[1] Nor was it lost on me that I was studying the *Divine Comedy* at this moment in my new life. As a young man in love I could catch the daring, even dangerous truth of what Dante was attempting in the figure of Beatrice: how *eros* could be transfigured into *caritas* without rejecting the body, how we might come to know the divine face, however tentatively or imperfectly, by looking deeply into the faces of those we are given to love.

The *Divine Comedy* was not the only text suddenly to tell my story; there was scripture too. Oddly enough, given my particular circumstances, it was not David's love for Jonathan "passing the love of women" (2 Sam. 1:26) that caught my breath, but other passages that used the language of intimacy to describe the relationship between God and ourselves. There was Hosea crying out over the faithless Gomer, or Jeremiah unable to resist naming the Lord even though it caused him pain to do so:

> If I say, "I will not mention him, or speak any more in his name," there is as it were in my heart a burning fire shut up in my bones, and I am weary with holding it in, and I cannot. (Jer. 20:9)

At long last the Song of Songs made sense! Indeed, as I was told more than once, my love was "terrible as an army with banners."

What strikes me now about this crucial period in my life, apart from the overblown romantic intensity of it all, was not only my ease in seeing my homosexual experience in the light of one of the greatest heterosexual models—Dante's Beatrice was a woman, after all—but also how readily I related what was happening to me in bed with the world of scripture and theology. It was as if by falling in love I had discovered a connection between the longings I felt for my beloved and that immense longing for God that utterly transcended the boundaries of my romance. I was everywhere leaping in faith.

After a year of this impassioned assault I was asked by my lover to cease and desist: my Beatrice had had enough. The misery I felt was predictably enormous and in my pain and confusion I sought out a psychiatrist. After hearing the ranting of my disappointment, he warned me that homosexual attraction was inevitably doomed to failure: "It's not a very gay life, is it?" Because good boys usually make even better analysands, I did not challenge my doctor by asking what precisely the element of homosexual doom was in my case, but I did not capitulate to his forecasts of misery either. I decided instead that it was simply time to get on with being a sexual person. This meant the hit or miss of several relationships, some serious and others less so, but in each of which I received gifts and sustained losses, was guilty of rank selfishness and given the grace to make genuine sacrifices. I wonder how anyone learns to love except through this messy practice: making mistakes, having to forgive and be forgiven, painfully discovering the intractable otherness of someone else. In any event, learning to love, both sexually and otherwise, was the way I grew up.

∞

Given the strong disapproval of homosexuality in the Christian tradition, together with my lifelong involvement in the church, I am amazed that I never felt religious conflict over being gay or saw any reason to assume God's displeasure with my sexual being. To be sure, as usual with scrupulous people, my sins were ever before me. But what I had to confess were particular instances of pride, envy, wrath, lust—not my homosexuality as such. "Coming out" was done gradually, tentatively, and friend by friend: my reticence had to do with a fear of making people unhappy with me. I think it telling that the first place I felt free to be openly a gay man was at church. The liturgy was where, week by week, I found my center; it didn't occur to me that anything as central as my sexuality should not belong there too.

From all the horror stories I have heard over the years, tales of hatefulness that span the full denominational spectrum of Christianity, I recognize that my experience puts me in a fortunate minority. Was this because I was not exposed to homophobia in my parents' only mildly religious household? Or because the urban parishes where I chose to belong were open to all sorts and conditions, and took people on as themselves, whatever they were? Or was it because, since my nature is both conservative and prone to please, I never called attention to myself as being gay? Was it perhaps too easy for me to "pass"? For whatever reason, the Episcopal Church, at least as I knew it, did what its street-signs everywhere advertise: it welcomed me.

Work was another kind of environment, however. While never lying about my sexuality there, I kept it a secret—not as something shameful, but as something that did not exist. I came up with many excuses: colleagues would disapprove; I would never stand a chance at getting tenure; female students would think I wasn't interested in them personally while male students would misinterpret my interest; I did not have time to be a gay scoutmaster for homosexual seminarians; besides, it was nobody's business. No doubt there were other justifications for silence: the closet always has its reasons.

After I fell in love with a man called Luis, who came to share my life as well as my home in 1983, this silence became more of a burden, in large part because I found myself at last so profoundly partnered. I was more "at ease" than I had ever been before, but still wary of breaking the good news at school—and the relationship *was* news. The two of us seemed to have nothing in common but the attraction of opposites that first drew us together. He was a doctor, an epidemiologist, a Mexican, and a former Roman Catholic with severe reservations about Christianity. In short, he was not me. But what we in fact shared in common was a profound sense of being at home with one another. And once again, as years before at the beginning of my active homosexual life, the experience of intimacy was joined inextricably to that of my faith. Now, however, the lesson was different. If my first taste of love had been to see the connection between my longing for another person and the larger human longing for God, what I found through Luis was the other side of things. In his unflappable daily commitment to me, whether I was being a "good boy" or was at my very worst, he showed me something of how steadfastly God loves us. More than a few times I would drive him to repeat a line that describes what is perhaps his greatest legacy to me: "Muchachito, you make me suffer but I adore you." Until Luis, I had never registered that I could be loved deeply even when I was not being especially loving in return. It seemed nothing would drive him away. It was an astonishing discovery.

So, too, was the fact that Luis was ill. Shortly after we established a home together he was confirmed in his self-diagnosis that something was wrong. The HIV virus, let alone the test to detect it, was not yet known; we only had evidence that his immune system was under stress. A couple of years later our worst suspicions were confirmed, so that we were thrust into the same nightmare that so many other gay couples have come to endure: the side effects of medication, a diarrhea that would not go away, falling T-cell counts, the fear of blindness or loss of mind. Roughly seven years after we met, Luis, at the age of thirty-five, was dead. The sustained loss of him, both before and after his death, remains my most powerful experience of the cross. It meant living Good Friday day after day, sensing at one and the same time that I had been abandoned by God but that I was nonetheless supported, even carried, in the void. This love was a far cry from the one terrible as an army with banners; much of the time it only seemed terrible. And yet, as the Song of Songs also says, it was "as strong as death."

It proved impossible—no, it even seemed shameful—to keep all of this a secret at work. While I made no general announcement to the Divinity School, where probably it would have surprised nobody very much, I nonetheless allowed myself to be known as a gay man. Luis's valor in dying was too precious to keep behind closed doors, in some private world where friends and family were allowed free access but from which my colleagues and students were excluded. It would be too much of a claim to say that AIDS radicalized me: I was still disinclined to make waves. But the epidemic did propel me out of the implicit "don't ask, don't tell" mode I had adopted only in the workplace. AIDS gave me, I suppose, the courage of my convictions. You could ask; I would tell.

∞

Because I came of age after the liberating effects of Stonewall, lived in urban and university worlds, and never sought the church's approval for ordination, I have existed in a kind of never-never-land. Somehow, and despite the fulmination of the Christian Right, crisp rulings from the Vatican, and the strong objections of some of our own bishops, I never felt the church opposed me—even though John Boswell's book *Christianity, Homosexuality, and Social Tolerance* vividly set before me a history of intolerance.[2] None of these events, current or ancient, seemed to touch me. Ignorance remained bliss. I was even slightly impatient with gay people, Christian or otherwise, who made such a production out of being different or feeling embattled. "Grow up!" was often the mutter under my breath. In time, of course, this innocence inevitably came to its long overdue end. In 1994, and in the workplace where I had long kept my sexuality under wraps, I encountered for the first time a formal "Judeo-Christian" rejection of what I had taken for granted as life.

The occasion was an article that appeared in the journal *First Things* in March 1994, "The Homosexual Movement: A Response by the Ramsey Colloquium."[3] It was signed by twenty-one men with various religious and institutional affiliations, one of whom was a Yale colleague. Had the Ramsey Colloquium only made its concerns known to the readers of *First Things*, my great awakening would no doubt not have occurred as it did. But an excerpt in the *Wall Street Journal* that included the twenty-one names quickly made "The Homosexual Movement" required reading at the Divinity School. Many students were in an uproar, prayer vigils were held, faculty exchanged xeroxed broadsides through the campus mail. After the two weeks of spring break, there was also a panel of professors who offered a variety of theological viewpoints. Although this was no doubt the historical moment my new-found "radicalism" was born for, I largely missed the crisis. The day the article was distributed I was in the hospital with John Boswell's mother and his partner of over twenty years, waiting with them to see if he would emerge from a coma and go on living with the AIDS-related brain disease he had borne so courageously. It was only later, after Boswell came out of his coma and the semester began to wind down, that I actually studied the document.

It shocked me. I felt as if I had discovered something like the *Protocols of the Elders of Zion*, except in place of the perfidious Jew of that anti-Semitic tract it was "the Homosexual Movement" that could be blamed for everything rotten in our common life, including "sexual promiscuity, depression, and suicide and the ominous presence of AIDS" (19). The Ramsey Colloquium was not addressing itself primarily to the church, so neither the handful of scriptural prohibitions or the checkered history of Christian tradition was invoked. Rather, the authors were concerned to speak to all of America about a national crisis, about the state of the family and an embattled "heterosexual norm," both of which were presented as endangered species, "fragile institutions in need of careful and continuing support" (19). To my surprise the document showed no interest in the larger social and economic forces that provoke change and therefore cultural distress—what *Time* has called "Twentieth Century Blues." Rather, its focus was limited to the dangers posed by homosexuals and the entire polemic animated by what the authors claimed almost proudly to be "a reflexive recoil from what is wrong" (19).

The "wrongness" of homosexuality, once one gets past the document's broad parody of a supposedly uniform lifestyle, is its alleged attack on marriage and the family. Only the heterosexual norm fosters "the continuation of human life, the place of difference within community, the redirection of our tendency to place our own desires first" (18). In the logic of the Ramsey Colloquium, either you are "with" the norm or you are against it. Ignored is the fact that, like everyone else, homosexuals belong to families, and in my experience spend a considerable amount of time in the ongoing support of parents and siblings, nieces and nephews. Gay people also make new families. Increasing numbers of them adopt the offspring of others; some sire or bear their own children. No gay person or organization to my knowledge has ever argued that tax dollars should be withheld from schools, hospitals, or programs established to assist the life of parents and children. Nor is "the Homosexual Movement" currently dismantling public welfare.

But then, who *are* the homosexuals in this movement? The Ramsey Colloquium does not descend to the level of Jesse Helms in his denunciation of "deliberate, disgusting, revolting conduct," but the picture it paints is not pretty. Like other sexual revolutionaries, gay people are said to suppose "that the body is little more than an instrument for the fulfillment of desire, and that the fulfillment of desire is the essence of the self" (17). Allegedly fearful of commitment, constitutionally selfish, and unable to embrace the difference that God placed at the heart of male-female creation, the homosexual gazes at himself or herself in the mirror of Narcissus and, morally speaking, wastes away. Someone more to be blamed, perhaps, than to be pitied. Entranced by momentary pleasure, as opposed to the "commitment to time and history" (17) that characterizes the heterosexual norm, the homosexual in this account essentially abandons the commonweal.

Whatever my own failings may be, no one would ever, I think, apply this devastatingly negative judgment on the lives of gay people to me. Nor can I extend it to any of the many homosexuals I know personally. The Ramsey Colloquium concocts a stereotype and then turns it into a movement, as if the libidinal mayhem of a Gay Pride parade in New York accurately represents the real life of homosexuals any more than a New Orleans Mardi Gras (or an afternoon of television) gives us an accurate picture of the heterosexual norm.

When slandered, there is the immediate temptation to defend one's own integrity by producing the proper trophies of citizenship. In my case, there are the nine godchildren, the sermons preached at other people's weddings, the record of contribution to the United Way, Nature Conservancy, and the parish church—all the documented evidence of commitment to time and history. To amass credentials, however, is to run the risk of being a "good homosexual," allowing myself to be construed as the exception to a rule that is used to defame others who do not share my benign experience or conventional style but who are no less worthy of honest treatment.

I suspect, moreover, that self-defense is not what the Ramsey Colloquium is looking for anyhow. What they want is confession, remorse, and amendment of life. Gay people like me who are judged "incurable" must resist the impulse to act on their desire for a sexual life, that is, for "homogenital gratification." Instead, we must discover "the reality and beauty of sexually chaste relationships of deep affectional intensity" (18). Why is such friendship the only acceptable way to be intense? And why this effort to avoid the passion, comfort, and humor that invariably play themselves out in sexual love? The answer, *tout court*, is Sin. Homosexuality is judged to be an objective disorder; it makes the unnatural seem natural while actually wreaking havoc with the natural world as God has ordained it. For this rea-

son, the only cure, at least for those who cannot function within a heterosexual union, is complete abstinence. Like the alcoholic who must not
drink or the pedophile who must resist the urge to have sex with a child,
the homosexual must be resigned to obey God's providential will by becoming celibate. As Cardinal Ratzinger put it in his 1986 letter "On the Pastoral Care of Homosexual Persons," gay Christians must accept a call "to
enact the will of God in their life by joining whatever sufferings and difficulties they experience in virtue of their condition to the sacrifice of the
Lord's cross."[4] In other words, Offer It Up.

Rehearsing the argument of the Ramsey report, and then taking into account the philosophical tradition it draws upon, I am reminded of a conversation from my boyhood. Contrasting the disrespectfulness of children
then, in the mid-1950s, with the way things had been in her own youth, an
older relative declared that if either of her parents had ever told her to say
that milk was black, she would have done so because they were her parents. More than forty years have passed but I still recall my reply, delivered
sheepishly but delivered nonetheless: "But milk isn't black, it's white." Like
Galileo, told by the church authorities that the earth was the stable center
of the universe but knowing that "it moves" all the same, I felt in my own
small way responsible to truth. My cousin Dorothy and her parents would
have been complicit in a lie. I simply couldn't join them.

Nor can I now. I would sooner allow myself to be dismissed as Invincibly
Ignorant—constitutionally unable to "get it," stone deaf to the call of nature and reason—than to have my personal history, the joy of my sexual being, and the quality of my relationships all dismissed as "distorted." On the
basis of what knowledge are such judgments made? What actually makes a
love distorted or, as this discourse also has it, "less than optimal"? In hind-
sight I can readily imagine having lived my life better, more wisely, more
lovingly. But as it stands, my experience of love and loss, pleasure and pain,
have together been none other than the way that I have come to know the
gospel, to live vitally within the Christian tradition, and, however inadequately, to love God.

The Ramsey Colloquium, or indeed some panel of likeminded Anglican
bishops, might pronounce that my homosexuality *per se* is a way of life that
"encourages sexual relations for pleasure or personal satisfaction alone"
(16), that it constitutes a turning away from "the disciplined community
that marriage is intended to engender and foster" (16), and that people like
me have willfully rejected the providential design that has been etched into
human sexual nature. Such accusations have echoed throughout Christian
history, and yet absolutely none of them ring true. I am not driven by pleasure alone. I live a highly disciplined life, though it is outside the community of marriage. And the supposed etching of providence seems not to

have left in me the desired heterosexual imprint. To say otherwise would be to tell a lie, as bold-faced as the claim that a glass of milk was black.

∞

I can imagine how easily my appeal to the evidence of my own life may be dismissed as special pleading, as yet another example of the misguided "autonomous self" promoting a hopelessly modern agenda that confuses the Good with what feels good. What then shall I say to this? I leave it to others to discuss the few but oft-invoked scriptural passages, as well as the natural law argument that fuels the Ramsey Colloquium. In some sense what I have to offer is the witness of my own life and that of other gay believers, people who acknowledge themselves bound not by some heterosexual mandate but by the far more rigorous demands of a gospel that stands above all of us. It is the Rule of Love, after all, that is normative—not nature or the family.

Does this mean, then, that God (and Western civilization) are mocked? I don't think so. Neither heterosexuality nor "heterogenital gratification" shows signs of going away, and if their norms are changing, as indeed they seem to be, there may be as many reasons to praise as to lament. Nor do I believe that the church's consultation with its gay and lesbian members about the actual facts of their experience will undermine family and society by acknowledging the validity of another form of sexual life. Why, after all, does difference need to mean opposition? Rather, genuine interest in the reality of gay people may bring about a long overdue conversation. Confronted with actual gay and lesbian Christians, it will be less easy for the church to think of us in the same light as temple prostitutes or coerced catamites, to brush away our reality as if it were all so much *porneia*. A window may very well be pried open that has been stuck for a long time. I can imagine the intake of fresh air as healthy for everyone. At the very least, it would making breathing easier and thereby change the atmosphere of the whole conversation.

The first steps in such a dialogue, however, will entail a certain measure of talking back. I can think of an analogous situation within the Roman Catholic Church: the opportunity for married couples to say to their guardians of the natural law that contraception does *not* necessarily nullify or render sterile the purpose of their marital union. Instead, it can make it practicable without fear or anxiety, because not every sexual act needs to lead to procreation. It can simply be for joy. So too among us Anglicans, for whom contraception has never been regarded as a sin but among whom homosexual acts are still officially prohibited, at least for anyone who wants to be ordained. It strikes me as sensible that those who condemn "homogenital gratification" should listen to seasoned practitioners of the same, to hear in human language, as opposed to the disembodied discourse that so often prevails in church discussion, how for some people such gratification can be a means of grace. Not only taking pleasure but making love. Not the only way, nor the way of the majority, but one way all the same.

Kierkegaard said that in his systematic rigor Hegel had managed to construct a perfect house; the trouble was that no one could actually live in it. One thinks in this regard of the church's many pronouncements on human sexuality, of the official edifice constructed over the years, and wonders not only how few are in current residence but whether, in fact, there ever have been very many. Could sexuality be the area of Christian life where hypocrisy has become most deeply institutionalized? Where we have all felt called upon to lie or remain silent in order to remain members incorporate?

In any event, I prefer to make use of another architectural metaphor that has an even finer pedigree: "in my Father's house are many mansions" (John 14:2). Here the emphasis is first of all on God, as opposed to the laws of providence or nature. This means that we are dealing with the One who made the rascal Jacob a patriarch, the harlot Rahab an ancestor of Christ, and a Jew like Paul none other than the apostle to the Gentiles. The divine will is quirky, disruptive, full of surprises, with a propensity to break human conventions rather than fulfill them. This God consistently makes room for those who, by law or custom, are not supposed to be there. Moreover, the Creator loves difference: day and night, male and female, Jew and Greek, slave and free, all opposites that find their complement not so much in one another as in God.

I struggle in vain to understand why such a Creator should not also count as good that other aspect of diversity which is homosexuality. If we are proportionally few in number, we are nonetheless found everywhere in time and history, and also show no signs of going away. Rather than negating "the place of difference within community," as the Ramsey Colloquium charges, gay people may actually serve to uphold it. We remind the majority that not everyone is the same, indeed, that diversity is not only the spice of life but its characteristic.

But does the fact of many mansions in one house involve humanity in needless confusion? Certainly, having only one way to enter, only one room in which to stand tall, has the virtue of simplicity. Even children can be taught to read its blueprint from an early age (although whether they will all be able to live inside that building is another question). Confusion, however, has never given the Maker of heaven and earth a moment's pause. God seems in fact to have a predilection for infinite variety, almost as if it were quite as much a reflection of the divine character as order and proportionality.

Second-guessing providence is always risky business. Still, I cannot help believing that the existence of gay people, far from straying from divine intention, is part of it—yet another mysterious manifestation of the Creator's taste for those myriad "dappled things" that together form the counterpoint of the world. Makers of systems have never been able to find a purpose for the existence of homosexuals. There is no discernible "use" in the natural order, no clear-cut "point" for the larger human community. I think, on the contrary, that gay people exist for no utilitarian reason whatsoever, but only as yet one more reason to give God thanks for a bounty that is full to overflowing, and mercifully beyond our control.

> All things counter, original, spare, strange;
>> Whatever is fickle, freckled (who knows how?)
> With swift, slow; sweet, sour; adazzle, dim;
>> He fathers-forth whose beauty is past change:
>>> Praise him.[5]

NOTES

1. Andrew Sullivan, *Virtually Normal: An Argument About Homosexuality* (New York: Knopf, 1995), 191.

2. John Boswell, *Christianity, Homosexuality, and Social Tolerance: Gay People in Western Europe from the Beginning of the Christian Era to the Fourteenth Century* (Chicago: University of Chicago Press, 1980).

3. "The Homosexual Movement: A Response by the Ramsey Colloquium," *First Things* 41 (March 1994): 15-20. Hereafter all parenthetical page references in my text are to this article.

4. Joseph Cardinal Ratzinger, "On the Pastoral Care of Homosexual Persons," *Origins, Catholic News Service Documentary Service* 16. 22 (13 November 1986). Cited by Sullivan, "Virtually Normal," *The South Atlantic Quarterly* 93. 3 (Summer 1994): 671-672.

5. "Pied Beauty," *Poems of Gerard Manley Hopkins,* 1948; 3rd ed. (New York: Oxford University Press, 1961), 74.

THE
CHRISTIAN
HOUSEHOLD

∞ *Cynthia S. W. Crysdale*

Christian Marriage and Homosexual Monogamy

One of the wonderful mystery novels of Ellis Peters, which are set in a medieval monastery and have Brother Cadfael as the central sleuth, is called *An Excellent Mystery*. This is an odd title, since all her novels are mysteries. It seems as if she has named this one as a means of self-congratulation. It is only as the novel unfolds that one discovers she has a different sort of mystery in mind. In fact, all the pieces fit together only at the very end of the story, when she quotes the *Book of Common Prayer*: "O God, who hast consecrated the state of Matrimony to such an excellent mystery...Look mercifully upon these thy servants."[1] The novel, it turns out, is not only about mystery as a puzzle to be solved by a sleuth, but, even more, about the mystery which is marriage.

A similar view of the unknown yet transformative depths of marriage is given in a different form by Rosemary Haughton in *The Transformation of Man*. While the whole book is a phenomenology of human development and transformation, the second chapter, "Encounter," is a description of an imaginary young couple in the throes of an emerging sexual intimacy. While Haughton chooses to tell the story of a non-Christian couple in a secular culture, her point is to illustrate how sexual encounter demands self-transcendence and transformation. Each step of the way each partner has the choice: to grow and expand, while inevitably becoming more committed to the other, or to close in on himself or herself, with the awareness that this closedness will ultimately terminate the relationship. This description shows not only how sexual intimacy is implicitly oriented toward marriage, but that such an encounter is ultimately oriented toward salvation:

> It is by seeing the sexual encounter striving to achieve its full stature that we may be able to see that it *can* be a saving encounter, and that this is most likely to be so in marriage, properly understood.[2]

I begin with these two examples because both describe an element that is often lacking in popular culture today. We have legal marriage, cohabitation, sit-com images of marital strife, romantic images of relational salvation without sin. But rarely, if ever, are the depth of intertwined selves, their struggles to forgive sin over the long haul, and the salvific element of monogamy portrayed. Even St. Paul's early recognition that the mystery of salvation is integral to the marriage relationship is often overlooked because of his patriarchal views.

Both Haughton's and Ellis's stories illustrate another element of Christian marriage, besides its depth and its mystery, that has to be understood in grasping its meaning. This further element is what social historians would call the "social construction" of marriage. However essential the notion of salvific encounter is to a theology of marriage, marriage is and always has been a social institution, in fact a very flexible one, structured according to the economic, political, and social needs of each era. Haughton demonstrates this by including as central to her story the psychosocial drama of each partner's past, what she calls *formation*. Transformation depends on this socially embedded formation, and marriage is meant to be a formative institution that makes transformation possible. Ellis illustrates the social construction of marriage by her medieval setting and the peculiar manner (to the modern mind) in which her protagonists' marriage vows are fulfilled.

The purpose of this essay is to hold two elements together and then to ask a challenging question. The two elements are the salvific mystery that *can* be (surely the institution does not make it so) part of marriage, and the social construction of such an institution. The challenging question is this: Might a theology of marriage that holds both these elements together have anything to say about the pairing of persons of the same sex? Is it possible for Christians to accept that the mystery of Ellis's novel and the salvific encounter described by Haughton can be and are experienced by persons of homosexual orientation? Can the institution of Christian marriage adapt in order to provide a framework in which homosexual love can thrive and develop?[3]

The first part of this essay consists of a brief history of Christian marriage, illustrating the ways in which our conception of marriage has changed through Christian history.[4] The point of this review is not to prove that there are historical precedents for homosexual marriage, but rather to indicate the flexibility and adaptation of the institution of marriage to various eras.[5] The second section of the essay raises the possibility that marriage might once again adapt—this time, to our modern understanding of sexual orientation—and reviews the theological obstacles to such an adaptation.

The Development of Marriage
in Western Christian History

Christian marriage, of course, has it roots in the Jewish tradition. Yet the history of Israel itself exhibits a variety of social arrangements, some of which seem shocking today. Most obvious are the Old Testament accounts of the many wives of the patriarchs. In a nomadic culture, proliferation of sheep, goats, and children was an indication of wealth and prosperity. The main purpose of marriage was procreative, to expand the husband's clan. The more wives one had, the more children. Children were seen as a gift from God and, especially for women, barrenness was a curse. Thus, although the story of the creation of Adam and Eve was known and recorded at the height of the Israelites' power in the tenth century B.C., it was not taken as an endorsement for monogamy, because Solomon and others kings had many wives.[6] The moral injunction to take only one wife developed in connection with the reinforced monotheism and moral reforms of the exilic and postexilic periods. The demise of polygamy was also political and economic: the forced exile of Judah and Israel by Assyrian and Babylonian powers and the entrenchment of urban life made the taking on of multiple wives impractical and unnecessary.

By the time of Jesus, polygamy was theoretically still allowable but rarely practiced. Nevertheless, marriage was seen as a duty, a vocation in which procreation and loyalty to spouse were part and parcel of loyal loving concern for one's clan, nation, and God. Celibacy was rare, and most marriages were arranged. Negotiations took place between two families, who sought spouses for their children from their own relatives, within the degrees of relationship specified by the Torah. When a young girl married she became a part of her husband's family and, quite often, the young couple lived in the paternal household. A double standard operated in which men could divorce their wives but wives could not divorce their husbands.

The elements of Roman culture that came to influence Christian marriage were equally patriarchal. The Roman father was not only head of the household but possessed all legal rights over his wife and children. As in Jewish custom, marriage was a family affair. Wedding ceremonies, for both Jew and Roman, were public and formal but not liturgical, in the sense of being conducted by religious authorities. The marriage ceremony would be conducted by a family member—the father of the groom—and priests were invited to offer sacrifices or bless the couple as an auxiliary aspect of the ceremony.

Little is known about Christian wedding and marriage customs in the first century. Most Christians were adult converts and many were already married, so that pastoral issues involved how to deal with unconverted spouses (see 1 Corinthians 7). Jesus' injunction against divorce obviously stood out in the nascent Christian communities since it is recorded in several gospels and alluded to by Paul, though Paul makes exceptions to it (again, see 1 Corinthians 7). Added elements in this context include both persecution and the expectation of the parousia, so that Paul's injunctions, as well as the recording of Jesus' harsh sayings about family in the gospels, must be read in light of an audience of converts struggling to maintain their convictions while awaiting Jesus' return.

The ensuing centuries of Christianity saw the institution of marriage as a civil affair, arranged and conducted by family members. Even after the conversion of Constantine in 313 the legal regulation of marriage and divorce was left to the government rather than to church officials. Marriage under Roman law was by the mutual consent of parties involved (or their parents) and cases came to court only when contested or involving disputes over property.

The fathers of the church, who were so influential in setting the course of theological doctrine in areas such as christology, had little to say about marriage, mainly because it incited no great controversies. Generally, they accepted marriage as a social institution under Roman law as well as a religious institution sanctioned by Christ. Christians were expected to follow the norms of the gospels and the epistles, and homilies abound recommending love and fidelity between spouses.[7] But these religious and ethical ideals were accepted as part of an existing secular institution.

One other important development during the patristic period had to do with the amalgamation of Christianity with Greek culture. In contrast with Hebrew scripture, some trends in Greek thought distinguished sharply between mind and body, and added to the distinction an evaluation such that mind (or the realm of spirit) ranked higher than body (the physical, material realm), which was regarded as a temporary prison if not as evil in itself. The influence of this perspective on Christian theology can be seen in the rise of asceticism, and in the way celibacy came to occupy a more honorable place in the spiritual hierarchy than marriage. Paul's comment that "it is better to marry than to burn" (1 Cor. 7:9) was taken to refer to those who were incapable of achieving the holier state of celibacy. Augustine and others justified married sexuality in its procreative purpose. Still, sexual appetite remained evil: "Those who use the shameful sex appetite in a legitimate way make good use of evil, but those who use it in other ways make evil use of evil."[8]

Thus, in the earliest centuries of Christianity marriage was accepted as a secular institution. Marital values such as fidelity were endorsed but, on the whole, the spiritual ideal lay with celibacy, while married sexuality presented an obstacle to be theologically justified. The Middle Ages brought a shift from marriage as a secular to an ecclesiastical institution. In the fourth and fifth centuries liturgical wedding ceremonies gradually increased, and by the eighth century church weddings were common but not required.

But by far the most important moment was the fall of the Roman empire and the juridical quandary that ensued. With the breakdown of Roman law, ecclesiastical authorities stepped in to settle disputes, including those regarding marriage, and the era of canon law was launched.

A particular dilemma arose over the definition of marriage. Under Roman law a marriage contract was legal and binding by reason of consent—either the consent of the parties involved or that of their parents. The Germanic tribes that overtook the Roman empire saw consent as merely a promise; a marriage did not exist until consummated in the first act of sexual intercourse. These two traditions led to multiple problems. Young couples would run off and get married against the consensual contracts made by their parents or legal guardians. Or individuals would try to get out of a marriage by claiming that they had previously made a consensual contract to marry another. Since marriage was as much an economic arrangement as anything else, often involving large assets and property, these civil suits—and the definition of marriage they entailed—had much at stake. In the twelfth century the church finally settled on the idea that a valid marriage involved both consent and consummation. It took the Council of Trent, in the sixteenth century, to abolish secret marriages by insisting that all marriages take place before a priest and two witnesses and that the intent to wed (the "bans of marriage") be published at least three weeks in advance.

The shift toward marriage as an ecclesiastical institution led to the creation of distinctively Christian rites and to the definition of marriage as a sacrament. Earlier, Augustine had declared the three ends of marriage to be procreation, union (that is, fidelity), and symbol (of Christ's relation to the church). This latter notion, combined with the relevant passages of St. Paul, was developed at the same time that distinctive marriage rituals were devised. Eventually, marriage was declared to be one of the seven sacraments in that it embodies the grace of Christ's redemption of the church.

The Protestant Reformation of the 1500s challenged both of these medieval developments. The corruption of ecclesiastical courts in the late Middle Ages led reformers to reject ecclesiastical jurisdiction over marriage as well as its sacramental status. Reformers held a high view of marriage and its permanence, but believed it should be under civil jurisdiction and did not see it as a sacred ritual instituted by Christ. The history of ensuing centuries bore out this shift back to marriage as a civil institution. After the fall of the French aristocracy in the late eighteenth century, the Napoleonic code of law put marriages back under civil jurisdiction. Other European powers followed suit, and the fruits of the secularization of the Enlightenment were written into the U. S. Constitution. Today, marriage ceremonies are legal, civil affairs of the state, and certain persons, including clergy, are designated as *ex officio* delegates of the state.

I have been sketching in broad strokes some of the stages that marriage, as a social institution, has passed through in the Christian West. From a secular institution with religious meaning for those who happened to be Christian, marriage became a sacrament at the heart of medieval Christendom. The Protestant Reformation as well as the political and social outcomes of the Enlightenment put marriage back into the secular domain. This brings us to the doorstep of the modern era. Before moving on, however, let me discuss three major elements that have been definitive in forming our contemporary understanding and experience of marriage.

First, there has been the influence of *industrialization*. In the colonial era of North America, homestead and workplace were synonymous. Whether agrarian or craft-based, the home was the place of production and family members—women and children included—were the producers. The rise of industrialization shifted all this. Small factories and, later, large industrial complexes gradually replaced the home as the locus of production. With this shift came the introduction of a wage economy, with profound effects on family life. Men were now the workers, who left home to bring back wages. Women became keepers of the home, servicing the men so that they could work and using their wages to manage the household.[9] The division between public and private life established itself and the sanctity of the home as "off-limits" for social control was accepted.

Second, at about the same time (early to mid-nineteenth century), *romance* entered into the arena of marriage. Whereas up until this point marriage was primarily an economic arrangement (under various forms of parental control), whose main purpose was producing and educating offspring, the Enlightenment endorsement of individual choice altered things. For the first time, in the late 1700s "lack of affection" began to be cited as a reason for divorce. Compatibility and romance grew as the commonly understood basis of a good marriage, whose partners chose one another of their own free will.

Thus, we in the twentieth century have inherited a model of family as economic consumer, not producer, in which two persons fall in love and choose to establish a household and family. Up until recently, it was simply assumed that the family worked with well-established gender roles. The husband left the home to be the breadwinner while the wife stayed at home to develop the potential of her children and secure a safe haven for all to return to at the end of the day.[10] This Ozzie-and-Harriet ideal has, of course, been challenged in the last thirty years, through both the women's liberation movement and structural economic changes, sending women, even mothers of young children, into the workforce in droves.

In the meantime, the role of children in families has changed dramatically. The shift to a wage economy came along with the discovery of human life cycles: until the early 1800s the notion of childhood as a discrete time of life did not exist. Whereas children were at first employed in the interests of the industrial enterprise, child labor laws were eventually passed while public education increased. The role of the child as an economic asset to household production ceased and the notion of childhood enrichment (resting squarely on the shoulders of the women at home) emerged.

Third, by the twentieth century, medical and technological advancements led to the intervention of *artificial contraception*. This development was embraced by the growing movement for women's right to choose, at the polls as well as in the home. In contemporary society it is overwhelmingly presumed that children are an option, a choice made by those involved in sexual intimacy. From children as biological necessity and economic asset (and, for many women, a dreaded inevitability), we have now come to children as a choice, and even—in the case of some reproductive techniques and adoption arrangements— a commodity.

A Contemporary Theology of Marriage: Including Gays (?)

What I have presented so far is no more than an outline of the main contours of developments that were far more intricate than my summary suggests. Given the cursory nature of this review, then, what conclusions might we draw from it? Some would conclude, with a thorough relativism, that when it comes to marriage there are no universal norms or values, leaving the future of Christian marriage quite open. That is not my position. I would say, rather, that my far too rapid overview of history indicates a difference between changing norms—the social roles, expectations, and customs prevalent at a given place and time—and the abiding *values* that undergird them. In other words, I believe that it is possible to discern basic tenets of a Christian theology of marriage which have been adapted and enriched as Christian history has unfolded.

As indicated by my reference to "mystery" and "encounter" at the beginning of this essay, I believe that one of the most basic values of marriage is that it calls two individuals constantly to grow beyond their own self-enclosed perspectives. The marriage relationship—in a whole variety of ways—demands that each person grow in both self-understanding and in self-sacrifice for the other. Marriage is thus a call to self-transcendence. As Haughton indicates, this vocation to self-transcendence is built into the very nature of sexuality itself, so that sexual intimacy without commitment and growth is a truncation of human potential. Further, this challenge to growth indicates the peculiar nature of sexual intimacy: it involves a depth of intersubjectivity that is not present, or is present in different ways, in other equally self-transcending relations, such as friendship.

In addition, this challenge to self-transcendence has a religious dimension. The point of marriage (and its sexual intimacy) is to draw persons out of themselves in order to grow closer to *God*. Self-transcendence is not just in the interests of the other partner, but also that each might become transformed into a deeper communion with the divine.[11] In addition, an adequate theology of marriage must take account of sin. Married, covenanted love is not exempt from hurt and injustice. Thus the religious dimension of marriage involves redemption and reconciliation. Without grace, without the gift of healing and renewal and forgiveness, no potential encounter of transformation will reach its fulfillment. Indeed, it would become a stifling idolatry.

In sum, sexual pairing is oriented toward long-term commitment and self-transcendence, and its potential is only fulfilled by ongoing acceptance of the grace of God. Thus far, what I have indicated as the perduring aspects of Christian marriage is *something like* what St. Paul, Augustine, and the medieval theologians meant by the sacramental aspect of marriage. While this notion itself developed into a technical category defined by canonical and liturgical mandates (which were then rejected and revised by Reformers), the basic *value* remains the same.

The institution of matrimony has always existed as a framework within which this ideal of commitment can be carried out. The openly proclaimed commitment and faith of a couple, combined with the support of a faithful and being-redeemed community, provide a public structure whereby promise-keeping has accountability and within which the oscillations of sin and forgiveness will not break the bond.

Now, as we have seen, many other "interests" have, in the course of history, formed and influenced the institution of marriage. Economic interests, familial, intergenerational interests, patriarchal culture, concerns for class or racial purity, all have infiltrated and affected the *form* that marriage takes. These are not evil in themselves; a further ethical analysis is required to determine the values and disvalues within the social structure of each era. But basic to each era, and perduring as the Christian ideal for today, is the notion of marriage as a deeply intersubjective union, consummated and held together by sexual intercourse, oriented toward the self-surpassing growth of each of the individuals as well as of the couple itself, made possible through the intervention of God's grace, and made public and supported by a community of faith.

It is at this point that my "challenging question" arises. In recent years the assumption that sexual intercourse between a man and a woman is the only legitimate form of genital intimacy has come to be questioned. Gay people are a fact, a presence within the Christian community as well as outside of it. While gays are often stereotyped as promiscuous, evidence exists that long-term monogamous partnerships are an increasing reality.[12] So now we have Christians forming monogamous same-sex partnerships akin to marriage. Thus the question arises: To what degree is gender-differentiation a core component of the basic ideal, mentioned above, of Christian marriage? Given the many ways in which this ideal has adapted and manifested itself through history, what is to keep the Christian tradition from once again accepting new forms to manifest the old ideals? If a same-sex partnership involves all the elements outlined above—deep mystery and self-transcending encounter, struggle with sin and acceptance of grace—why deny it the community of faith and an institution analogous to marriage that can be a formative structure in which transformative growth can take place?[13]

In making an adaptation of this sort, an obstacle is raised by each of the two chief foundations on which Christian ethics bases its precepts and arguments: the Bible and natural law. We will examine these two sources for Christian ethics in order to see how the arguments derived from them are made. The point here is not to build or refute specific arguments regarding homosexual pairing as much as it is to point out methodological issues; that is, concerns about the assumptions on which these arguments rest.

The Bible

Clearly, the Bible assumes that marriage involves heterosexual couples and nowhere does it indicate any openness to alternate arrangements. In fact, biblical injunctions against homosexual activity are some of the most direct ethical prescriptions that Christian theology can glean from the Bible. Since arguments over particular passages abound elsewhere, let me simply highlight the problems involved in accepting biblical injunctions or norms at face value.[14]

The issue here is none other than that with which we have been dealing all along. The Bible, as a group of writings from many historical and cultural contexts, must be historically located in order to be adequately understood. The issue in interpreting the Bible, very simply put, is how to separate the earthen vessel—which we can dispense with—from the gospel message it contains—which is the core of our salvation.

Examples abound in which biblical perspectives, or even mandates, have been either rejected or pastorally adapted to new situations. Most obvious is the patriarchal context of both Testaments. Paul's injunctions for women to be silent or cover their heads in worship are no longer considered central to salvation or even to faithful liturgy. Less obvious, perhaps, is the New Testament's acceptance of slavery, or biblical laws against usury (that is, the taking of interest on loans). Even Jesus' words against taking up the sword have been adapted into what is now the long history of the just war tradition.

Even within the New Testament we find pastoral adaptation of the very strong words of Jesus. His rejection of divorce in favor of the permanence of marriage is acknowledged in 1 Corinthians 7. Yet Paul is facing a pastoral dilemma of his own: how to deal with married couples in which one spouse has converted and the other has not. Paul, while espousing the ideal of permanence, and knowing full well Jesus' position on the issue, nevertheless ultimately insists that the *form* of marriage should give way to more basic gospel values. If the unconverted spouse is unhappy with her partner's conversion, they should separate, since "it is to peace that God has called you" (1 Cor. 7:15).

The modern era, with its recognition of individual rights as well as the unmasking of false consciousness by Freud and Marx, has led to new insights into the New Testament's sexism, acceptance of slavery, and even anti-semitism. In each case, these new insights must be held in counterpoint with the demands of the gospel: recognizing St. Paul's patriarchal bias need not lead to the dismissal of his profound insights into law and grace. In each case, core gospel values, such as love for sinners or acceptance of those rejected by society, and the call for a radically new vision occasioned by following Jesus, take precedence over the cultural milieu that comes with the first-century locus of Jesus and the early Christians.

It goes without saying that discriminating what is essential from what is not is a difficult and perilous undertaking. But, as the examples I have given indicate, Christians have had to exercise just such discrimination time after time, and there is reason to think that they must do so again today. For there is no question but that we have entered into new understandings of sexual orientation in recent decades. Much work still has to be done to understand the role that nurture and nature play in the evolution of individual sexuality. However, enough is known to indicate that sexual orientation is not *simply* a conscious moral choice. It seems to be something that happens to an individual rather than a lifestyle for which one opts.[15]

Given this new understanding of homosexuality, which includes the distinction between homosexual orientation and homosexual acts, as well as the difference between promiscuity and fidelity, what aspects of biblical revelation are relevant to our question? If one's concern is for recognition of the deep mystery and encounter that can occur over a lifetime of homosexual monogamy, are the biblical passages dealing explicitly with homosexual acts adequate for forming a position on homosexual marriage? As many have pointed out, the cultural context of these passages reveals that the moral issues at stake in them have more to do with rejecting pagan religion and distinguishing Jews from Gentiles than they do with devising a sexual ethic.[16] What about the gospel values of love, fidelity in marriage, openness to the other, conversion to God's radically different view of the world? In this light, sin gets redefined at a deeper level, as the failure to follow Jesus or the taking on of other "masters" or both, rather than as particular acts involving another person of the same sex.

The point here is not to *dismiss* the Bible as a resource for theology or ethics but to ask how the Bible is used. Is it not more important to glean from the New Testament the strong call to conversion and the importance of fidelity in marriage than it is to adopt a cultural perspective ignorant of sexual orientation as given?

Natural Law ②

Some more compelling arguments, perhaps, against homosexual marriage come from commonsense observations of "nature." This appeal to "the way things are" or "the order God has established in nature" are the basis of what has classically been called natural law. The argument appeals to the facts of morphology, the structure of our gendered bodies and the natural biological purpose of sexuality. According to this view, persons are created as men or women, with the clear purpose of mating and producing children. Homosexual coupling is "unnatural" or "disordered," given this obvious created order.[17]

This argument is, I believe, a serious one. But a few observations should be made about assumptions behind and within this position. Just as the Bible cannot necessarily be read and taken at face value, so too sexuality cannot be simply interpreted as the obvious outcome of bodily structures. The point here is that, as the review of history indicates, human sexuality has cultural meaning. That is, human sexuality, while involving a set of biological urges, is much more than animal instinct. Human sexuality is always sexuality that *means* something, because it involves *persons* who bring to their sexual encounters a whole way of looking at the world, themselves, their partner, their future. Inextricably bound to sexual intercourse are the memories, hopes, expectations, and blind spots of the persons involved, all of which may be more or less inarticulate.[18] In other words, just as marriage as an institution is socially constructed, so too is sexual intimacy, and explaining the purpose of sexuality merely at the level of morphology or biology is reductionism of the worst sort. Just as one cannot read the Bible literally, one cannot "read" biological facts literally: one must defend one interpretation as more adequate than another.

But what does "more adequate" mean here? Once again one is thrown back to the question of what is most basic to the meaning of human sexual intimacy. Is it the heterosexual nature of it? Is it its biological production of children? Or is it the self-transcendence spoken of above, a self-transcendence that includes and finds its complete fulfillment in the love of God? Does one determine the meaning of sexuality according to its biological orientation or according to its spiritual meaning and its unitive purpose, that of drawing two persons into a deep intersubjective bond? Throughout

Christian history those who have chosen a life of celibacy have insisted that the ultimate spiritual orientation of sexuality supersedes even its biological ends. "Reading" bodies literally runs the risk of biological reductionism or a fundamentalism of nature, or both.

Still, just how fluid can this spiritual nature of sexuality be? Can it disregard the biological ordering of creation altogether? In other words, what about children and procreation? The *lack* of procreative possibility has for centuries been cited as a major argument against homosexuality, and continues to be a central issue in Roman Catholic ethics. According to official Roman Catholic dogma, the unitive and procreative ends of marriage are inseparable, and must be present in every act of sexual intercourse; hence the ban on artificial contraception. But the connection between the unitive and the procreative is not iron-clad. In fact, throughout history, the church has accepted that the sexual activity of sterile couples and post-menopausal couples is valid. More recently, non-Roman communions, including the Anglican, have accepted the separation of the unitive and procreative dimensions of sexuality entailed in using contraceptive devices.[19] And, lest we speak of procreation in the abstract, remember that the role of children in marriage has shifted dramatically in the last century and a half. The biological necessity of children issuing from sexual unions has been curtailed, though not eliminated. Likewise, the meaning of having children has shifted from children as economic assets, who were simply smaller versions of adults, to children as emotional investments demanding concentrated years of nurturing and education. In other words, parenting, like marriage and sexuality, is constituted by meaning, not simply a reproductive process.

The point here, once again, is that it is the *meaning* of having children or not having them that matters. The criteria of a healthy Christian marriage is the self-transcendence involved in "reproducing" the love between spouses, not the mere *fact* of biological children. While I do not want to dismiss the biological ordering of creation into male and female as inconsequential and of no import, I do want to insist that the *meaning* of both marriage and children lies in the intersubjective bonds developed and the growth in love, loyalty, and faith in God involved rather than in the mere biology of male and female reproduction.[20]

Conclusion

This essay has covered a lot of territory in exploring the possibility of Christian homosexual marriage. My whirlwind tour through Christian history bears on the topic indirectly, in that it illustrated the fluidity by which Christian ideals of monogamy have developed in different times and places. I have also tried to stress what I consider to be the most basic gospel values of Christian marriage: marriage as a deep mystery of intertwined persons in relation to God, on a journey of encounter and redemption. I have explored the possibility that this deep mystery can be the core of homosexual as well as heterosexual committed relationships, to the extent that we can adapt Christian marriage once again to a new context, a context in which homosexual orientation is understood as a given rather than as a moral choice.

While there is much more dialogue needed over how to interpret biblical revelation and God's created order, my point has been to pay attention to the ways in which these sources are or can be used. To overlook the cultural distance between ourselves and the biblical world, or to "read" the created order merely on a biological level is, in both cases, to miss the deeper spiritual meanings of the gospel and of marriage as mystery and encounter.

Having made this case, there are still further issues to be explored. Though I began by illustrating the social construction of marriage, I have ended by endorsing an abstract ideal, a theological theory of marriage. We must return to the concrete manifestation of marriage today. As both a legal and religious institution it embodies strong cultural mandates that are heterosexual. Marriage, as it in fact functions today, excludes same-sex partnerships totally. To change church polity and liturgy as well as legal spousal rights in order to accommodate same-sex monogamy is a matter of praxis, not just theological possibility. Accepting something at a theoretical level is a long way from reconstructing social meaning and praxis.[21]

The question at the end of all this, then, is whether homosexual monogamy is the same as homosexual marriage. Is marriage the right category for describing or endorsing faithfulness in homosexual couples? Perhaps all the ideals and values I have articulated are important aspects of committed relations among homosexual Christians, but nevertheless "marriage" is not what is called for. This question needs dialogue with and within Christian gay and lesbian communities. Some would insist that homosexuality is so different from heterosexuality that it must generate its own standards, values, and norms. To some, an adaptation of Christian marriage to homosexuality constitutes an imposition of heterosexual norms onto the homosexual community. Here, the gay and lesbian communities, especially those who profess themselves Christian, must sort out their own expectations. To what degree does Christian marriage as outlined here offer an ideal, or even an institution, that is helpful or transformative for gay and lesbian Christians?

What lies ahead is necessarily further dialogue. There are those who may contest the flexibility of marriage as I have outlined it historically. There are surely those who will balk at the adaptability that I propose for our current theology of marriage. Undoubtedly, some will take issue over methodology in Christian ethics and my treatment of the Bible and natural law. Finally, even those who might accept my positions on all these points will not agree on whether and in what ways the social institution of marriage ought to adapt itself—liturgically and legally—to same-sex partnerships. The way forward involves, once again, mystery and encounter—in this case, the mystery and encounter of the wider Christian community. We are called to have faith, not in our own convictions, nor even in the dialogue itself, but in the Divine Mystery to which we are all committed and which transcends our differences. This faith necessarily includes an openness to serious encounter with faithful Christians of all sexual orientations.

NOTES

I am indebted to several people who helped me formulate my ideas on the issues in this essay. A presentation on this topic by Mary Stewart Van Leeuwen at West Point Grey Baptist Church in Vancouver, B.C. in July, 1995 proved to be seminal in my thinking. Conversations with Theo DeBruyn and Julie Burke contributed to my grasp of the social construction of homosexual partnerships today.

1. Ellis Peters, *An Excellent Mystery* (London: Future, 1985), 190.
2. Rosemary Haughton, *The Transformation of Man: A Study of Conversion and Community* (Springfield, Ill.: Templegate, 1967), 42.
3. One further note should be made before I proceed. This essay is addressed to the theological *status quo*, to heterosexuals who accept the mainline Christian theological tradition on marriage. A further and different issue—not addressed directly here—is whether homosexuals involved in monogamous partnerships would want to adopt *marriage* as the institution that would be formative and supportive of their relationship. The alternative would be to devise some new institution that would serve homosexual partnerships as marriage serves heterosexual monogamy. This question is not the central focus of this paper, but I shall return to it again briefly at the end.
4. The section on the development of marriage in history draws on the following articles, published in K. Scott and M. Warren, eds., *Perspectives on Marriage* (New York: Oxford University Press, 1993): M. G. Lawler, "Marriage in the Bible," T. Mackin, "The Primitive Understanding of Christian Marriage," and J. Martos, "Marriage."
5. In this essay I treat the social construction and history of Christian marriage. In the 1994 bishops' pastoral study document several paragraphs are dedicated to the history and social construction of homosexuality. See *Continuing the Dialogue: A Pastoral Study Document of the House of Bishops to the Church as the Church Considers Issues of Human Sexuality* (Cincinnati: Forward Movement Publications, 1995), 66-67. See also the work cited there: David F. Greenberg, *The Construction of Homosexuality* (Chicago: University of Chicago Press, 1988).
6. Martos, "Marriage," in Scott and Warren, *Perspectives*, 33-34.
7. For example, see the homilies of St. John Chrysostom, *On Marriage and Family Life*, trans. C. P. Roth and D. Anderson (Crestwood, N.Y.: St. Vladimir's Seminary Press, 1986).
8. *On Marriage and Concupiscence* II, 21, as quoted in Martos, "Marriage," 43. See the discussion of this history in *Continuing the Dialogue*, 48-50.
9. Note that this pattern became a cultural ideal for all classes, but was a lived reality only for women of the middle and upper classes. Lower class women and children were forced into the workforce because of financial needs. Black women and immigrant women served as

domestic labor for the upper classes so that the "cult of domesticity," the ideal of the home as a haven of peace and leisure, might be a reality for white women.

10. Note that the New Testament passages on domestic relations—Colossians 3 and Ephesians 5—were adopted during this period as religious sanctions of this arrangement. Thus, what were the developments of economic and cultural conditions (the industrial revolution) came to be seen as "God's order" as specified in biblical revelation.

11. See Rowan Williams, "The Body's Grace," included in this volume. Williams takes the same phenomenological approach to a theology of sexuality that Rosemary Haughton does, as discussed above.

12. See Robert Williams's discussion of this in "Toward a Theology of Lesbian and Gay Marriage," *Anglican Theological Review* 72 (1990): 138-139. He cites the following studies: David P. McWhirter and Andrew M. Mattison, *The Male Couple: How Relationships Develop* (Englewood Cliffs, N.J.: Prentice-Hall, 1984) and Betty Berzon, *Permanent Partners: Building Gay and Lesbian Relationships that Last* (New York: E. P. Dutton, 1988). See also *Continuing the Dialogue*, 62-78.

13. Two thorough attempts from within the Anglican Communion to delineate a theology of and rationale for same-sex marriages include Robert Williams, "Toward a Theology of Lesbian and Gay Marriage," in *Anglican Theological Review* 72 (1990): 134-156, and Jeffrey John, *Permanent, Faithful, Stable: Christian Same-Sex Partnerships* (London: Affirming Catholicism, 1993).

14. See *Continuing the Dialogue*, 23-37. See also John, *Permanent, Faithful, Stable*, 5-10.

15. See Eric Marcus, *Is It a Choice?* (San Francisco: Harper and Row, 1993), 13-14, quoting a man's response to the question of choice: "Why would I choose to be something that horrifies my parents, that could ruin my career, that my religion condemns, and that could cost me my life if I dared to walk down the street holding hands with my boyfriend?" For this reference and several other helpful citations I am indebted to a student, Julie Burke, and her paper, "Same-Sex Marriage: A Moral and Philosophical Presentation." See also *Continuing the Dialogue*, 62-78.

16. See *Continuing the Dialogue*, 31-34 and John, *Permanent, Faithful, Stable*, 6-8.

17. See John, *Permanent, Faithful, Stable*, 9-13 and Stephanie Brooke, "The Morality of Homosexuality," *Journal of Homosexuality* 25 (1993): 77-99 for refutations of natural law arguments. For a defense of natural law in reference to homosexuality, see John Finnis, "Is Homosexual Conduct Wrong? A Philosophical Exchange," *New Republic* (15 November 1993).

18. See Williams, "The Body's Grace" and Haughton, *Transformation*. See also Timothy F. Murphy, "Homosex/Ethics," *Journal of Homosexuality* 27 (1994): 9-25.

19. See Robert Williams, "Toward a Theology," 145, where he points out that the changes in the 1979 Episcopal marriage liturgy make procreation less central to the marriage rite, if not entirely optional. See also *Continuing the Dialogue*, 50-54, in which the 1958 Lambeth Conference is quoted:

> The procreation of children is not the only purpose of marriage. Husbands and wives owe to each other and to the depth and stability of their families the duty to express, in sexual intercourse, the love which they bear and mean to bear to each other. Sexual intercourse is not by any means the only language of earthly love, but it is, in its full and right use, the most intimate and the most revealing; it has the depth of communication signified by the Biblical word so often used for it, "knowledge"; it is a giving and receiving in the unity of two free spirits which is in itself good (within the marriage bond) and mediates good to those who share it. Therefore it is utterly wrong to urge that, unless children are specifically desired, sexual intercourse is of the nature of sin. It is also wrong to say that such intercourse ought not to be engaged in except with the willing intention to procreate children.

20. See Williams, "Toward a Theology," 144, where he discusses the number of gay and lesbian couples raising children. Many of these children are from previous heterosexual marriages. Nevertheless, this raises the issue of new reproductive technologies and their use by gay and lesbian couples to "reproduce" the fruits of their love. The ethics of the various types of reproductive technologies is a discussion beyond the scope of this essay. Suffice it to say that, just as I believe that our answer to homosexual marriage has to go beyond a "fundamentalism of nature," so too I believe that our position on reproductive technology needs to be nuanced beyond restricting procreation to that which results from genital intercourse.

21. Nevertheless, such reconstructions are beginning to happen and are not likely to disappear. State legislatures are beginning to consider legislation over spousal rights for same-sex partners and liturgical forms are being written and used to recognize, in a religious context, the commitment between homosexual partners. While I have said here that it may be difficult to move from theological theory to institutionalized and accepted praxis, the opposite is also true: *if* social "reconstruction" is underway in some sectors, theologians had better begin rethinking their theologies of marriage in order to contribute constructively to such reconstruction as it unfolds rather than doing "catch-up" decades later.

∞ James Robertson Price III

Christian Parenting and the (Gay) Child

Prologue

"You know not what you ask," Jerry hissed, and then threw down his napkin and called for the check. It was December. We were having dinner in a restaurant just off Tompkins Park, not far from his apartment in the East Village. I was in town for a visit and hadn't seen Jerry in six months. His partner, Robert, had died of AIDS two years earlier—so with fear and trembling I had asked what I had been meaning to ask for some time: Was he HIV-positive?

"I know what I ask," I replied. "We've been friends for over twenty years. I need to ask. I need to know."

"I promised myself I would never lie to anyone about this. I won't lie to you." Then, abruptly, Jerry stood, turned, and headed for the door. I caught up with him and we walked to his apartment in silence. The phone was ringing. It was Catherine, my wife, calling from home in Washington, D.C.

"Jamie, William has told me he is gay. I feel completely cut off from him, like I've lost him. Christmas is going to be very difficult."

It was time to go home.

Preliminaries

As I write, it is Christmastide again. Three years have passed, Jerry with them. William is now seventeen and a senior in high school. He entered my life when he was ten, and I became his stepfather two years later when Catherine married me. Catherine and I also have four other children, all by previous marriages: two girls, Caitlin and Megan; and two boys, Devon and Pierce. Their ages range from twelve to seventeen, and like William, they are all in one stage or another of adolescence. Our family is endlessly challenging and wonderful, and Catherine and I are active, devoted, and rather exhausted parents.

My title is "Christian Parenting and the (Gay) Child." I punctuate it as I do because despite my focus on William, the fact that he is gay is not essential to the issues I discuss. What's more, despite the universalizing pretensions of my title, my interpretation is shaped by the concrete details of our family and filtered by the vantage point of my place in it. For example, most of the pain and much of the drama associated with William's being gay is concentrated in his relationship with his mother. So, although I play active parental roles in William's life, because I am his stepfather and a relative latecomer to his relationship with Catherine, I am inevitably one step removed. Thus I speak for only myself, not for Catherine or William, but they have graciously given me permission to write this essay, and my hope is that they will recognize themselves in it.

I have framed my topic as a response to a question I find important: If, as a heterosexual parent, you discover that the sexual identity emerging in your child is different from your own, what difference does being a Christian make? Or, to rearrange it somewhat: If, as a Christian parent who also happens to be heterosexual, you discover that the sexual identity emerging in your child is lesbian or gay, how might the teachings of the tradition help you respond to the potential conflict with your child?

By framing my topic this way, I take for granted rather than argue the position that homosexuality is "natural." However, since this vexed term is pivotal in current discussions of homosexuality, I want to pause briefly to clarify my assumptions on the point.

It was not really a surprise for me to learn from William that he is gay. Over the years there had been various indications—taunting by children at the local pool the previous summer not least among them. Still, we never anticipated he would "come out" at fourteen; nor did we anticipate the conflict this would precipitate.

For his part, William asserts that he did not "choose" to be gay, and by this he means two things. One is that his desires have a spontaneity and intentionality, a narrative character all their own. As happens with all of us, a combination of genetic and historical factors have converged to shape the fundamental character of William's desires and spontaneities.

The second thing he means is that he wouldn't choose to be gay if he could help it. I am saddened by this meaning, and unlike the first, it strikes me as profoundly "unnatural." What he wouldn't "choose," of course, is his daily dose of homophobia—the labeling, the ignorance, the specter of violence. Unavoidably, William has internalized the images and stories that legitimate homophobia in our culture, and these in turn manifest in him as the feeling that if he didn't have to choose himself, if he didn't have to choose the intentionality of his desires, he wouldn't.

∞

What if, as a heterosexual parent, you discover that the sexual identity emerging in your child is different from your own?

Parenting and Sexual Identity

As I think back on the emergence of my own sexual identity, I remember it as a spontaneous yet gradual process, an unfolding of myself from within that felt integral to the developing story of myself: of growing up, figuring out who I was, becoming an adult. I don't mean I never felt anxious or confused or surprised, but I don't remember feeling any fundamental dissonance or disjunction within myself. With my parents and teachers, yes; within myself, no. I don't know if my experience is common; it may be different for many women and gay men. For me, the internal dissonance and disjunction has come with being a parent of children who are coming of age.

The difficulty, I think, is that when my children were children, I (with my wife) was a principal actor, narrator, and interpreter of the story of their growth and development. Now, as they move into adolescence and young adulthood, not only do other actors appear, but I find myself required to relinquish the control that comes with being principal narrator, and to let them begin to tell the story for themselves. I find myself inhabiting a story I never imagined, required to develop ways of thinking, feeling, and acting that can make me very uncomfortable.

Sometimes I don't like the role in which I am cast; sometimes I refuse to go along with a plot line one of my children wants to explore; sometimes I am cut out of the story entirely. These are all moments of friction, and the friction is magnified if the story you have been telling for yourself and your child is largely heterosexual, and the emerging sexual identity of your child is not.

Stories, after all, are the basic stuff of human living. "All the world's a stage, and all the men and women merely players." Stories frame our questions and orient our experience; they shape our feelings and direct our actions. They provide the framework in which we interpret the growth of our children and live out our hopes for them. We imagine them happy, safe, productive, successful. As heterosexual parents, we readily conjure marriages, grandchildren, holiday gatherings, and much more. This story—our own special combination of images, feelings, and hopes—is not simply held within us in narrative form. It is the form that meaning takes in our lives. On that day in December, at fourteen years of age, William declared himself the teller of his own story, and tore Catherine's story to shreds.

Stories and Conflict

Conflict is the clash of mutually exclusive stories. It is also the negation of one storyteller by another. In a conflict, friction and dissonance are at their highest, because the differences involved are fundamentally not negotiable. At stake is a story that grounds one's identity and meaning. To surrender it is to surrender one's self; to be negated as a legitimate voice is to feel negated oneself.

Fortunately, conflict is comparatively rare. Most friction between parents and children over issues of sexual identity arises in disagreements and disputes.[1] My daughter Caitlin and I once had a running disagreement over whether a particular boy should be her boyfriend. ("He doesn't treat you well," I would say. "He does too," she would reply.) Despite the friction, this was not a clash of mutually exclusive stories. We held in common the cultural story that anticipates a boy and a girl being drawn to each other and developing a special relationship. The disagreement was about the details of the narrative goal—who the boyfriend should be, not whether there should be one.

Disputes run deeper. My son Devon and I engaged in a dispute about whether he and his girlfriend could take a two-week road trip to Florida. ("You're too young; I'm not comfortable with this," I said. "I'll pay for it myself; I'll be careful," he replied.) Again, the common narrative framework was the cultural story that legitimates boyfriends and girlfriends. The friction came from differences about the appropriate means for developing such a relationship.

The conflict with William is complex. It is not a disagreement over whether a particular person should be his boyfriend (though we have had that disagreement). It is not a dispute about what behavior is appropriate in such a relationship (though we have had that dispute too). Nor is it a clash over gay *versus* straight versions of the story about two people being attracted to each other (that is not a source of conflict in our family). The conflict is rooted in the difficulties of being an adolescent and being gay in our culture.

Being Adolescent; Being Gay

In American culture, adolescence is the time when a child begins to insist upon having a voice in the story of his or her identity. It is a trying time. For the child, it means trying on new or different narrative possibilities, and learning how to make them one's own. For the parent, it means trying to move toward an adult relationship with one's child, and learning how to let go of narrative control. Despite the inevitable friction, it is a gradual, mutual process, typically mediated by the rituals that mark key narrative moments in the story of growing up in mainstream America: entering high school, extracurricular activities at school, sweet sixteen parties, proms, getting a job, graduating from high school, going to college, and so on. As a gay adolescent, the difficulty for William (and Catherine) is the absence of a viable, mutual narrative of growing up, complete with public roles and rituals.

William was a model child—bright, polite, helpful, sociable—but when the time came, he was simply unable to identify with the mainstream story of American adolescence. Of course, he could not simply dismiss or ignore the story, like some library book dumped through the return slot. Like his siblings and peers, William internalized it. As it did for them, it framed his experience, shaped his feelings, and directed his actions—except that he experienced it as a fundamental negation of himself. This negation gave rise to a conflict within him: a conflict of stories manifested in his rejection of the public rituals of the mainstream story, and his active search for a viable alternative.

In the middle-class, urban, professional spectrum of American culture our family inhabits, the public rituals of the mainstream story are enacted principally in terms of school activities and preparation for college. William has rejected these. He has an active personal life and many friends, but he refuses to engage in socially recognized roles at school. Now a senior, he has never participated in a club, theater production, or sports team. As often as he can manage, he sleeps during the day and stays up at night. Regular reports from school indicate that academically he is "not working up to his potential," and that he is cavalier about school rules and protocol. He has opted out of the school's college advisory program, and his application to a school of design in New York City has been on his terms and his schedule.

William's awareness of the conflict within him, combined with his courage and personal integrity, led him to "come out" at fourteen years of age and to launch a search for a viable narrative that continues to this day. This search for narrative integrity is healthy, natural, and a tribute to the values with which he was nurtured as a boy by Catherine and his father. Concretely, however, William's search has been marked by two fundamental problems. First, in Washington there are very few self-acknowledged gay adolescents, not enough to make a viable community. The gay community is adult and engages in adult activities, both personal and professional. It has yet to figure out how to mentor gay adolescents. Second, more profoundly than an adolescent who can find narrative alternatives in the mainstream culture, William had learned to identify himself by being "different." Consequently, he was powerfully drawn to that subgroup within the gay community which also defines itself by being different. He began sneaking out of the house, frequenting the gay club scene, and for over two years was deeply involved with a group who engaged in elaborate costume, dance, cross-dressing, and pageantry.

Inevitably and immediately, the clash of stories in William led to conflict with Catherine. His rejection of the mainstream story and its public rituals have made it impossible for Catherine to participate in William's life. His participation in the gay club scene, and his search for an alternative story—carried out largely in adult venues—has been impossible for her to approve for her adolescent son. The issue for Catherine is not William's sexual orientation; it is his safety and well-being, her concern for the kinds of choices he has made, and her desire to be a responsible parent. To their mutual pain, William and Catherine find themselves caught in the clash of mutually exclusive stories and the negation of each other as legitimate storytellers.

Catherine's conflict with William is a parent's dark night of the soul. She is not a mother required by the demands of adolescence to release narrative control; she is a mother who has been cut off and denied narrative legitimacy. The story Catherine lived and told as she raised her son has been annihilated. She has been plunged into a fearsome cloud of unknowing: cut off and powerless as a parent; unable to recognize the child who stands defiant and combative before her; finding to her shock that the story she has been living no longer provides her with meaningful direction, but serves instead only to escalate the conflict with her son.

∞

What difference does being a Christian make?

Intermediaries

I come now to the Christian part of my topic. Frankly, this is a difficult task, partly because of the secular tenor of our times, which makes it difficult to identify and talk about the religious dimension of our personal and cultural stories, and partly because of the singular nature of religious stories themselves. As I define it here, a story is a "religious" story if it provides us with the narrative framework that holds, critiques, and transforms all the other stories we tell. As "religious," such stories tell our deepest, most comprehensive story; and as will become clear below, such stories need not be associated with a particular religious tradition. The point, however, is that religious stories are difficult to talk about. For just as it is easier to talk about what we see than about the power of vision itself, so it is easier to talk about our personal and cultural stories than about the narrative ground of our storytelling.[2]

All of us live inside a religious story, and faith is our acceptance of that story as the ground of all our storytelling. My interest here is in exploring what difference being held by a Christian story might make, especially for parents who find themselves in a clash of conflicting personal and cultural stories with their gay or lesbian child. I will be drawing on Catherine's conflict with William for illustrative purposes only. This religious exploration is my own.

Christian Story

I will begin by retelling one of Jesus' stories, the parable about the man who attempted the journey from Jerusalem to Jericho (Luke 10:30-35). To appreciate this story as a religious story, it is important to enter imaginatively into the narrative world Jesus presents.[3]

The journey from Jerusalem to Jericho passes through notoriously dangerous countryside. No one makes this journey if he or she can help it. So as the man sets out we are filled with foreboding and identify imaginatively with his peril. In the next scene our fears are realized, and with the man, we are attacked, robbed, beaten, stripped, and left half dead in the ditch at the side of the road.

In the third scene a priest comes along. Our expectations rise. Imaginatively, we get out of the ditch, identify with the priest, and prepare to rescue the man—a much happier role than lying there half dead, the victim of a brutal assault. But the priest doesn't stop. He passes by on the other side of the road and disappears from the story. The same thing happens when a levite comes along. Narratively, we remain abandoned in the ditch with the wounded man.

In the next scene a third man comes along, a Samaritan. Nothing could be worse. Samaritans and Jews are bitter enemies, divided by seven centuries of antagonism stretching back to the separation of Israel into the northern and southern kingdoms. Imaginatively, it is impossible to identify with this Samaritan. Unlike the others, he does not disappear from the story. Instead, he comes across the road toward the man in the ditch. Our anxiety rises. The man—and we with him—is completely vulnerable to the attack of the approaching Samaritan. There is only one way to imagine the ending of this story: we are going to die. We shut our eyes.

Of course, in the final scene, Jesus surprises us. Our enemy is not an enemy after all. The Samaritan picks up the wounded man, puts him on a donkey, takes him to an inn, and provides for his care and healing. The implacable face of tragedy is in fact the face of healing and grace.

It is easy to let the religious character of Jesus' story slip away and to reduce it to another interpretive framework: for example, to read it as an interesting artifact of the broader cultural story of Jewish-Samaritan relations in the first century of the common era. But it is important to stay with this story as a religious story, and to pay attention to the way it works.

In the story of the journey to Jericho, Jesus plays to our basic fears about safety, survival, and control. He sets up the terrifying dilemma in which we, through our identification with the protagonist, are left abandoned in the ditch—wounded, threatened, and powerless. He then subverts our fears and expectations with a surprise ending, which reveals that he is in fact telling a different story than we thought.

"Surprise" is our recognition that Jesus' story is challenging our spontaneous faith in a quite different story: the one that tells us that whenever we find ourselves "in the ditch," we are locked into a tragedy in which only bad things can happen. This is the religious story told by the "realist" in us all. Jesus' challenge is an invitation to a new religious story and a new faith.

Christian Story and the Ditch

In her conflict with William, I submit that Catherine is "in the ditch." She is powerless to participate in his life, in pain at feeling cut off, and terrified by the threat of what could befall him. William's search for an alternative story includes Catherine's worst nightmare—an adult club scene, with its specter of alcohol, drugs, AIDS, and gay bashing. For Catherine, it is all too easy to imagine herself in the grip of a tragedy in which only bad things can happen. The question is, What difference would it make if she were to allow the religious story told by Jesus to hold, critique, and transform her conflict of stories with William?

On one level, of course, it would make no difference. William would still be gay; still be seeking an authentic, alternative story; still be refusing to participate in the public, predominately heterosexual rituals provided by the mainstream cultural story. Catherine would still be in the ditch, wounded, powerless, and afraid.

On another level, however, it would make a profound difference. To be held by Jesus' story is to be reminded that despite the ditch, a larger story of healing is being told. Despite the crush of Catherine's worst fears for herself and William, to be held by Jesus' story is to be reminded that healing and grace, not tragedy and annihilation, are the deepest reality. Again, this doesn't mean tragic things don't happen (my friend Jerry is dead of AIDS). It doesn't mean that all fears are groundless (William has been physically threatened and harassed both in and outside school). Nor does it mean that someone who looks like your worst enemy is necessarily an agent of healing and grace, though it may be so. Like all religious stories, Jesus' story operates at the ground of our narrative consciousness. It doesn't make suffering and misfortune either justifiable or intelligible, any more than it makes the road to Jericho free of robbers; it simply tells us that they are not the last word. But this makes all the difference in the world. For as a religious story, it holds, critiques, and directs all our storytelling, and thus provides the ultimate frame for our questions, experiences, feelings, and actions.

To clarify my point, it will help to compare Jesus' story with the "realist" story he seeks to subvert, the one that tells us that when we're hurt, afraid, and not in control, we're locked into a story in which only bad things can happen. The gospel of this story proclaims that if there is no direct and perceptible link between what we can do and what is happening to us, all will be lost. To be held by the "realist" story is to be reminded that enemies are enemies, that being in the ditch is the worst possible circumstance, and that only two basic options remain: to fight for control or give up; to struggle or flee.

In her conflict with William, for example, if Catherine's storytelling were held by the "realist" story, she could fight for control of the conflict. Coercion and anxiety would then mark all her attempts to hold William accountable, monitor his social life, and engage him in activities at school. Or, she could give up and quit the struggle entirely. In this case, cold resignation and numbed detachment would permeate all her dealings with him. In either case, the conflict with William would stand. Inside the "realist" religious story, the clash of mutually exclusive stories is confirmed, not resolved.

The story told by Jesus opens up a different world: one in which people in the ditch are reminded that a larger, healing story is at work; one in which enemies may be friends, despite appearances and expectations to the contrary. The memory of a larger, healing story undercuts and diffuses the urgent need for a direct and perceptible link between what we can do and what is happening to us. It enables people in the ditch to find their center in the experience, to attain an active state of balance, rather than to fight the ditch itself.

In her conflict with William, for example, if Catherine's storytelling were held by Jesus' story, she could more easily accept the vulnerability and powerlessness of being in the ditch. She could be present to the loss of her dreams and the negation of her story, and grieve these losses simply and cleanly. She would not need to deny them or project them angrily onto William. Likewise, she could wrestle directly with her fears for William, without feeling she needed to act them out, whether coercively or in resignation. Her conflict with William would loosen. Amidst the friction and clash of their personal and cultural stories, held by the memory of a larger, healing story that could include them both, Catherine could find an active state of balance, free from the need or expectation of control. This balance would mark all her dealings with William.

Change and Christian Story

Being a Christian, then, would make at least this much difference: in a situation of pain, fear, and powerlessness such as that experienced by Catherine in her conflict with William, it becomes possible to find one's center, to attain an active state of balance, free from the expectation or need to be in control of the outcome. The question, however, remains: Is this difference only in the consciousness of the person whose storytelling is held by Jesus' story, or does it make a difference in the wider world of the parent and child? To put the question another way: Is Jesus' story just a helpful narrative placebo, or does a good Samaritan really come along? It is one thing to suffer well. In fact, it is no small thing. But it is quite another to get out of the ditch and become engaged in a story of healing.

This question raises the issue of causality, and how it operates in light of Jesus' story. In seeking an answer, two things must be kept in mind. First, change is a function of doing, and Christian stories, in and of themselves, don't do anything. We do. Second, as a religious story, Jesus' story sets the ultimate frame, not the particular activities, of our doing. As discussed earlier, this "doing" is an active state of balance, a centeredness in situations of pain, fear, and powerlessness that enables a person to grieve, to wrestle directly with loss and fear, to withhold projections, and to act, free of the desire for control or any felt need for a direct and perceptible link between one's actions and the results of those actions. Again, the question is, How does this "doing" change anything? And what is the correlation between this "doing" and the arrival of the Samaritan?

In answering, it will help to compare the idea of causality operative in Jesus' story with the one operative in the "realist" story. According to the "realist" story, you can't change what you can't control, and to be in the ditch is to be without power or control. The logic of this image is so strong that, once we slip inside it, it is very difficult to imagine how Jesus' story, which severs the link between activity and accomplishment, could have anything real to say about causality and change. If healing takes place, what else besides dumb luck could bring it about?

As Jesus tells the story, healing change is not a function of power and control. To grasp the causal efficacy of his story, consider the image of a lighted match burning a piece of paper. The paper is changing: the flame is burning it up. But the flame is not doing anything special to make this change happen. It is simply "doing" what flames always do, which is to burn. For its part, the paper is burning because it has the capacity to burn. The flame is not in control of the paper. The change taking place is a function of the *relationship* between the paper and the flame—in this case, physical proximity. Take the paper out of the fire—change the relationship—and the changing stops.

Consider now the conflict between Catherine and William. As the flame is to the paper, so the parent is to the child. Jesus' story changes things because it promotes a certain kind of "doing": a centeredness in the face of loss, an ability to grieve while withholding projections, and a freedom to act without the need or expectation of control. Like the flame burning the paper, Catherine (or any other parent) need do nothing other than the "doing" promoted by Jesus' story. Why? Because change is a function of relations, not control. In the case of material objects like paper and flame, the relation is physical distance. In the case of human beings—here a mother and her son—the relation is the telling of a common story in which they can recognize both themselves and each other. Like the paper withdrawn from the flame, their conflict is a clash of mutually exclusive stories, a negation of each other as legitimate storytellers.

The story they seek is as yet unknown, and the experience of unknowing is the dark night of their conflict. Yet the "doing" promoted by Jesus' story sets the conditions for the emergence of the new story. It does not provide the new story itself, which must emerge concretely in the mutual telling. But it does undercut the spontaneous tendency to determine a story in advance and impose it on the other.

The "doing" Jesus' story calls forth is not easy, and it does not come without cost. For a parent like Catherine to remain centered in the ditch—to feel the pain of being cut off from her son, to feel negated as a teller of their mutual story, to feel the loss of grandchildren he will never give her, to go to bed each night trembling for his safety—to feel these things without going numb, to grieve these losses without rancor and controlling projections, is to experience what Christians traditionally refer to as an experience of the cross.[4] It is to establish the conditions for change. For even though Catherine has been negated by William as a mutual teller of their story, being held by Jesus' story would enable her to avoid responding in kind. Negated, she would not negate in return.[5] I hasten to add that such "doing" is neither masochistic nor passive. Nor does it counsel surrendering the hard parental work of setting limits and establishing expectations. It can, however, transform a conflict into a set of disputes and disagreements.

As the parent of an adolescent, the burden of this "doing" is properly Catherine's to bear. The principal work of adolescents in American culture is to begin to discern their authentic narrative voices, and the responsibility of parents is to help them find it. Obviously, for parents of gay or lesbian children, this task can be unusually trying and painful. Yet, in my view, it is too much to expect William—or any other (gay) child—to suspend his quest for an authentic story of his own and to closet his spontaneities in the mainstream of cultural history. I do not deny, of course, that William's quest for a viable story, like that of many other adolescents, has lacked a certain balance in the last several years. Nevertheless, like the paper in the flame, William has the capacity for change.

Indeed, the time may come, and now is, that William will bear his mother's burdens with her, will be able to experience her fears without defensiveness and projection, and will grieve with her the loss of the children he will never have. This is the arrival of the Samaritan, the birth of a new story. Catherine, held by Jesus' story, can hold William. One day, they will hold each other. That is the difference being a Christian can make.

NOTES

1. The distinction among conflicts, disputes, and disagreements is drawn from John Burton, *Conflict: Resolution and Prevention* (New York: St. Martin's Press, 1990).

2. For an excellent discussion of the use of "story" as an interpretive category, and particularly in relation to the New Testament and the history of the early Christian community, see N. T. Wright, *The New Testament and the People of God* (Minneapolis: Fortress Press, 1992). For another, related exploration of this topic by the present author, see James R. Price III and Charles H. Simpkinson, "Sacred Stories and Our Relationship to the Divine," in *Sacred Stories*, ed. Charles Simpkinson and Anne Simpkinson (San Francisco: Harper, 1993), 11-26.

3. In my retelling of this story I rely on the work of Bernard Brandon Scott, *Jesus, Symbol-Maker for the Kingdom* (Philadelphia: Fortress Press, 1981).

4. For a theological discussion of the experience I am describing in narrative terms, see Charles Hefling, "A Perhaps Permanently Valid Achievement: Lonergan on Christ's Satisfaction," *METHOD: Journal of Lonergan Studies* 10 (1992): 51-76.

5. For a very helpful discussion of a Christian approach to power and nonviolence, see Walter Wink, *Engaging the Powers: Discernment and Resistance in a World of Domination* (Minneapolis: Fortress Press, 1993).

∞ *Sheryl A. Kujawa*

How Might We
Teach Our Children?

K*ids*, Larry Clark's recent film about teenage sexuality, has been reviewed widely as a no-holds-barred journey into the world of modern adolescence. Written by nineteen-year-old Harmony Korine, this urban drama centers on a group of teenagers who hang out on the streets of New York, relentlessly trying to entertain themselves during the course of a single day. In the opening scene one of the main characters of the film, a boy named Telly, who is in his mid-teens, is seen seducing a younger and sexually experienced girl in her parents' home. After skipping down the steps and outside the door, Telly meets his best friend, Casper, and gives him a complete description of the recent seduction along with his reasons for wanting to deflower as many young virgins as possible. Later on, Casper beats another boy almost to death and has intercourse with Jenny after an all-night party in another friend's home. Though Jenny protests, she passes out and is unable to resist his advances. What Casper doesn't know is that Jenny found out that same day that she is HIV-positive.

Kids is a profoundly disturbing film. It was written by a young person, and presents young people from their own perspective. The realities of life faced by Telly, Casper, Jenny, and their friends are a threat to our notions of polite society. Certainly not all teenagers today are sexually active, and not all drink or take drugs. Nor are all young people so graphic and articulate as the characters in this film. Yet before we dismiss *Kids* as just another example of urban nihilism, it is important to ask ourselves if we are in collective denial. Just how much do we know about the sexual behavior of the young people in our lives?

To be sure, part of my discomfort in watching *Kids* was that it was hard to remain detached while watching someone less than sixteen years of age discuss sexual matters in a detailed way that would have been unthinkable when I was that age. But what is more painful to me is the realization that the Tellys, Caspers, and Jennys of the world are in our midst; they are not someone else's children, nor can we assume that they are outside the Episcopal Church.

On the minds of many Christian adults today who hear the current religious debates surrounding issues of human sexuality[1] and who love and are concerned about young people is the question: How might we better help and teach our children? This basic and key question concerning the role of the church in the healthy sexual development of our youth is raised in the document *Continuing the Dialogue: A Pastoral Study Document of the House of Bishops to the Church as the Church Considers Issues of Human Sexuality.* There the discussion of adolescent sexuality is raised within the context of "discontinuities"—"the experience of those who have received God's gift of sexuality but are outside of the covenant of marriage."[2] No doubt, as *Continuing the Dialogue* suggests, abstinence is an appropriate sexual standard for teenagers, whether or not they eventually find themselves called to the married state, as many will. Sexual intercourse is not an indication that one has achieved adulthood, and there are other ways within romantic relationships that young people can express their feelings.[3] Yet adults do not always take into account that young people do have sexual feelings, and that many act on those feelings. Adolescence is a time of change and exploration for young people, and an interest in sexual matters is a sign of healthy growth. So the discontinuity between the sexual standard taught by the church and the reality of the lives of many young people, particularly now, when adolescence is prolonged, is a matter of pastoral concern.

Our pastoral role as a church is "to help all youth, whatever their sexual identity and behavior, navigate the difficult journey from adolescence to adulthood."[4] Yet how we are to fulfill this role is far from evident. Exactly what part should the church play in relation to the healthy sexual development of young people? How do we provide moral teaching and guidance as a way to form their sexual decision-making, while at the same time continuing to welcome those young people who will fall short of our moral standards? Lastly, what can young people teach us about their own experience of human sexuality that can inform the church?

The problem of discerning the role and nature of the church in the sexual development of young people is exacerbated by the lack of consensus among educators about the success of sex-education programs in general and of abstinence-based programs in particular. Traditionally most sexuality educators have argued for abstinence in their curricula and agreed on the value of helping teenagers postpone sexual intercourse until they are ready for a mature relationship. These same professionals also believe, however, that approaches which teach only abstinence, without also including information on family issues, sexual decision-making, and sexually transmitted diseases such as HIV/AIDS, are not effective, and that the "Just Say No" solution is simplistic. No data suggest that having young people pledge to abstain until marriage is effective, and they themselves have stated that "Just Say No" is not a deterrent to teenage sexual activity.[5] Though it is generally agreed that religiously observant youth tend to refrain from early sexual activity, it has also been argued that sex education has been most successful at reinforcing abstinence among young people who are already refraining from sex. Overall, we have been much less successful in educating teenagers who are already having sex about the consequences of their actions, or influencing them to become abstinent.[6]

A review of the current literature the field of sex education shows that a number of religiously-oriented curricula support abstinence through fear tactics, reinforcing feelings of guilt and shame in young people rather than offering more positive views of human sexuality. Some of these programs include lists of what will happen to young people—ranging from the loss of communication skills to death—should they decide to engage in premarital sexual behavior.[7] Fear-based approaches to human sexuality can be particularly damaging to young people because they reinforce negative attitudes and double messages about sexual relationships. In other words, "Sex is dirty, save it for the one you marry."[8]

∞

How can the church become a place of dialogue, compassion, concern, and safety for young people as they explore what it means for them to be sexual beings? At least part of the answer to this question lies in our ability as a church to come to terms with who young people are today, rather than who we would like them to be. Each generation has a way of laying claim to its own experience: certainly we see that truism realized among contemporary young people today, who are quick to point out what makes growing up in 1990s distinctive. In listening to them it is hard not to notice how readily and casually they are able to talk about sexual matters like HIV/AIDS,[9] the rising incidence of pregnancy and suicide among their peers, and the degree to which many have already experienced some form of sexual violence.

It is painful for me to realize that, as an adult, I have been complicit in the forces working against young people in our society. Young people are who they are because they have been shaped by our culture and have lived in an adult world where they have known indifference, neglect, abuse, violence, racism, addiction, and abandonment. We are responsible for their devalued status in our society. A 1994 telephone survey about the attitudes toward sexuality of teenagers in grades nine through twelve from across the United States found that fifty-two percent have had more than one sexual partner, while just eight percent said they had no sexual experience whatsoever. More than half of the sexually active young people surveyed said that they should have waited until they were older, and nearly three-quarters reported that they usually had sex in their parents' home. While almost all the young people who were interviewed had talked about sex with their parents at some time, at least half indicated that they would like to speak more openly.[10] The sad reality is that youth at every economic level are often neglected by adults who should care for them.

Adults often find it difficult to relate to teenagers because for some of us the teenage years represent our own painful and unresolved past, or the death of our childhood. To other adults, young people may represent unwanted change or complete chaos. Close proximity to young people may threaten our image of ourselves as "together" adults. We may even envy them their youth. Yet we cannot hope to build emotional bonds with young people—much less discuss feelings as intimate as those involved in sexuality—unless we have resolved our own adolescence and are ready to relate to them from our strength. All teenagers could benefit from the support of caring and secure adults as they face the many physical, spiritual, emotional, social, and intellectual challenges ahead.[11]

Perhaps more than any other age group, teenagers believe that their own experiences are unique, as expressed in statements such as "No one knows how I feel," "I can't talk to anybody," or "You just don't understand." This belief in their own uniqueness may lead young people to underestimate the consequences of their actions and to take dangerous risks, or not to think about consequences at all. That is why the effectiveness of a warning about the dangers of unprotected sex is lessened when young people have already tried it and have managed to avert disaster. Even if they have a friend who got pregnant or was diagnosed HIV-positive, teenagers may still believe that it could never happen to them.[12]

Moral education for teenagers needs to be current, ongoing, and related to their own issues. An important task of adolescence is to develop and strengthen one's own ability to make decisions with integrity. Young people need adult encouragement, trust, and support in this process. They face choices with life-changing circumstances, yet have little experience making difficult decisions. For teenagers, standards of behavior are determined largely outside themselves—by family, friends, the culture, and the church. They respect and use others as reference points in deciding about the rightness and wrongness of particular actions, and they value personal acceptance and approval by others as critical to their personal sense of self-esteem. The challenge for families and the church is to provide strong and healthy communities where young people can nurture their own integrity.[13]

Just as young people's identity formation takes place in relationships, so does the formation of their faith and spirituality. In listening to the faith experience of youth we need to be alert to their personal experience of God's active presence in the lives. This does not mean that we have to abandon our tradition or standards, but that we must make a concerted effort to connect the experience of young people to a broader understanding of how God is acting within the church. Young people look to the church for love and for a sense of meaning and commitment. The most powerful human influence on the spiritual life of young people is that exerted by Christian people, family and friends of all ages, who are living with them and are expressing their own faith.[14]

For some young people, the developmental tasks of adolescence are particularly challenging. As part of the establishment of his or her own identity, a teenager must come to terms with what it means to become a woman or man in our society. In some communities, equality between the sexes is not widely accepted, and we need to be aware of the effect that rigidly imposed sex roles can have on both boys and girls. Deeply ingrained gender biases afflict our institutions, including the church, and these biases can damage the fragile self-esteem of young people, as well as cause them great personal pain.[15]

Many girls become aware during adolescence of the dangers of being female, and have to face the reality of sexual trauma. By late adolescence, if a girl has not herself faced some type of sexual trauma or assault, she is likely to know others who have. For this reason, many parents feel more physically protective of daughters, and come into conflict with a girl desiring more independence. Indeed, there are causes for legitimate concern. Girls face sexual harassment on the street, in school, and in other public arenas. A higher proportion of girls are sexually abused than of boys, and the perpetrator is likely to be either a family member or someone known by the family. One of the most difficult developmental tasks girls must face is that of becoming the "sexual subjects" of their own lives, rather than spending their lives as the sexual objects of others. Teenage girls who manage to stay true to themselves become optimistic, idealistic, spiritually grounded, and committed to making the world better. Conversely, those who are not encouraged to act from their true selves become cynical and lose hope.[16]

Teenage boys, too, are challenged by the need to form a secure gender identity, at times without the example and guidance of healthy male role models. Youth violence has grown increasingly deadly over the present decade, and young black males have suffered an epidemic increase in deaths due to firearms.[17] Young men need the assistance of individuals and the church to protect them from sexual abuse, and to help them develop healthy sexual identities, free from damaging sex role biases and informed about the ways their sexuality affects them other than through unwanted pregnancies.[18] Young people of both sexes need to be encouraged to develop a sense of their gender identity that is consistent with the Christian faith.

For lesbian and gay youth, the assumption of heterosexuality in many of our approaches to adolescent sexual development causes increasing alienation among teenagers who already may suffer from a deeper lack of self-esteem than their heterosexual peers, and who may also be the victims of ridicule and violence. It has been argued that because of the sense of judgment they feel from their religious communities, young gay and lesbian people who are religious experience a greater lack of self-esteem than those who are not.[19] Moreover, they are two to three times more likely to attempt suicide than heterosexual young people, and it has been estimated that thirty percent of all completed suicides are committed by lesbian and gay youth. Many gay and lesbian youth are further endangered when they run away from home because of the conflicts their sexual identities have caused there, and when some of them are then forced to turn to prostitution to support themselves. The parents of lesbian and gay youth are also in need of the church's pastoral concern. They frequently experience feelings of guilt and humiliation, and fear religious reprisals as well. At the same time, they are concerned about the well-being and happiness of their children, the possible vocational limitations imposed on gay and lesbian people by society, and the prejudice and violence that may be part of their daughter's or son's life.[20]

∞

How might we better help and teach our children? To be sure, there is no easily definable answer to the role the church is called to play in regard to teenage sexuality. Some would like to show pastoral concern for young people by proclamation or fiat. Personally, I believe that the possibility of having an effect on young people in this way is long past. To insist on such an approach to issues of human sexuality only reinforces what too many of them already believe to be true—that the church is determined to be irrelevant to them, that it refuses to address issues of importance to them, and that adults are hypocrites willing to lay down moral standards but unwilling to engage in dialogue about how and why those standards were formed. Contemporary opinion mistakenly holds that it is natural for young people to leave the church for a while, and that it is the church's role to wait until they decide to come back (which does not necessarily happen!). Our acceptance of this assumption prevents us from looking seriously at the issues of belonging for young people within our faith community.

It has been my experience that young people want to talk with adults openly about their concerns and want to be in dialogue about our differences. They want to discuss who they are, spiritually and sexually, and they want to know what the Episcopal Church has to say about both. They are interested in Jesus Christ, and want to know more about the gospel in terms that relate to them. Young people are looking for a great deal from the church: identity, purpose, affirmation, healing, authenticity, community. We must decide whether we are committed to them or not. Many young people today have suffered disillusionment and betrayal at the hands of adults, so if we as a church say we have a commitment to their health and well-being, we had best keep our promises. Our credibility as an institution depends on it.

As I stated earlier, *Continuing the Dialogue* sets a challenge in regard to adolescent sexuality: "to help all youth, whatever their sexual identity and behavior, navigate the difficult journey from adolescence to adulthood." I want to conclude by focusing on some basic ways we can begin to address this challenge.

The church can begin to address teenage sexuality in theological terms that young people can relate to and understand.

One effective method has been developed by a group of youth ministers in one diocese who came together in a focus group to discuss those aspects of their own sexual experience that have been "holy," and those that have been "broken." The result of these discussions was a list of five foundations of Christian human sexuality that make sense to young people, and that were successfully tested at conferences and training events:[21]

> You are holy.
> Sexuality is good.
> Sexuality is powerful.
> You are not alone.
> You must take responsibility.

The idea here is to give young people a visible and practical demonstration of the ways the church takes seriously all aspects of human life, including human sexuality.

Adults in the church can begin to get in touch with the holiness and the brokenness of their own sexuality, and can be willing to share that experience with young people.

Young people need adult role models. If we hope to be able to relate genuinely with young people, we need to face our own sexual histories, and we need to commit those experiences to prayer and reflection. We also need to come to terms with the realization that not all adults in the church act in a responsible way toward young people. If the church is to be a safe place for young people, we need to take a clear stand against all sexual harassment and abuse, and protect young people from all forms of sexual trauma and violence.

3 *The church can become a place where young people receive accurate information about human sexuality, as well as the teachings of the Episcopal Church.*

In spite of the efforts of sex-education programs, many young people continue to need accurate information about human sexuality. In addition, adults in the church should be knowledgeable about the content of Episcopal and Anglican documents on human sexuality. Often young people assume, because they do not have access to the information, that the church has not responded to a particular issue. Adults in the church must provide them with the information they need in order to make responsible decisions.

4 *The church can begin to reach out to young people who are at risk and to their families.*

Though all young people are marginalized within our society, some are more at risk than others. Young people who have fewer personal and societal options are at greater risk for early sexual activity and pregnancy. They are often part of families that have few options for assistance. While a teenager's sexual development is highly influenced by family environment, and while some congregations have provided parent education programs, comparatively little has been done by the church on a large scale. In communities where young people have few recreational and educational options, the church can provide these within a Christian context, thereby helping young people to build a values base for making decisions about sex. Efforts to reach out to at-risk youth and their families also need to include gay and lesbian youth and their parents, who frequently feel isolated within our congregations.

5 *The church can engage in a dialogue with young people about human sexuality, listen to them, and incorporate their experience into its teachings.*

Though we are aware that it is important for the church to come to terms with teenage sexuality, much of what has been published on the topic—including this article—is written from the perspective of adults interpreting the experience of young people. More needs to be done to include young people themselves in the dialogue, and to create the conditions in which they would feel comfortable in discussing their sexuality issues.

An honest approach to teenage sexuality forces the church to take the humanity of our young people seriously, and to relate to them as brothers and sisters on the journey of faith. We are called to walk among young people, as Jesus did in his ministry, to listen deeply to what they have to say, to establish bonds of caring for them, and to be willing to treat their experience as legitimate. Only then can we relate with integrity the church's teachings to them, and only then can we begin to lead them into the deep mystery of Jesus Christ. One of the main reasons so many of our education programs for teenagers fail is that many adults want to "teach them religion," but few are willing to enter their lives with the kind of patient presence that Jesus exemplified.

Entering the lives of young people is something that will take our time, as well as demand a quality of presence. The presence needed is a healthy, open, adult presence that is willing to speak the truth, even the painful truth, but always in the spirit of compassion. As we begin to talk and listen to young people about their feelings, their bodies, their hopes, and their fears, we will learn more about Christ in the process. Only in this spirit do our prevention programs have any chance of being effective. For young people who have honest, caring, and decent adult support, much can be resisted and overcome. Perhaps then we can shift the focus away from shame and blame, and toward the realization of God's love for each of us.

NOTES

1. The definition of human sexuality used for the purposes of this paper is the following: "Human sexuality encompasses the sexual knowledge, beliefs, attitudes, values, and behaviors of individuals. It deals with the anatomy, physiology, and biochemistry of the sexual response system; with roles, identity and personality, with individuals' thoughts, feelings, behaviors and relationships. Humans sexuality addresses ethical, spiritual, and moral concerns, as well as group and cultural variations." (From SIECUS, "SIECUS Position Statements" [New York, 1989].)
2. *Continuing the Dialogue: A Pastoral Study Document of the House of Bishops to the Church as the Church Considers Issues of Human Sexuality* (Cincinnati, Ohio: Forward Movement Publications, 1995), 55.
3. *Continuing the Dialogue*, 56; National Guidelines Task Force, *Guidelines for Comprehensive Sexuality Education*, 34.
4. *Continuing the Dialogue*, 58.
5. SIECUS, "Adolescents and Abstinence," *SIECUS Report* (August/September 1994). This report suggest that as many as two-thirds of the young people surveyed reported that "Just Say No" was not, in their estimation, an effective approach toward encouraging abstinence.
6. Barbara Dafoe Whitehead, "The Failure of Sex Education," *The Atlantic Monthly* (October 1994), 69, 72.
7. Leslie M. Kantor, "Scared Chaste? Fear-Based Educational Curricula," *SIECUS Report* 21 (December 1992/January 1993), 1-2.
8. J. Ingrid Anderson, "Normal Sexual Development: An Overview," in Dorothy Williams, ed., *Yes You Can! A Guide For Sexuality Education That Affirms Abstinence Among Young Adolescents* (Minneapolis: Search Institute, 1987), 111.
9. Though this article does not specifically address HIV/AIDS education for young people, it is important to note that in this area of human sexuality education the Episcopal Church has already made important contributions. See Gene Robinson and Thaddeus Bennett, eds., Al-

tagracia Perez, writer/consultant, *The Episcopal Guide to TAP (Teens for AIDS Prevention)* (New York: The Domestic and Foreign Missionary Society, 1994); Altagracia Perez, "Oh My! I Have To Talk About HIV/AIDS, Too!," in Sheryl Kujawa and Lois Sibley, eds., *Resource Book for Ministries with Youth and Young Adults in the Episcopal Church* (New York: Domestic and Foreign Mission Society, 1995), 289-293.

10. *Teens Talk About Sex: Adolescent Sexuality in the 90s: A Survey of High School Students*, commissioned by Rolanda, a KingWard Production in association with the Sexuality Information and Education Council of the U.S. (New York: SIECUS, 1994), 4-5, 16, 22, 35-36.

11. For a comprehensive discussion of adolescent development written from the perspective of the Episcopal Church, see *Called to Teach and Learn: A Catechetical Guide for the Episcopal Church* (New York: The Domestic and Foreign Missionary Society, 1994), 137-154. Also see Fredrica Harris Thompsett, *Courageous Incarnation: In Intimacy, Work, Childhood and Aging* (Cambridge, Mass.: Cowley Publications, 1993), esp. ch. 2 and ch. 5.

12. *Called to Teach and Learn*, 145.

13. Dorothy L. Williams, ed., *Human Sexuality: Values and Choices* (Minneapolis: Search Institute, 1991), 103.

14. *Called to Teach and Learn*, 146-148; Les Parrott III, *Helping the Struggling Adolescent* (Grand Rapids: Zondervan, 1993), 296-302.

15. Lisa Kimball, "Gender," in Kujawa and Sibley, eds., *Resource Book*, 106-109; Williams, *Human Sexuality*, 95-101; also, Carol Gilligan, *In a Different Voice: Psychological Theory and Women's Development* (Cambridge, Mass.: Harvard University Press, 1982), 1-23.

16. Mary Pipher, *Reviving Ophelia: Saving the Selves of Adolescent Girls* (New York: Ballentine Books, 1994), 65-71, 205, 210, 280-281.

17. *The State of America's Children Yearbook* (Washington, D.C.: Children's Defense Fund, 1987), 54, 56.

18. George H. Gallup with Wendy Plumb, *Growing Up Scared in America: And What the Experts Say Parents Can Do About It* (Princeton: The George Gallup International Institute, 1995), 21-22, 28; Benjamin P. Bowser, "African American Male Sexuality through the Early Life Course," in Alice Rossi, ed., *Sexuality Across the Life Course* (Chicago: University of Chicago Press, 1994), 127-150.

19. *Continuing the Dialogue*, 57-58, 62-69; Report of the Standing Commission on Human Affairs, in *The Blue Book: Reports of the Committees, Commissions, Boards, and Agencies of the General Convention of the Episcopal Church* (August 1994), 111; Gene Robinson, "Whose Kids Are These, Anyway!," in Kujawa and Sibley, eds., *Resource Book*, 176; Jane Spahr and Chris Glaser, "Mission within the Lesbian/Gay Community," in *Breaking the Silence, Overcoming the Fear: Homophobia Education* (New York: Presbyterian Church U.S.A.), 53. See also Williams, ed., *Human Sexuality*, 91; Frederick Borsch, *Christian Discipleship and Sexuality* (Los Angeles: Episcopal Diocese of Los Angeles, 1992), 26-27, 32.

20. Merrill and Muriel Follansbee, "Pastoral Care with Parents and Friends of Lesbians and Gays," in *Breaking the Silence*, 35. Also, Mary V. Brohek, *Coming Out to Parents: A Two-Way Survival Guide for Lesbians and Gay Men and Their Parents* (Cleveland: Pilgrim Press, 1993); Leroy Aaron, *Prayers for Bobby: A Mother's Coming to Terms with the Suicide of Her Gay Son* (San Francisco: HarperSanFrancisco, 1995).

21. For an explanation of this process see Lisa Kimball, "Human Sexuality: Teenagers and the Church," in Kujawa and Sibley, eds., *Resource Book*, 102-105. This model was also tested and refined as a workshop, "Human Sexuality: Holy and Broken," at the Youth Ministries Leadership Academy in 1994, co-sponsored by the Youth Ministries Office at the Episcopal Church Center and the diocese of Southwest Florida. The facilitators were Lisa Kimball, Altagracia Perez, and Richard Harris.

SCRIPTURE
AND
TRADITION

∞ Marilyn McCord Adams

Hurricane Spirit, *Acts 10-15*

Toppling Taboos

To say that church and society are in the midst of a major crisis about human sexuality is by now platitudinous understatement. Over the last fifty years, traditional sexual mores have unravelled with accelerating rapidity. The divorce rate has sky-rocketed. Extramarital sex beginning in teen years has become commonplace. Living together "without the benefit of clergy" is accepted in most circles. The gay and lesbian liberation movement has "come out" and organized for political action. Gender roles have significantly shifted. Over the last dozen years, sexual abuse of children at home has been successfully prosecuted in courts of law.

The question raised by the present and impending chaos is not only how to weather it, but how to use it creatively and constructively. Happily but not surprisingly, the New Testament offers us a model for negotiating institutional crises in the power of the Spirit. In this paper I take my cue from Acts 10-15, the story of how the church dealt with the shocking surprise of Gentile conversions in her earliest years. I begin with a schematic overview of that story. Later sections will draw out some of its implications.

I.
Institutional Crisis, New Testament Paradigm

The narrative in Acts 10-15 unfolds in four stages:

1. At the outset the social context with its taboos carries unquestioned authority.

Tradition counted it unlawful for Jews to enter a Gentile house or receive Gentile guests or eat with them (Acts 10:28; 11:3). Peter had taken such regulations for granted and observed them (Acts 10:14; 11:7). Likewise, refugee preachers began by speaking to Jews only (Acts 11:19).

2. The taboo is challenged by experience.

Peter receives a set of heavenly visions forbidding him to count as unclean what God has cleansed, and is given instructions by the Spirit, which match those Cornelius receives from an angel (Acts 10:1-6, 9-16, 19-20). Moreover, Peter "sees" the Holy Spirit fall on Gentile converts as they listen to preaching (10:44-46; 11:15-17).

3. Over a period of time, the institution "learns from the Spirit" and changes its policies.

Peter obeys heavenly instructions, receives Cornelius's messengers as his guests, accompanies them to Caesarea, and stays there with them (Acts 10:21-23, 48; 11:10-12). Jerusalem refugees accept the fact of Gentile conversions, and Paul and Barnabas go to minister to these emerging congregations (Acts 11:21-26). The Jerusalem council officially decides that Gentile Christians do not have to be circumcised, but have only to obey the covenant with Noah (Acts 15:1-22).

Gentile conversions raised no minor issue. The radical nature of this change reverberates through the New Testament. The book of Acts itself records persistent, even violent opposition to it within the mother Jewish community, whose plots on Paul's life launch his final journey toward Rome. Paul's own letter to the Galatians contains a diatribe against the circumcision party within the church. Deutero-Pauline letters refer to the Spirit's toppling of this taboo as the mystery hidden through the ages (Eph. 3:4-6). Yet—

4. The Spirit's taboo-toppling was the key to the spread of the gospel.

"The word of God grew and multiplied" (Acts 12:14; 16:5; 19:20), and reached to the ends of the earth.

II.
The Notion of Taboo

The outline just presented makes use of a term that needs to be explained: *taboo*. Notice the evaluative language Peter uses after his vision as he protests, "No, Lord, nothing *unclean* has ever entered my mouth" (Acts 10:14; 11:8). Anthropologist Mary Douglas teaches us that purity and defilement are social metaphors, part of the system of evaluation erected to enforce existing social definitions and boundaries.[1] "Holy" means "separate, having clear and distinct boundaries"; "clean" signifies being wholly and completely a paradigm instance of a given kind; dirt is stuff out of order. There are many relevant orders: natural, social, liturgical. What falls between the cracks of any such order is bivalent—it carries two values or powers—and therefore it is regarded with ambivalence. On the one hand, it seems dangerous because disruptive to the establishment; by being out of order, it reminds us that the order oversimplifies, rules things out—things which, if they should get too powerful, might overturn the present regime. At the same time, on the other hand, these "misfits" *attract,* because they represent surplus power from the margins, over and above what we might expect in the normal course of things. Thus witches, mediums, astrologers, and desert hermits are the subject of both fear and fascination.

Because other orders also function as metaphors for the social whole, threatened societies tend to develop elaborate rules about purity and pollution that draw on these other organizational principles as well. To take a biblical example, animals that do not fit perfectly into crude biological categories are unclean (Lev. 11). Similarly, walls that are partly mildewed and persons partly leprous are unclean because they are not wholly and completely one thing or the other (Lev. 13; 14:33-57). Moreover, these categories of evaluation are "objective" in that they are utterly independent of the knowledge or intentions of the agent. All that matters is whether the boundary has been violated. Thus, in *Oedipus Rex* the king is ruined because he has in fact married his mother; that his deed was unwitting, that indeed he had spent all his conscious effort to avoid this tragic destiny, is irrelevant. Likewise, the person who unknowingly steps on an unmarked grave or touches a dead body is unclean all the same. So are the lame, the blind, and the mutilated, because they—usually quite involuntarily—fail to be perfect specimens.

Taboos are social institutions that wall out behaviors and conditions that are deemed most potentially disruptive. Threats to social order come in degrees, both concretely and symbolically. The refusal to respect private property or the physical safety of fellow tribe-members or citizens is a "concrete" menace. Insofar as the sexual purity of women is an important metaphor of social integrity, a woman's failure to observe the dress code by wearing the veil may be treated as a violation of the sacred, even though its concrete disruptive potential is quite small. When "unclean" conditions are not seriously disruptive, either concretely or symbolically, matters are easily set right by prescribed rituals. Men who have bodily discharges or who touch menstruous women may take ritual baths (Lev. 15:16-28). Contaminated porcelain dishes or silverware may be buried for a period of time.

Another reason why taboos are erected is to prevent attacks on the social foundations. Taboos aim to make the excluded behavior or condition "unthinkable." For that reason they are not rationalized or explained; anyone who would dare ask "why" is already on the brink of violation. That there is no remedy for taboo-violation reflects the fact that these are behaviors and conditions participation in which makes one "unfit for polite society." They are so traitorous to social aims that the group is permanently unwilling to rehabilitate anyone who crosses that line. For example, several years ago in

California the man who had not only raped his victim but axed off her arms could find no community that would accept him after his release from prison. Similarly, known incest used to put both perpetrator and victim outside the bounds.

Pollution and taboo legislation are readily translated into divine sanctions, for society counts itself sacred, God being the commander and enforcer of what makes for its survival and well-being. Thus, portions of the Hebrew Bible (the Holiness Code in Leviticus, for instance) represent God as the absolute monarch and author of the pollution legislation, the erector and maintainer of taboos.

Sexual mores have almost always been prime targets of taboo enforcement, for two closely related reasons. Psycho-spiritually, sexuality is one of the most powerful forces in human personality, interlocked as it is with the individual's creative energy. Careful channeling is thus key to bringing a child up in the way she or he should go. Sociologically and biologically, human sexuality is tightly linked, through procreation, with the future of families, tribes, and nations. It is therefore something in which society has a vigorous, even desperate interest.

One significant consequence of sexual taboos is that they make our approach to human sexuality inarticulate. A range of gender roles, complete with sharply defined contexts for managing sexual expression, is presented as the normative range of "forced choices." Inevitably violations stain; if discovered, they may cast offenders "into outer darkness." Insofar as social taboos get transposed to divine sanctions, sexual transgressions threaten to separate one not just "from the people" but also from God.

III.
Toppling the Taboo Mentality

Even if it is human nature to invent taboos and enlist God to enforce them, Christians have many reasons to deny that God operates that way. Taboo-thinking is theologically unsound in at least three ways.

1. Taboos are untheological because human social schemes oversimplify.
Scripture does include the Holiness Code and the revisions of *Haustafeln*, or lists of domestic rules, in the deutero-Pauline letters (Eph. 5:21–6:9; Col. 3:18–4:1). Nevertheless, the general drift of the Bible is to suggest that God does not set the divine seal of approval on any merely human social system. The reason is that the Realm of God is utopic; perfectly integrating the good of individuals and the good of the whole, it is comprehensive in a way no human society can be. Human nature being what it is, sanity and social stability require us to project and enforce some grid of categories on reality. But even with the best of intentions, human capacities for social or-

ganization are limited. We are inveterate oversimplifiers. Any scheme we come up with will be crude, leaving out something interesting and valuable. The story from Acts shows how the church discovered that God had "broken down the dividing wall of hostility between Jews and Gentiles" (Eph. 2:14-15), founded a Realm that would cancel exclusionary distinctions between "male and female, Jew and Greek, slave and free," integrating them all into the Body of Christ (Eph. 3:4-6; 4:1-16).

2. Taboos are untheological because they are immoral, in several ways.

In the first place, the system of purity and defilement with taboos at its extreme fails to be congruent with morality, because its criteria are different. As noted above, classifying someone as clean or unclean does not take account of that person's knowledge or intentions; it does not even confine itself to what is within his or her power. Characteristically, a double standard applies, so that consequences for the perpetrator have often been less than for the victim (of rape, for example, or parental incest). Likewise, many "unclean" states are utterly involuntary. The woman with the issue of blood, the blind, the lame—these are biblical examples. By contrast, our Lord denies that externals defile, declaring instead that "God looks on the heart."

Moreover, enforcement of taboos *qua* taboos is unjust because it forces persons who straddle existing social categories to pay a disproportionate price for the common good. To them the disingenuous message is: "Our social scheme is working well for most of us. It excludes you. We're afraid your integrity must be sacrificed for the sake of society at large. Indeed, it would be selfish of you not to forgo your own interests for the greater good." Unless there is strong evidence to think the lines have been drawn not arbitrarily, but for good moral reason in particular, this is unjust.

In the third place, taboo enforcement is usually cruel, because its consequences for the violator are very severe—social discrimination, exclusion, loss of personal dignity and wholeness, loss of community and concrete well-being. This harshness is amplified when sanctions against conditions one is powerless to remedy are imposed, not because one *is*, but because willy nilly one *symbolizes* a threat to society. Suicide rates among gay and lesbian teenagers, horrendous though they are, give only a feeble measure of the mountains of self-hatred and oceans of misery caused by taboos against homosexuality. Even before we get to the bottom of current issues about human sexuality, the cruelty of taboo enforcement, its violation of the love-commandment, should convince us to stop.

3. Taboos are untheological because they are based on human fear and incompetence.

We humans are naturally and reasonably terrified of social dissolution. We know from experience that our capacity to justify social policies with articulate reasons is limited. Sometimes we correctly sense that something would be socially ruinous, but find ourselves unable to explain why. Isn't it better to enforce these intuitions with taboos than to be too permissive and put our community at risk? Once again, the problem is that fear exaggerates our sense of what would be catastrophic, and so tightens our grip on the status quo. But whereas taboos are the flying buttresses propping up human society, the story in Acts 10-15 combines with Pauline and deutero-Pauline texts to assure us that the Body of Christ is animated and coordinated by an all-wise and almighty Holy Spirit whose methods of social and cosmic integration do not require taboos.

I have been arguing that a "taboo mentality" is indefensible on Christian grounds. One result of this argument is that it puts the church in the business of perpetual self-subversion. Because the church is *human* as well as divine, she is shaped by limited human capacity for social organization, and consequently pressured to buttress her own structures with taboos. This temptation is heightened by her claim to speak for God, and so to package her own norms as authoritarian dictates that need no further explanation or warrant beyond "Thus saith the Lord!" Since the church is *divine* as well as human, however, she is constantly called to renounce taboos. Inasmuch as humans are personal, made in God's image, and uniquely (among things here below) capable of thought and choice, the church is always called to trust the Spirit and dare to bring what is feared, said, and done in the dark "out of the closet" and up to full consciousness, into the intimacy of the Spirit's classroom, for rational and prayerful examination.

IV.
Sexual Taboos: Uniquely Pernicious

For centuries the church has imitated human society at large by approaching the topic of sexuality in the modality of taboo and authoritarian dictates. She has recognized two options for managing sexuality. One is monogamous, lifelong, heterosexual marriage. The other is celibacy. Her rules and regulations have sent her members the message that even to contemplate other options could ruin their reputations, stain their characters, even count them out of divine society and endanger their souls. In the Victorian era the very topic of sexuality itself became taboo. Translations of the early church fathers, for example, left their theological discussions of sexual sins in Latin, so as to be accessible only to scholars. In Roman Catholic circles, the theology of marriage got reduced to "Do it only with each other," "Do it only to produce children," and "Wives, be ever-available lest your husband be tempted to adultery." Protestant opinion was simply summarized: "If you want to be sexually active, get married"; "What you do in your own bedroom is your own business"; "Just don't talk about it." And it goes without saying that on both sides homosexual activity was officially banned.

The church has, in sum, confused discipline with repression, and the consequences have been bitter. Keeping everybody's sexuality in the closet has distorted the church's picture of human nature and obscured her social vision. It has allowed her to turn a blind eye to sexual abuse of spouses and children within the institution of marriage. On the other hand, because sexuality is woven into the heart of human personality, her enforcement of sexual taboos sends the message that those who violate them are unacceptable, not because of something that could be altered, but at the core of their being. Her participation in such cruelty disqualifies her for the task of spiritual formation, aborts her vocation to care for souls, and indeed borders on apostasy by flirting with the lie that some people and conditions are beyond divine redemption.

In fair weather, all this goes unrecognized; only philosophers lament the operation of taboo-mentality with its lack of reasons why. As Acts 10-15 suggests, unchallenged taboos retain our unreflective allegiance. Even if we violate them, our sense of stain, guilt, or self-loathing pays tribute to their legitimacy. For better or worse, however, the last fifty years have battered away at the wall of taboos governing sexual mores. Centuries of complacent complicity in those taboos, to the neglect of theological and spiritual homework, has left the church at an embarrassing loss to explain why conventional rules and role expectations were supposed to have been a good thing.

V.
Choosing the Questions

Now that liquefying social institutions have forced the issue, the church must become more articulate about human sexuality. In so doing, it is of paramount importance to identify which are the questions that it would be most fruitful to pursue; and here models can make all the difference. In this section I will consider a number of different ways of modelling the church's vocation where sexuality is concerned.

One way to become more articulate about sexuality would be to inquire after a new set of *rules* about what is prohibited and permitted. Taboos dressed up as divine commands were often promulgated as thou-shalt-nots; recent civil law has attempted to formulate rules that are reason-based by focusing on individual rights, deploying the category of fully consensual adult behavior, and attending to subtle as well as flagrant abuses of power within the workplace and the home. To her shame, the church has been caught off-guard by these secular developments, and forced by the courts to scramble to clean her own house. Indeed, there is some danger that the church's creative energy for pursuing the topic of human sexuality will be drained off by negotiating and fending off lawsuits, leaving none for the constructive task of discovering and formulating norms.

In any event, the church's vocation is inadequately modelled by the portfolio of the liberal democratic state. For if the state is charged with the social task of maintaining collective peace and safety with fairness and minimal interference in individual lives, the church is responsible for the spiritual formation of individuals. Accordingly, she must press beyond prohibitions and permissions to discover and commend wholesome ways of being sexual persons in community with God and one another. As with any good parent or teacher, her deepest reasons for sponsoring any set of prohibitions and permissions will be rooted in considerations of what is fruitful or damaging to her children's spiritual health.

In this regard, it seems the church might have something to learn from Aristotle, who focused his ethics not on rights and obligations but on the good life. What makes for a truly choiceworthy life, Aristotle thought, could not be codified by any set of rules, but rather was a matter of discernment by good people. Accordingly, he investigated what the virtues or habits are that shape human beings into persons who can discern and live the good life. But the identification of these virtues presupposes some ideal, some criterion of what the good life consists in. Aristotle takes human flourishing as the ideal, recognizing that actual choices presuppose some concrete conception of that in which human flourishing consists.

The search for such an ideal seems a promising way to begin fresh thinking about human sexuality. It allows for flexibility, insofar as most ideals can be approached or approximated in a variety of ways. Moreover, ideals may be more and less abstract, and in principle there can be a plurality of ideals. Current institutions already recognize a pair of sexual ideals: monogamous heterosexual marriage, and celibacy. Likewise, the effort to identify ideals in principle could acknowledge that not just any and every lifestyle is wholesome, while at the same time opening the possibility of (not begging the question against) recognizing a wider variety of models for homosexual as well as heterosexual expression.

Despite these advantages, however, I doubt that asking after ideals of human flourishing provides the best focus for Christians who are rethinking human sexuality. In the first place, Christian spiritual formation is particularized in *calling*. It is not charted from the bottom up, targeted simply on what it is to be an ideal human being, but aims higher—at life together with God. A focus on ideals would have to be a focus on ideals of divine-human relationship. In the second place, though, concentrating on ideals seems too optimistic. To be sure, expectations could be modified by noting that ideals are difficult if not impossible to reach. But putting ideals front and center can lend the impression that we ought to be able to get close to them, and this suggestion underestimates how badly the taboo-modality has damaged most people's sexuality (whether heterosexual or homosexual). When the sexuality of many is so badly broken, Christian hope for it seems poorly expressed by talk of measuring up to ideals.

On balance, I think, the church can best become more articulate about human sexuality if she takes neither *rules* nor *ideals* but *sacraments* as her model. The old Prayer Book catechism defined a sacrament as "an outward and visible sign of an inward and spiritual grace." More broadly, though, all creatures reflect divine being and goodness; our common call is to express the image of God impressed on us, to be outward and visible signs of divine love in a broken and confused world. From this sacramental perspective, the fruitful question to ask would be: *How can we live as heterosexual or homosexual persons so as to be sacraments of divine love in a broken and confused world?* This approach would acknowledge the relevance of human well-being, because all creatures are more or less distant likenesses of God, designed to focus the image by flourishing. At the same time, a sacramental approach has the flexibility to allot dignity and significance to what is so broken that flourishing in that dimension is humanly impossible. For Christians, the paradigmatic sacrament of divine love is the crucified body of the Lord, a symbol which shouts that utter ruin, the antithesis of human flourishing, can still become sacramental, even before the ruin is "fixed" from a natural, merely human point of view.

At the creaturely level, sacraments in the more restricted sense involve material (water, oil, bread, and wine), a form of words, and a liturgical drama enacted on purpose; at the divine level, God's promise to bless and sanctify by divine presence. My suggestion is that human sexuality becomes sacramental when our lives as sexual human beings are "watched and prayed." This exercise begins where we are, as we "come out" to God as sexual beings, honestly pouring out our desires, frustrations, and confusions in prayer. My assumption is that wrestling with and before God for our sexuality will win the blessing of sacramental sexuality, and will eventually evolve a variety of Christian models, wider and richer than was ever imagined under the bondage of taboos.

VI.
Hurricane Spirit, Taboo-Free Zone

What we have received in Acts 10-15 is an official retrospective on the church's first institutional crisis. As with most authorized reports, this one is deceptively bland. Like Peter's vertigo at the heavenly vision, at welcoming Gentiles, at eating with them the first time, so too the heat of controversy with the circumcision party has been toned down, largely though not entirely, by what we now have as well-packaged form-critical units, formulaic stories repeated until they seem self-evidently true. The reliability of Peter's visions is not questioned. The correctness of his discernment, that what had fallen on the Gentiles was indeed the Holy Spirit, is not challenged. He has only to voice his testimony for hearers to accept his conclusion and rejoice in the Spirit's bold new idea. At the time, however, Peter—and later the refugee preachers and the Jerusalem council—had to tread the stormy waters of controversy, praying hard and trusting that they were looking to Jesus and not just some ghost.

What is obvious at present is precisely stormy controversy, the deep divisions within the church over the issue of human sexuality. Everyone agrees that recent social and political movements—the sexual revolution, feminist and gay/lesbian liberation, movements for children's rights—have mounted frontal and foundational attacks on conventional and ecclesiastical sexual mores. But many Christians reject the analogy with Acts 10-15. On one hand, the more strident diagnose such developments as open rebellion against divine commands, as the work not of holy but of unclean spirits. They remind us how the Right and the Good have been attacked, and God's commandments laughed to scorn, in every generation. They make their own appeals to scripture and tradition to pronounce these movements un-Christian and declare participants' experiences of wholeness and release inauthentic. The more extreme accuse Christians who beg to differ of apostasy, insisting that the church would be unfaithful in listening to secular movements instead of heeding the "clear" testimony of revelation. The more generous give their opponents credit for sincerity, while pointing out how easy it is to be honestly yet disastrously wrong. In my experience, these Christians are confident that they are right and usually not open to discussion, much less compromise.

On the other hand, still others (often those who hold positions of ecclesiastical authority and responsibility) are moved not so much by their own entrenched views about sexual mores as by fears about the institutional consequences of the church's attempt to press forward while its membership is so divided. They counsel delay, recommend progress by "ministeps"—such as discussion articles that at least bring the general topic of sexuality "out of the closet"—while insisting on conformity to old standards—no priestly blessings of same-sex partnerships, for example—until some future point at which the issue has become less volatile.

My disagreements with both groups are rooted in my conviction that justification by faith applies to our beliefs and not merely to deeds and choices. I agree that sincerity is no guarantor of truth. God alone is infallible. All human opinion is fallible, whether the collective mind of secular social and political movements, or the efforts of biblical writers and the church to discern God's purpose. All merely human perceptions are very much shaped by our thought-worlds and our social positions in them. Surely our Creator knows our cognitive limitations: God wrestles daily with formidable divine-human communication problems. Yet God respects our personhood, includes in our vocations our growing up to our full cognitive and emotional stature as persons. My conclusion is that the all-wise God no more demands that we always hold the right beliefs at every stage of our spiritual development than good parents demand it in rearing infants through childhood and adolescence to adulthood. I take it, then, that God will work with messy discernment processes, with honest attempts to orient ourselves to the divine point of view.

Thus my own conviction is that Christ our teacher and the Holy Spirit within us are constantly active, designing particularized syllabuses for individuals and groups, nudging and pushing us ahead on varying spiritual fronts, depending on where each is ready to move. Although we may be working on quite different assignments for years and seasons, we will all be progressing toward the goal of seeing as God sees and loving as God loves. For these reasons, we in the church have to consider the possibility that, confronted with our stubborn deafness on the subject of human sexuality, the Shekinah Spirit has taken these lessons out of the Temple to teach them to those who will listen. At the very least, God may use secular social movements as attention-getters, warnings against confident complacency and fearful digging in.

Moreover, I do not see how it is possible, given human nature, for church or society to learn anything very new about sexuality while demanding that everyone maintain the behavioral and normative status quo. Rather, a fresh "take" on human sexuality requires us to suspend judgment, really to listen, to enter into contrasting and even revolutionary points of view, to learn from those who have "tried them on for size." Listening with the aim of applying taboos in order to condemn makes us deaf; insisting on the presumptive rightness of traditional mores makes us hard of hearing. If we insist on the authority to judge and lack the humility of a pupil, how can we persuade those from whom we need to learn to speak? To repeat, sexuality goes to the core of a person. Data relevant to the wholesomeness of heterosexual and homosexual practices and lifestyles involve participants' most intimate feelings and self-estimates. Why should anyone share these with a hostile audience? Sadly, the church's lack of respect has silenced her own members, leaving them largely unwilling to share with the church their discoveries about what helps and hinders.

Fears for institutional stability need to be weighed against the risks of social irrelevance and irresponsibility. The world will not grant us an extended time-out. Many people in the pews have not waited, any more than Roman Catholic couples have generally observed the blanket ban on birth control. Lesbian and gay Christians, who have borne the brunt of taboo-enforcement, deserve not to wait. For better or worse, the power of past gender-role definitions and sexual mores is broken past simple recovery. The choice lies between *laissez-faire* and prayerful, reflective attempts to discern a subtler variety of wholesome patterns.

Ironically, the church's very divisions over human sexuality create a situation in which it is safe for some of us to go ahead. When the disciples saw Jesus walking on the water, not everyone got out of the boat—only Peter did, and only in Matthew's version of the story. The others stayed on board to row. First-, second-, and third-hand experience has already convinced many of us that nonconventional lifestyles are sacramental material. Some of us have seen too much to impose such burdens of proof as even our more moderate church leaders suggest.

My immodest proposal is that we find many and various ways to create taboo-free zones within the church where human sexuality can be openly and prayerfully explored. To do so is not tantamount to the conclusion that "anything goes." At mid-century, when the church found her blanket prohibition of divorce and remarriage pastorally indefensible, she did not thereby sanction any and every divorce as a good thing. Rather, pastoral experience evolved criteria, among them, whether a marriage was destroying the image of Christ in the partners. Nor am I suggesting a smorgasbord where people are urged to sample sexual practices new to them. The initial point of removing the taboo against "coloring outside the lines" would be to create an atmosphere in which Christians can prayerfully evaluate the ways of life they have already tried and share their insights with the church. What things were liberating? Which were confusing? Which were destructive of the image of Christ in everyone concerned, and which nourished it? Over time, one would expect evolution: the sunlight of a taboo-free zone, the fresh air of prayer, would be a climate where closeted plants could flourish, blossoming into new and better styles of integration. Likewise, the results of taboo-free discernment would shed light on why conventional institutions (which also have their good points) are so rapidly unravelling. What human conditions are they failing to consider? What needs are they failing to accommodate? What Christ-like potentials are they repressing?

This unravelling of our institutions, I might add, is why I am suspicious of the rush to tuck homosexual relationships into conventional cubby-holes by making gay marriage the norm. Not that marriage analogues aren't a good move for some gay and lesbian couples, or even an interim model for many. My objection is that intentionally short-circuiting the messy process of thinking afresh, in hopes of minimizing institutional disruption, actually aborts a process that could reform and revitalize our present institutions. We dare to get out of the boat, by faith in our Lord Jesus, to walk on the water, because experience has convinced us that in the area of human sexuality church and society need fundamental reform, not superficial adjustments. Current institutions of heterosexual marriage and celibacy have evolved through long use enforced by taboo. When taboos are toppled, we should not expect them to remain exactly as they are.

Walking on the water feels dangerous. Precisely because human sexuality lies at the core of human personality, alternative lifestyle experiments are costly to those involved in them. Mistakes run the risk of damaging and distorting the person at every level—physical, psychological, and spiritual. Yet, I ask, What forward-looking alternative is there? For homosexual activity there has been none for centuries; role models have been hidden and difficult to recognize. Individuals have had to choose between creativity, assimilation, and despair. Many experiments have been, and continue to be, performed anyway. When we "just say no" to nontraditional alternatives, we abdicate Christian responsibility for discernment: where all is taboo, all is likewise permitted; no distinctions have been drawn, no guidelines prepared. Christians who dare to approach human sexuality in a taboo-free zone embrace the task of identifying saints, painting icons, distinguishing the stuff of sacramental relationships, offering their failures on the altar to be taken up into the sufferings of Christ, transformed into the Bread of Life for the church and the world. My own sense is that within the church itself there are many discoveries waiting to be made, and many more to come when individual and collective praying-through becomes the obvious thing to do.

Meanwhile, I suspect that climbing overboard is no more dangerous than staying in the boat; merely human powers can no more conquer chaos than they can still the Spirit's wind. I believe that the Spirit is implicated in the present crisis, permitting the old order to unravel, indeed huffing and puffing it down, because our current social and ecclesiastical grid over human sexuality is a cruel and unjust oversimplification, increasingly sterilizing those who live within its norms. By the grace of God, watched and prayed sexuality within a taboo-free zone will participate in the Spirit's re-creative power.

NOTES

1. Mary Douglas, *Purity and Danger: An Analysis of Concepts of Pollution and Taboo* (London: Routledge & Kegan Paul, 1966).

∞ *B. Barbara Hall*

Homosexuality
and a New Creation

 How might the Bible inform the current discussion among Christians about homosexuality and the church's position and attitude toward gay men and lesbians? There is not an obvious answer to this question. On the one hand, what the Bible says explicitly about the matter seems uniformly negative. On the other, the Bible says *very little* on the subject. And it is clearly the case that those who wrote our biblical documents had no conception of the notions which routinely inform our conversation on these issues: the idea of "sexual orientation," the conviction that some persons are "constitutionally" (that is, "naturally") homosexual, the existence of long-term monogamous relationships among gay people. For those who take the Bible seriously, but not in a simplistic or uncritically "literal" way, it is difficult to know how the Bible can help us.

This essay suggests that Paul may be our best entry into fruitful discussion. At first glance, he is an unlikely partner in this conversation. What seems to be the clearest and most categorical condemnation of homosexuality in scripture occurs in Paul's letter to the Romans (1:26-27), and so I begin with a brief consideration of this text. In subsequent sections, we will look at Paul's notion of a *new creation*, in order to see whether his understanding of God's action in Jesus Christ might suggest some helpful possibilities for modern Christians.

∞

References to homosexuality in the Bible are extremely rare. The passages in the Old Testament and two of those in the New (1 Cor. 6:9, 1 Tim. 1:10) are seen, with good reason, as being largely irrelevant to the present discussion. Either they form part of a code long since discarded, or the texts are themselves unclear, or the social and cultural conditions in which references are found are obviously far removed from contemporary life. Romans

1:26-27 is the real problem. Here Paul declares in a clear voice that homosexual practice is "unnatural," "dishonorable" ("shameful," "degrading").

When these verses are read, what does the modern reader hear? The emphasis falls on the term "unnatural." The "dishonorable" description is too vague; the term is used in too many different ways to make it a particular stumbling block. But "unnatural" is as sharp a condemnation of homosexuality as one can imagine.

When Christians look at what seems to be the immediate context of these verses, Romans 1:18-32, the situation gets worse. Careful analysis will reveal nuances, perhaps, but the dominant impression is the right one: homosexuality is here associated with a long list of offenses which begins with idolatry (1:23) and includes a great many negative-to-terrible things. Paul starts this dire passage by referring to the wrath of God and ends it by declaring that those who commit the offenses listed deserve to die. The modern reader concludes that, for Paul, homosexual acts are sinful and those who commit them can have no place in any Christian community he would recognize.

But if that response is likely enough for a modern reader, how would the first-century Roman Christians to whom Paul wrote have heard this text? First, they would not have picked out these verses for special attention, nor would they have isolated them, as modern readers tend to do. They would have listened eagerly to the *whole* letter (probably read aloud in various church gatherings) and then studied it carefully. It was their first direct contact with the famous apostle to the Gentiles, who was coming to Rome to meet them. Moreover, some of them were not at all sure they could welcome Paul. What exactly was the gospel he preached? Was it the gospel they had received and were living out? In seeking answers to these questions, they would have pored over the entire letter, trying to hear what it said as a totality.

Second, the first readers of Romans would easily have recognized Paul's argument in Romans 1:18-32. It is very similar to descriptions, typical of Jewish teachers, that pictured dramatically the degradation of Gentile life without God and the consequences of human rebellion against God. What began as idolatry multiplied into every sort of evil imaginable. Jewish teachers who used this argument in sermons or discussions sometimes adopted the language of secular ethicists, especially those influenced by Stoic philosophy. It was a basic precept of Stoicism that one should do what is "natural." The ancient literature gives examples that show that homosexuality, in particular, was declared by some to be "unnatural." We can be fairly confident that Paul's first readers recognized a language and a style they had encountered before, here used by Paul in drawing his picture of the world prior to God's sending Jesus Christ.

Paul's readers in Rome would also surely have made the link between his argument and the well-known and well-loved stories of creation in Genesis 1–2: "male and female he created them," "be fruitful and multiply" (Gen. 1:27-28; see also Gen. 2:18-24). As these accounts have it, God's original purpose was to crown his creation with the man/woman who together and before God would live out the purpose of creation. It is not surprising that homosexuality would appear "unnatural" in the light of the images in these passages. It clearly does not conform to the creation stories in Genesis.

In Romans 1, then, Paul was not writing in his own characteristic vocabulary and style. He did not create an argument that was new to his readers. On the contrary, he deliberately espoused a version of Jewish ethical discussion that his readers already knew. It is not clear until almost the end of this long letter *why* Paul would argue in this way. In Romans 12-15, however, we learn that all along Paul has been appealing to a strongly Gentile church to welcome its Jewish members. Indeed, just prior to these chapters, in Romans 9-11, there is an extended passage on God's relation to the Jews, which makes clear that for Paul the church includes *both* Jew and Gentile. In Romans 1, then, Paul begins his letter by speaking *as a Jewish teacher would*, in describing the human situation. The underlying message is: "I, apostle to the Gentiles, the one who is on your side, you Gentiles—I argue as a Jew would, as I begin to spell out my gospel." The fact that Paul could expect his readers to follow the line he is taking is important if we are to notice the real dynamite of the whole passage—his claim that *no one*, Jew or Gentile, is exempt from the consequences of human rebellion against God.

For purposes of the present essay, there is another important point to note. In Paul's thinking the original creation, in which heterosexual was "natural" and homosexual was "unnatural," was irrevocably lost in the human rebellion against God. There is no going back to the way life was, as originally created. Thus, although Paul certainly speaks of homosexuality in a negative way in Romans 1:26-27, he does not provide a rationale for those who would argue that heterosexual behavior alone is acceptable to God, because it is "natural." There may be other grounds today for adopting a "natural"/"unnatural" line of reasoning on this issue, but those who do so cannot claim Paul's blessing.

The question remains, however: given his negative assessment of homosexuality in Romans 1:26-27, is there any possibility of fruitful exchange between lesbians and gay men and their supporters, on the one hand, and Paul, on the other? Does he have nothing to offer that will inform our search for the way of God's obedience today? I believe there is an important way that he can guide our quest. For Paul, what God has done in Jesus Christ about humanity's plight, as described in Romans 1:18–3:20, is to inaugurate a new creation.

❦

"New creation" is one of many terms Paul uses to express what God's action in Jesus Christ has accomplished. "Justification" or "righteousness" (the same word in Greek) and "reconciliation" are others. His vocabulary is very diverse. For purposes of this discussion, "new creation" is an apt notion to explore, since "new" suggests heretofore unknown or untapped resources and "creation" is, of course, our home, the arena in which we live all our lives. It is also a useful notion as we explore *Paul,* because the term has not been domesticated, so to speak, by constant use in the Christian theological tradition. It retains something of its original freshness and power.

It is not obvious what new creation means, however. As we look at the world, it does not strike us, and would not have struck Paul's first readers, as a *new* creation. If the old world still exists as it always has done, where is the new creation? It is not clear how one experiences, participates in it. How did Paul understand it?

Paul writes of the new creation in two places. The first is Galatians 6:11-16. In this paragraph at the end of his letter to the Galatian churches, Paul makes one last, emphatic attempt to argue strongly for the inclusion of Gentile Christians in the church, apart from any requirement that they become Jews in the process. That is, the question under discussion is, Does one have to be a Jew in order to be a Christian? It is hard for Christians today to be exercised by this debate, since Gentile Christianity is the only kind we have had for many centuries. But it was not so in Paul's day. Then, his Jewish-Christian opponents had a strong and cogent argument: Jesus, the Messiah, the Christ, was a Jew, sent to the Jews, who were the people who expected, awaited a Messiah from God. If Gentiles were to be included in the Messiah's community at all, *of course* they had to become Jews.

Paul saw another vision of what God had done and was doing in the church. He saw a *discontinuity* between God's long history with the Jews and God's act in Jesus. God has not renewed Judaism in Jesus; God has not elected to expand Judaism to include Gentiles through Jesus; God has not restored humanity to its original purpose in the first creation, by way of the long history of faithful Judaism, culminating in the faithful Jew, Jesus. All these ways of interpreting God's act in Jesus Christ were used by some early Christians. But in contrast to those other early Christian thinkers, Paul's conviction was that God had initiated a new creation. He spoke of a very sharp break with any and all past experience with God. "New creation" suggests that in Jesus Christ, God has started everything all over. It is a very drastic claim.

The first of the two passages in which Paul speaks about this new creation, Galatians 6:11-16, is a very rich paragraph, about which I shall note only two things. The first is that the new creation is the opposite of that arena in which the distinction of circumcision/uncircumcision (the equivalent of Jew/Gentile) is a serious and important issue. The new creation does not take such polarities as the defining terms of anything significant.[1]

The second point to note in this paragraph, for our purposes, is the mention of crucifixion. Paul makes a second drastic claim here: in the cross of Jesus Christ, *Paul* has been crucified to the *world* and the *world* has been crucified to *Paul*.[2] The modern reader automatically "spiritualizes" or "interiorizes" this notion, since the world is as obviously still with us as the old creation is. Indeed, they are the same thing. But there is no indication whatever that Paul meant to refer solely to an inward or strictly spiritual reality. He not only saw the new creation as the opposite of "world," he understood that the way from world to new creation requires a *death* to the old. He could hardly have put it in a more forceful way. Thus, in Paul's first mention of new creation, the very radical character of the image is established. The new creation is what all that is familiar to us is emphatically *not*.

The other paragraph in which Paul speaks of a new creation is 2 Corinthians 5:16-21. The modern reader usually understands this passage in an individualistic way: in Christ, God has reconciled us, one by one, forgiving our individual sins, and creating a spiritual relationship between God and me. We two are reconciled. The next step is that each one of us is to be a reconciler, again bringing people one by one to Christ. We do not *see* the words "*everything* old has passed away, *everything* has become new!" We rarely note "in Christ, God was reconciling the *world* to himself"—the same world to which Paul said in Galatians that he had died. We miss Paul's clear intention. While it is true that each one in Christ is a new creation (verse 17a), this reality depends on the *corporate* new creation to which each one is called and in which each belongs. The new creation is to replace the old one, not to be a collection of individuals within or alongside the old.

But now, in writing 2 Corinthians, Paul says the transformation has not taken place completely, with finality (as we, reading some two thousand years later, can readily attest). Paul is (surely, deliberately) imprecise about the new creation. On the one hand, he declares that "everything old *has passed* away, everything *has become* new." On the other hand, he advises his readers, "Be reconciled to God," and he insists that there is work for *Christians* to do in building the new creation: we have been given the ministry of reconciliation, we are ambassadors for Christ. That is, the new creation both is and is not a reality in the present time. God's power has broken into the world in such a decisive and radical way that it is possible to speak of a new creation. But it is also true that Christians have something compelling to do in relation to it. Is there a new creation or not? There is and there will be, based on God's continued work among faithful Christian ambassadors.

I have discussed the two passages where Paul explicitly refers to a new creation. But there is another text, Galatians 3:26-28, that also bears on the discussion. Although the term itself is does not appear, there is a strong link with the notion of new creation. So much is clear from Galatians 6:15, where, as we have seen, new creation is the opposite of the antithesis circumcision/uncircumcision or its equivalent, Jew/Gentile. The same polarity is mentioned in Galatians 3:26-28, along with two others. All three pairs are used by way of contrast. That is, they describe what the new creation is *not*.

There are two very important points about these verses in chapter 3, which modern readers need to know in order to understand their impact in the early church. The first is that the verses constitute an early Christian *liturgical formula*, almost certainly from a baptismal service. They can be set out as follows, in order to show the characteristic form of an early liturgical piece:

In Christ Jesus, you are all children of God;
You who were baptized into Christ have clothed yourselves with Christ.
There is no longer Jew or Gentile,
There is no longer slave or free,
There is no longer male and female.
All of you are one in Christ Jesus.

New Christians, coming up out of the waters of baptism and receiving a new garment, symbol of their new relation to Christ in the church, heard these words spoken—a solemn declaration of their membership now in the new creation. We are not dealing therefore with a series of sayings that Paul invented as he dictated his letter to the Galatians. He was quoting words his readers would have had good reason to remember with awe.

The second point for understanding the impact of these verses is that the polarities are not arbitrary. Paul, or whoever first created the baptismal formula, chose a set of contrasts well-known in their world. The newly baptized would certainly have found them familiar. There are various versions of these polarities known to us from Paul's time. A Hellenistic man would commonly thank his god or gods that he was a Greek and not a barbarian, free and not a slave, a man and not a woman. A similar set of three existed within Judaism. Rabbi Judah, from the end of the first century of the Christian era, is remembered to have said, "One ought to say three blessings every day: Blessed is he that did not make me a Gentile; blessed is he that did not make me a woman; blessed is he that did not make me a slave." Some Jewish visions of the final victory of God in the future included the overcoming of one or more of these same polarities. With all this in mind, one can better imagine the strong impact the words would have made on the newly baptized Christians. They announce the day of fulfillment, when the polarities that define and divide people are no more. They announce that God has won the final victory.

For those of Paul's readers who knew their scripture, the baptismal formula would carry yet another meaning, an echo of Genesis that explains an oddity in the way the formula is worded. In order to contrast two things, one normally says, "no longer this *or* that." Indeed, the formula says, "no longer Jew or Greek, no longer slave or free." Why then does it say "no longer male *and* female"? Clearly, this expression recalls the first creation story, "male *and* female he created them" (Gen. 1:27). In the new creation, the old polarities are eliminated. Not only so, but even the crown of God's creative work, the creation of man and woman, is superseded.

Even with these understandings of the associations the formula would have aroused in newly baptized Christians, it is not at all clear what the formula *means*. It is odd, to say the least—and would have been so even to the first generation of Christians, who expected the return of the triumphant Christ at an early date—to claim that fulfillment *has already happened.* Or, if it does not mean that, what does it mean?

∞

How did Paul understand the baptismal formula? He never spelled out in an explicit way what he thought it meant. However, a way to know his mind on the subject is to inquire *how he worked in practical ways in his churches, in order to bring into reality a community where these distinctions* (Jew/Greek, and the like) *were unimportant.* A passage which deals specifically with sexuality would be especially appropriate for our discussion and so I have chosen 1 Corinthians 7. Nowhere in his letters does Paul so clearly tackle the question of what is entailed in living out in the real world the affirmation "no longer male and female."

1 Corinthians 7 is a very hard passage for modern readers to hear with any understanding. Most people see that Paul commends celibacy (vss. 7, 8, 28b, 32-34, 37-38, 40) as the best way to live. Further, they see that marriage is solely for the purpose of abating passion in an acceptable way, and that this is a grudging concession on Paul's part (vss. 2, 9, 36). Beyond this, few modern Christians are interested enough to proceed. Closer scrutiny, along with a dash of imagination, however, provides an intriguing picture of the events which led Paul to write the chapter.

In this passage on sexuality, one part of the baptismal formula, namely "no longer male and female," is specifically under consideration. We can infer this because in the middle of the discussion of sexuality (vss. 17-24), Paul suddenly takes a detour away from his subject to speak briefly about

Jew/Gentile, slave/free. Why would he do such a thing? How would his readers in Corinth have made sense of what he says? The obvious answer is that the issue of sexuality under discussion between Paul and the Corinthians is specifically related to the interpretation of "no longer male and female." The other two polarities in the baptismal formula (Jew/Gentile, slave/free) come to mind, because one polarity in the baptismal formula suggests the other two. These latter offer Paul appropriate analogies in a discussion of the third, "no longer male and female." The Corinthians, then, have been working on the meaning of "no longer male and female" and have written Paul about it (1 Cor. 7:1).

Here is what *they* thought "no longer male and female" entailed: some believed that being Christian meant living completely celibate lives. The rationale was simple and clear. What does it mean to say that in Christ believers were no longer male and female? Clearly, these Corinthians reasoned, it means that Christians have been transformed so that they are no longer sexual beings. They have moved beyond (or above) the normal human condition of sexuality into a new state. The way to express this is obviously to live publicly as celibates. Such an interpretation of sexuality in the new creation would have fit neatly into some hopes current at the time. There were, in both Hellenistic society and Jewish thought, notions that in some ideal future the distinction between the sexes would be overcome. Some of the Corinthian Christians saw "no longer male and female" as a clear affirmation that this promise was now fulfilled. This was one of the specific marks of the *new* creation, which superseded the old.

In such a situation, judging from Paul's response to their letter, we can surmise that those Corinthians who were married to other Christians were being urged to live in the marriage as celibates; those married to unbelievers were being urged to divorce them; those widowed or not yet married were being urged to remain as they were. It is also likely that some individuals in the church had taken public vows of celibacy and that, among these, some now wished they had not done so. There was some controversy in the church about these matters, and they had been raised in a letter written to Paul. Paul, the known celibate, could be expected by those advocating celibacy in Corinth to side with them.

I have attempted a reconstruction of the situation in Corinth that prompted Paul to write chapter 7. The evidence to support the reconstruction is in the chapter itself. It appears when one asks the question: under what circumstances would Paul have written this chapter? Several points are worth attention, even in this brief discussion. I will mention five.

The first is that the chapter appears to address two sets of readers, those who are married and those who are not. The first verse begins: "Now concerning the matters about which you wrote...." Paul then quotes from their letter and speaks against what they have written, speaks strongly in favor of marriage. This part (vss. 1-16, with 39-40 as a kind of postscript) is addressed to married people. Next comes the detour on Jew/Gentile, slave/free, referred to above (7:17-24). Paul then resumes the thread of his discussion: "Now concerning virgins...." The phrase "now concerning" repeats the opening words of chapter, and is found frequently elsewhere in 1 Corinthians. It introduces Paul's response to something his readers had written to him. In 1 Corinthians 7:25-38, Paul addresses the unmarried, perhaps those who have taken vows of celibacy. The reconstruction of the discussion in Corinth I have suggested above explains why Paul urges marriage in one section and celibacy in the other.

A second point to notice is that Paul argues strongly *against* an interpretation of "no longer male and female" as a change of state for Christians, from normal humanity into sexlessness. The comments on sexual passion and controlling it (vss. 2, 5, 9, 36) are Paul's attempts to insist that Christians have not passed beyond sexuality into some superior state. There is a perfectly sensible, this-worldly way to know whether you have been called to celibacy in the Christian life. If you are consumed by passion, you have not been so called! Another way to argue against a change in the human state is to speak about "calling," as Paul does in his detour (vss. 17-24). These verses are often interpreted as Paul's advice to Christians never to change anything. That is a ludicrous interpretation, of course, since Paul was forever urging his readers to change in various ways. What he clearly meant is that one is acceptable to God (and therefore in the church) just as one was when God called him or her, *with regard to the three polarities*. In effect, "You do not have to change in order to be God's. You already belong to God, just as you are—Jew/Gentile, slave/free." And in terms of sexuality, you already belong to God just as you are, married, single, about to be married, widowed. Paul is saying, "Contrary to what some in Corinth are urging, you do not have to be celibate in order to show forth the new creation."

A third point to note is that Paul, supposedly a dried-up, grumpy old celibate who had no use for sex in the Christian life, sees sex as *sacramental*. In verse 14, often overlooked, he claims that the unbelieving partner in a marriage is consecrated, "made holy," by the sexual relationship with a believing partner, and the children in such marriages are holy. Thus, Paul recognizes the *power* of sexuality in life and claims this power for the new creation—surprising, to say the least, from one who supposedly thinks celibacy is the superior way.

Indeed, a fourth point to note is that Paul insists that there is no one right way for Christians in this matter. As to the married, he counsels that they stay married, though if an unbelieving spouse wants it, divorce is all right. As to the celibates, he counsels them to keep the vow, if possible; but, if not, it is perfectly acceptable to get married. Paul clearly wants a church with *both* married and celibate people, but does not make rigid rules for either.

Finally, a very important note is struck with regard to the new creation in verses 29-31. Here Paul broadens the discussion to include much more than the male/female issue under consideration. What does it mean to deal with the world as if one had no dealings with the world? It does not mean: "Do *not* deal with the world. Create another sphere you can call a world and pretend you live there." That is what some Corinthian Christians wanted to do, with their claims about celibacy. Paul rejects that vision of the new creation. It also does not mean: "Deal with the world the way you did before your baptisms," for then the new creation means nothing. It may be that discerning the meaning of "as if...not" is the church's most important task in any given time and place. For Paul, at least, it meant something like: "The world is still very much with us and we *must* deal with it. But the power of God's new creation is also now with us and available to us. That means we are no longer *governed* by the powers of the world, compelled by the options given by the world." Normal life in the world is not obliterated, but it *is* transformed.

What is Paul saying about the meaning of "no longer male and female" in the new creation at this time? To summarize: there is now no "change of state" effected by baptism (a possible interpretation of the statement "no longer male and female"). What is true now is that there is in the church a *diversity* of expression of sexuality, within a community in which each one is accepted and honored for the gift that he or she brings and offers. What is new about such a creation? Not anything dramatic or even noticeable at first glance. But something profoundly different from the way life works in the old creation is suggested. Those who are different from others (from the "norm," whatever that is in a given community), who even hold different convictions about what the Christian life is, live in a community with one another in which each one is built up and supported by the others.

The interpretation I have offered is all of a piece with what we know of Paul's attitude on other issues. Again and again in his letters, his way of working in his churches is to stimulate and support diversity. Three examples will help to show this. One of these appears just after the chapter I have been discussing. In 1 Corinthians 8-10, the quarrel Paul had to address was between those who believed that one can eat anything with impunity and those who were afraid to eat meat that had been sacrificed to idols. Paul's counsel to the first group was: do not eat if it offends or frightens your Christian brother or sister. To the other group he said: eat what is sold in the market without asking questions. Each group was to move a step toward the other. There was no one right way for everyone; diversity was encouraged and each one was to support the other.

A second example of Paul's way of working comes later in the letter. In 1 Corinthians 12-14, the issue was a sort of hierarchy of "spiritual gifts." For some, clearly, speaking in tongues was the premier gift. Others were distinctly inferior. Paul argued that there is a multiplicity of gifts and it is the *Spirit* who gives them. *Each* is to be honored because each serves and builds up the new creation.

Paul's letter to the Romans provides a third example. Even though he was not thinking of the notoriously contentious Corinthian church, Paul took enormous pains in Romans to affirm that *both law-observant Jewish Christians and law-free Gentile* Christians were equally members of the new creation, in which they upheld and supported each other.

For Paul, a church where everyone is the same is not the new creation. In the context of a discussion of "no longer male and female," he said clearly that whether married or celibate, a person is acceptable. One did not have to change one's sexual status or practice in order to be a Christian. Indeed, one is to be married, celibate, widowed, whatever, as if one were not in that situation, not counting one's sexual status as a mark of any distinction, but, liberated from such status-givers, free to love and serve everyone.

∞

The possibilities for fruitful conversation between Paul and those who support the full inclusion of gay men and lesbians begin to emerge. But sober judgment is called for. Consideration of the new creation in Christ, as Paul named and worked on it, might encourage some to declare straightaway that in Christ there is "no longer straight or gay." But that impulse is, in its own way, as "literalistic" as any other. That is, one does not want to seize on *any* text, wrench it from its first literary context in Paul's letter, and claim it as a slogan on *either* side of the debate about homosexuality. With regard to Romans 1:26-27, discussed above, I argued that the issues about what is and is not "natural" must proceed without Paul's help, since for him what was natural in the original creation has, with human rebellion, been lost for good. That means that Romans 1:26-27, often cited in the current debate as a key text, does not offer a serious point of entry into the matter. In a similar way, the existence of the slogan "no longer Jew or Gentile" does not *in itself* warrant the expansion into "no longer straight or gay."

Before claiming "no longer straight or gay," then, it is well to note what we are and are not trying to do. We are not trying to get Paul to say something he did not say and would not have said. We must allow Paul to function in his own time and place; he must not be pressed into speaking directly to issues defined in ways so alien to him that we cannot imagine how he would respond. At the same time, however, we are not asking

Paul's permission to take a path not explicitly authorized by him. On the contrary, we are attempting a *conversation* with scripture, and more particularly with one of its authors, Paul, in which we will listen seriously and with openness to him, and in which we will learn from him, but in which we will also speak and act as Christians intent on following the Holy Spirit's lead in our own time.

To speak of a new creation offers both exciting prospects and difficult problems. On the one hand, new creation suggests that everything and anything is now possible. What has held authority in the past (indeed, the past itself as authoritative) is made relative. To quote Paul: "everything old has passed away, see, everything has become new!" In relation to the discussion going on in the church, this should suggest that the long history of the church in dealing with homosexuality is *not* automatically authoritative for Christians today. It is odd that this point even needs to be made, given the church's long and iniquitous history with slavery, but it must be said explicitly: that Christians in the past have rejected homosexuals and homosexuality is not a sufficient reason for them to continue to do so today. In Paul's notion of the new creation (as well as elsewhere in the Bible), there is clear warrant for taking a new look at old positions, indeed new positions too, on issues, when there is compelling reason to do so. The old is not valid because it is old. God can and does do new things.

Of course, it is not the case that everything in our prior experience is to be jettisoned. Paul did, after all, bring his own scripture and his tradition to bear on the arguments he presented and the decisions he made. The operative criteria by which he honored some traditions and rejected others are complex and impossible to demonstrate in this essay. Suffice it to say that "everything has become new" does *not* mean that all scripture, tradition, authority prior to Christ are illegitimate after Christ. Testing of what is old and also of what is new is clearly required. New creation offers a fruitful way forward, and openness. But it does not declare that any particular new approach is an expression of the new creation, just because it is new.

The chief difficulty raised by the notion of a new creation is that, more than nineteen hundred years after Paul's declaration of it, there seems to be little support for its existence, not to mention its power to change things in a tired old world. There is certainly no convincing empirical evidence of a new creation. Where does one see the old creation transformed? Christians sometimes answer with an individual person of note, with a momentary piece of wonderful news, such as peace where there has been war, or with examples of goodness that occur. But few of us believe, with Paul, that "the present form of this world is passing away." On the contrary, in most of what we do, we take our cues from a secular notion of what reality is and where power is to be found, which has little to do with Paul's claim that in Jesus Christ, God has brought a new creation.

What might it mean for our discussion of homosexuality to take Paul seriously about the new creation, keeping in mind the obvious difficulties involved after twenty centuries of Christian experience? First, a negative comment. It is no part of Paul's thinking to suppose that any and every polarity which defines life is negated by the new creation. "No longer male and female" yes, but not "no longer parent or child." So we do not want to claim in too facile a way that one can insist on "no longer straight or gay."

It is also not the case that we can spell out principles or guidelines by which we will be assured, in advance, which polarities are declared irrelevant. *Any* seriousness about a new creation *must* allow that no set of rules will guarantee our faithfulness to the new creation. There is a necessary sense in which things are up for grabs. Assurance in advance that our positions will be secure and correct is not at all what we are likely to get from the adventurous apostle to the Gentiles. Quite the opposite. Because Paul was sure that God is in control of creation, he felt entirely free to try out different things and see what happened. What might it mean if we were to follow in his footsteps?

A number of things come to mind. First, Paul wrote in 1 Corinthians 7:29-31 of what is sometimes called his "as if...not" ethic. He counseled his readers to live in the world as if they did not participate, were not obligated, by its claims. Surely this suggests that we ought at least to lower the temperature in the current debate. That is, Paul says in effect, "Do not give the issue more importance and more power than it has. Find ways to live *as if* there were *not* a debate on homosexuality." It might help us to hear each other more clearly and with greater charity if we discussed the place of homosexuals in the church as if everything were *not* at stake. Paul calls us to trust that God is in charge and therefore we can sit a little loose to the current battle.

Paul's insistence on diversity in the church for the period before the End may also offer a pointer. The clearest and easiest path for Paul, given the many issues about sexuality in the Corinthian church, was to lay down a rule or two. It is really astonishing that he did not do so. Instead, he not only insisted that both married and celibate people had honored places in the church; he also allowed for a change in either status, given the need. In the face of such flexibility, we would do well to note that we will not make church policy with regard to homosexuality by fiat, or by discussion and argument alone, but only by living through, together, the days ahead—listening, learning, and being willing to change, to be flexible. Such a process requires that we embrace diversity, and that we develop a high tolerance for the inevitable difficulties diversity brings to community life. There is no other way by which the church will come to its mind on this matter. Living with diversity, genuinely honoring those with whom we disagree, might generate some creative possibilities for moving forward, as a whole church, that no one has thought of yet. To tolerate, even celebrate, diversity is not so very difficult for those who truly trust that God is the one who directs the process. We might even remind each other that, through this debate, God is bringing yet another part of the new creation into being.

As we proceed, there are two things about Paul's approach to issues of sexuality in particular that we would do well to keep in mind. The first is his recognition of the power of sex and the fact that he claimed it as a way of *holiness* in the new creation. In a society where sex is so much overvalued and so much feared—depending on your perceived need for freedom to experiment and to indulge, or your perceived need to control the young—we can be grateful not only for Paul's earthy realism, but also for his earthy vision of the new creation. Of course sex is powerful, and it has always been and will always be controlled in communities. Christians now, as in Paul's time, will have a part in working out those controls. But the exciting and intriguing notion Paul offers us is that sex functions powerfully to create *holiness* in the new creation. In relation to the issue of homosexuality, we might expect new light to be shed in the church by asking lesbian and gay Christians how their sexuality nurtures their own holiness and that of the Christian communities in which they participate.

The second point about Paul's approach to sexuality that we would do well to remember is his insistence to the very spiritual Corinthians that they were not now beyond sexuality. Whatever the new creation is, it does not mean that the ordinary terms of life for all other people have changed for Christians. The test for a call to celibacy was therefore obvious. If one's passion was strong, one was not called to celibacy. In the discussion about homosexuality, then, we may legitimately suggest that, given the normal community controls on decency and responsibility in sexual expression, if one's sexual passion is for someone of one's own sex, that may be an acceptable, nay, a good way to express one's sexuality in the new creation. In other words, in Christ there is no longer straight or gay.

A study of Paul's notion of God's new creation has reminded us of some biblical claims we tend to lose in the daily round of coping with life. One is that God is finally in control of the world and all of us. There is power there which is in the end more powerful than anything else. Another is that in Jesus Christ, God has done something new about the human plight. Power for a new creation is now present in the world, according to Paul, as it was not before. Among other things, this means that people are no longer fated, destined to be victims of old polarities that have separated, dominated, and alienated them. The whole "us and them" mentality is open to transformation in Christ. In our time, this means that we are called to explore seriously the call to proclaim with the earliest baptized Christians, "In Christ there is no longer Jew or Gentile, slave or free, male and

∽ *Charles Hefling*

By Their Fruits

A Traditionalist Argument

The glory of God," said the Anglican poet Charles Williams, "is in facts. The almost incredible nature of things is that there is no fact which is not in his glory." Now homosexuality is a fact. Presumably it always has been. But if there is any fact for which Christianity has never found a place in the "pattern of the glory," as Williams called the ordered majesty of the universe, that fact is the existence of gay people. Somehow it does not belong. At best, it has been regarded as unseemly; at worst, as incongruous with creation and Creator alike—so much so that, in the memorable words of a placard protesting the ordination of a gay Episcopalian, THERE IS NO GOD IF HOMOSEXUALS ARE ALLOWED INTO HEAVEN.

By dismissing as unthinkable the very idea that God might welcome into everlasting joy lesbians and gay men who neither abjure nor make a secret of their sexuality, that protester was taking a stand in keeping with Christian tradition. There is no reason here to rehearse the litany of condemnations which make up that tradition, but there is every reason to keep in mind how strong and consistent a tradition it has been. No doubt many individual Christians have taken a different view. No doubt what official teaching outlaws has often been tolerated in practice. Yet even if all the gay-positive evidence unearthed by John Boswell and other historians were less debatable than it is, it would show only that there have been eddies, now and then, in a stream that has been flowing in much the same channel for nineteen hundred years. As to how *gravely* wrong homosexuality is, there have been different opinions; as to whether it *is* wrong, only one.

Nothing less than the consensus of Christendom, then, is being challenged by ordinations such as the one just mentioned, as it is by the liturgical blessing of same-sex partnerships. The problem is not simply that a decent Anglican reticence about the fact of homosexuality is no longer possible; nor are these innovations simply pragmatic problems that adjusting the ecclesiastical mechanism will solve. The issues at stake are issues of moral theology too big to admit of *ad hoc* solutions such as Anglicans have so often made do with, and the tradition that is being defied is a tradition of theological reasoning too serious to dismiss without a hearing. What the church should be asking is whether there are any reasons, equally serious theological reasons, for change. A moral judgment as long-standing and as nearly uncontested as the traditional position on homosexuality has been makes a claim on Christian conscience that is not to be set aside "unadvisedly or lightly, but reverently, discreetly, advisedly, soberly, and in the fear of God." Intelligence then, not expediency, should be the ground on which the church takes, if it does, a stand different from the one it has traditionally taken.

This is not to say that theology is the one thing necessary. It is not. The question about homosexuality is a question about persons, not abstractions, and deciding that question concretely requires not just the intellectual knowledge generated by theologians but the personal knowledge that comes from acquaintance and friendship with lesbian and gay individuals, from hearing their stories, from being part of their lives. Without the cooperation of this kind of direct, personal knowing, theology has not much power of its own to change anyone's mind, still less the mind of the church. But though there is only so much that theological argument can do, that much does need to be attempted. Another Anglican poet, T. S. Eliot, defined theology as finding good reasons for what is already believed intuitively. It may be that Christian intuition in regard to gay people is changing, but by acting on that ground alone the church risks falling into what Eliot called the greatest treason: to do the right thing for the wrong reason.

$$\infty$$

To take a stand different from the one it has traditionally taken would in one sense be a traditional thing for the church to do. It has, with good reason, changed its mind more than once on an important issue, and would be following precedent by changing its mind on a similar issue for similar reasons—the greater the similarity, the stronger the precedent.

Anglicans, of course, have not far to look for a conspicuous example of departure from unbroken catholic tradition. Their communion has determined that women can minister as bishops, priests, and deacons, and this decision is sometimes cited as a precedent that bears on one aspect of the current discussion of homosexuality. To exclude people from holy orders because they are gay—so the argument runs—is as unjust as excluding people because they are female. But the analogy is not very strong, and so neither is the argument. Even supposing that ordination is a matter of justice, the two disqualifications, though each has something to do with sex, are not the same at all. On the one hand, to judge from the Episcopal Church's current policy, it is not that homosexuals *cannot* be ordained; they can, although only those who maintain celibacy *should* be ordained, since it is only as celibates that they can provide the "wholesome example to all people" that befits the Christian clergy. On the other hand, the traditional view was not that ordaining women would be harmful, but that it was impossible in the first place. The impediment lay not in anything a woman did but in the fact of her being a woman. It had nothing to do with wholesomeness and nothing could remove it.[1]

In a general way, then, the ministry of ordained women does go to show that ancient traditions on matters of moment can change, but a closer analogy to the change that is now under discussion, and hence a stronger precedent for making it, would be the case of a *moral* prohibition, consistently maintained for theological reasons but at length rescinded. That is essentially what is in dispute in regard to gay Christians, laity as well as clergy: whether the church can now judge that something its own tradition has always forbidden is not, or not necessarily, wrong. Has a comparable change in Christian moral teaching ever occurred?

It has. Anyone who opens a savings account is, by that commonplace act, judged, as the church would have judged it from earliest times and for many centuries, guilty of wrongdoing—not of some peccadillo, either, but of mortal sin. Its name is usury. Today, if the word is used at all, it means something like "charging too much interest," but that is not what all Christendom condemned under the name of usury down to modern times. Usury meant taking *any* profit on a loan of money, any interest beyond the principal. So defined, usury was denounced by saintly theologians such as Ambrose, Augustine, and Jerome, denounced by bishops and solemn church councils, denounced *ubique, semper, et ab omnibus.* Nor was the doctrine that usury is always wrong "some obscure, hole-in-the-corner affectation, but stood astride the European credit markets" and governed both the church's own practice and its influence on civil law.[2] If anything, it was a stronger and more consistent teaching than the one about homosexuality.

As *Continuing the Dialogue,* the study document presented to the Episcopal Church by its House of Bishops, mentions in passing, Christians no longer regard interest on investments as sinful in and of itself, biblical prohibitions notwithstanding. A very significant shift has evidently taken place, and examining it will, I think, shed light on the possibility of revising the traditional judgment on homosexuality, which in many respects is remarkably similar.

To begin with what scripture has to say about taking interest, probably the most familiar passage is in the psalm that asks what sort of person would be worthy to "ascend the hill of the Lord" and answers by describing someone who has never "given money upon usury."[3] That verse reinforced explicit prohibitions in the Law, as did Jesus' exhortation to "lend freely with no hope of gain."[4] All this is plain enough. Yet it raises two questions. In the first place, the Law includes a great many prohibitions, some of which the church has never held to be binding. So, if the prohibition of usury is one that does apply to Christians, *why* does it? Where does the difference lie? In the second place, given that it applies, exactly what does it apply to? Usury is profit on a loan, but not all profit is usury and some profit-making loans are blameless: renting a farm, for example. Again, what makes the difference? Both these questions come down to the same thing: What does the wrongness of usury consist in? What makes it wrong?

The answer that was taught and accepted throughout the Christian world for centuries ran as follows. The wrongness of usury lies in the character of what is loaned. If I lend you my bicycle and you ride it to work, I may fairly ask you not only to return it to me but also to pay me something in exchange for the use you got out of it. Similarly, if I lend you a piece of my land and you use it to grow vegetables for your table, I may fairly charge you rent. Why? Because in each case I have loaned something that produces something else—rides, food—so that there is nothing wrong in my getting back more than I loaned, in making a profit, provided it is not exorbitant.

Not so with money. If I lend you a sum of money and you use it by spending it, nothing new is produced. The money is gone. That is the nature of money: it is a medium of exchange, nothing more. It does not grow or breed. To use it is to use it up completely. Were I to demand from you a greater sum of money than you borrowed, I would be treating the money I had loaned as though it were something it is not, as though it could do something more than purchase other things, as though it were fruitful or productive in itself. Because it is not, taking interest amounts to robbery.

On this argument, to profit from a loan of money is wrong because it is an enacted lie. Taking interest contradicts the facts of what money is, what it does, what it is for. The traditional case against usury depends on how money is understood, and because it does, the acceptance of a different, more adequate way of thinking about the nature of money could—and eventually did—overturn the whole argument. The traditional reasoning makes sense only if money is best thought of as "barren" or "sterile" in the sense that putting it to use consumes it entirely. But no economist today understands money in this simplistic way. Already at the time of the Reformation Calvin was pointing out that of course money locked in a box is sterile—any child can see that—but who borrows money to keep it in storage? Put it to work, and it can be as fruitful as many kinds of merchandise.[5] Where does that leave the biblical commands and exhortations? They are to be construed, says Calvin, in light of the Golden Rule. Generosity and regard for the poor are still Christian virtues; cupidity and avarice are still vices; interest is still sinful if it hurts one's neighbor. But moderate interest is not in any and all circumstances wrong, and accordingly the word "usury" is to be taken, as it is today, as referring not to interest as such but to interest that is excessive or injurious.

Such, in brief, was the traditional argument and its gradual, but in the end complete, reversal. For purposes of the discussion that follows, there are four points to note. First, the traditional position on usury takes the Bible seriously, but it goes on to seek an intelligent explanation of biblical prohibitions. The presumption is that reason and revelation complement and reinforce one another. More specifically, in the second place, the old argument about usury is based on matters of fact—on what money actually is and does. Change in the way these facts were understood, more than anything else, is what brought about a revision in the church's teaching. This leads to a third point. The new understanding of money as productive or fruitful on its own, though everyone now takes it for granted, is very counterintuitive. Coins and bullion do not *look* fruitful. That "money breeds money" is a fact that intelligence can grasp, but grasping it means going beyond imagination's simple picture of money as inert metal. Finally, in the fourth place, abandoning the traditional prohibition of usury did not and does not mean that taking interest is morally good. It means only that particular cases, investment policies for instance, have to be judged in a wider context that takes their circumstances and effects into account. Calvin's attitude is instructive: although he denied that it was always wrong to take interest on a loan of money, he also held that the situations in which it could be taken without doing harm were very rare.

It will probably be clear already that the traditional argument for prohibiting the practice of usury bears a strong likeness to the traditional argument for prohibiting the practice of homosexuality. Here too there are biblical condemnations; not many, but all of them pointing in the same direction. If the story of Sodom is ambiguous, the epistle to the Romans is not, still less Leviticus. But here again it has to be asked exactly what scripture does prohibit and what the wrongness consists in. As with usury, moral theologians have tried to interpret scripture in the light of the best available understanding of the relevant facts, and as with usury they have found that the prohibition of homosexual conduct makes sense. In the case of usury, what had to be understood was the natural use of money, the way of using it that is in keeping with its nature, and usury was ruled out for being an unnatural use. Homosexuality has been condemned, both within and beyond the church, for the same reason: the behavior it involves could not be understood as natural. "Barren coitus" is the phrase St. John Chrysostom hurls against homosexuality, and its echo of the "barren metal" account of money is significant. Dante draws the parallel explicitly, associating usurers with homosexuals in the eleventh canto of the *Inferno*.[6]

Money, however, is no longer understood in such a way that lending it at interest contradicts its nature. Developments in trade and commerce, and corresponding developments in economics, have made it necessary to revise the theological account of how money may and may not be used. Can the parallel be taken further? Are there sound reasons for revising the traditional account of what the wrongness of homosexuality consists in? Is the idea that physical intimacy between men or between women can only be unnatural an idea that the best available understanding of the relevant facts will no longer support?

That, I am convinced, is the question the church needs to ask. The other, more obvious and more pressing issues all lead sooner or later to the question of what makes homosexuality wrong. To declare without further explanation that it is wrong because the Bible says so is not to answer but to dismiss the question, and the catholic tradition of Christian theology has preferred to address it, explaining the wrongness in question by appealing to matters of fact. On that explanation the church's policy and practice have always rested, directly or indirectly, and there they rest still.[7] Is it still a valid explanation?

It would make things easier—much easier—if the whole quagmire of controversy and confusion about what is and is not "natural" could be avoided. But I see no way to avoid it. Long before the word "homosexual" was invented, theology and common parlance alike spoke of "unnatural vice" or "the sin against nature," and did so with New Testament precedent. The fact that we now speak differently does not mean the line of thought represented by these antique phrases has disappeared. It has not. As the proverb says, you may heave nature out with a pitchfork, but it will just keep returning. In the contemporary debate about homosexuality it returns again and again, sometimes under other names. Why? Because the traditional way of thinking asked the right questions. Untraditional answers may now be called for. I think they are. But they will be answers to questions that are permanently valid.

∞

What it means to assert or deny that homosexuality (or anything else) is natural depends on what "nature" means. Unfortunately, there is hardly a slipperier word in English, and the same is true of the corresponding Greek and Latin terms. For present purposes it will be enough to sort out three basic meanings, which these sentences illustrate:

(1) They are moving out of the city in order to be closer to nature.

(2) Her beauty was the work of nature, not art.

(3) Glass is brittle and transparent by nature.

In the first sentence, nature is the world minus human civilization—earth and sky, plants and animals. In the second, nature is what a person is born with as contrasted with anything learned or acquired or imposed. In the third, nature is the essential properties and characteristics that make something what it is. The third sense is the one I have used already, in discussing the nature of money. If I point out that the nature of language is such that these three meanings overlap, I am again using "nature" in sense three.

The only way in which nature in the first sense, nature-as-the-environment, could be relevant to the present topic would be in an argument that because homosexual behavior does (or does not) occur in nature, say among other mammals, it is (or is not) appropriate for humans. Either way it is a very unconvincing argument. Christian theologians have used it, but it is seldom heard today and almost never in theological contexts.[8] The other two senses of "nature" do figure in contemporary debate, in ways that unfortunately tend to blur their difference. Where moral theology is concerned, it is finally the third sense that matters, but to show why it matters I will have to start with nature in sense two.

Sense two, nature-as-heredity, comes into nearly every discussion of what causes homosexuality. It is an important question in many respects. There is reason to think, for one thing, that people are more likely to be tolerant of lesbians and gay men the more they are convinced—say, by genetic research—that homosexuality is innate and in that sense natural. If it is not of their own doing that some people are born gay, refusing to accept them as the persons they are can only be bigotry. But while anything that promotes toleration is all to the good, the rule-of-thumb distinction between nature and nurture, heredity and social conditioning, does not really address the questions that Christian moral theology has to ask.

Suppose, for the sake of argument, that a single, definitive "gay gene" is there waiting to be discovered. Its discovery could have significant consequences. It would establish that homosexuality is no more a matter of choice or training than eye-color. It would confirm the testimony of lesbian and gay people who insist that their affections have always drawn them toward others of their own sex. It would put to rest any lingering doubts about the reality of "constitutional" homosexuality. It would explain why psychological "cures" seem to be few and ineffectual. It would mean, in short, that being gay is natural in the same sense—sense two—as other innate conditions, being left-handed for instance.[9] All this might change cultural perceptions of gay people and influence the making and administration of civil law. Would it affect Christian moral theology's traditional judgment? Not necessarily.

It is quite true that if there is such a thing as constitutional homosexuality, gay people are no more responsible for their sexual orientation than straight people are for theirs. And from this it does follow that no moral blame can fall on a person whose condition happens to be homosexual, any more than on one whose condition happens to be heterosexual. But that is all that follows. It does not follow automatically from the blamelessness of the homosexual *condition* that homosexual *conduct* is just as blameless as heterosexual conduct, and conduct has always been the object of Christianity's traditional judgment on homosexuality. Upholding that judgment is not incompatible with acknowledging that homosexuality is constitutional. It is quite possible to hold that their sexual orientation puts gay people at a moral disadvantage for which they are not personally responsible; to hold, in other words, that the fault is not theirs, but the fault is in them. As to themselves, they are to be accorded every dignity as persons, indeed as gay persons; as to their sexual conduct, it is as wrong as it always was.

Such a compromise with tradition has its appeal. It seems to conform with St. Augustine's advice about loving sinners while hating their sins. It is evidently the official position of the Episcopal Church, in so far as there is one.[10] Yet there is something odd about it. Andrew Sullivan devotes a long stretch of his recent book *Virtually Normal* to arguing that it is not so much a compromise as a paradox. He finds it self-contradictory to think that there could be, on the one hand, a natural, blameless condition which, on the other hand, leads only to actions that are gravely wrong.[11] But this idea is paradoxical, properly speaking, only if there is reason to assume that nature (sense two) always gives rise to actions that are morally good or at least neutral—and that assumption is very doubtful. More and more of the way human beings behave has been found to be more and more deeply influenced by genetic inheritance, less and less by deliberate choice. While it is a vast oversimplification to think in terms of "selfish genes" or "promiscuous genes," there seems to be no question but that behavior of every kind, good, bad, and indifferent, has a biological component for which no individual can be held accountable. Yet the fact (if it is a fact) that human beings are selfish by nature, that they have an inherited predisposition to act selfishly, does not make selfishness good. It explains why people find it difficult not to act selfishly, but the obligation to overcome the difficulty—in older language, to resist the temptation—is not removed by discovering that selfishness is a natural condition. And much the same thing could be said, without self-contradiction, about people who are homosexual by nature.

Much the same thing *is* said in the official statement on matters of human sexuality recently issued by the bishops of the Church of England. Their carefully reasoned document notes that evidence for a genetic origin of the "homophile orientation" has been welcomed by some Christians, on the supposition that it "would confirm homosexuality as an alternative condition within creation of equal validity with the heterosexual." The welcome is ill-advised, however, and the supposition a mistake. The bishops do acknowledge that homosexuality is a condition, distinguishable as such from homosexual behavior. What they deny is that genetics—scientific knowledge of nature (sense two)—has any decisive bearing on whether such a condition is good or bad. Neither this explanation of what makes some people gay, nor any other explanation that science might arrive at, can settle the *moral* question about homosexuality.[12] What matters, from that standpoint, is not the beginnings of homosexuality but its ends, not where it originated but where it is going, not what causes some persons to be so oriented but what they are oriented toward. *end*

The English bishops have thus taken a stand on the role of reasoning in moral theology which, as they well know, rules out the seemingly plausible argument that if homosexuality has its origin in nature (sense two) it must not be wrong. In their view, sexual orientation, whatever its cause, cannot be considered morally good or bad in isolation from the sexual conduct that it is an orientation *toward*. So far, surely, they are right. If the very idea of sexual "orientation" is the idea of being headed or drawn in one direction rather than others, then however that direction may be *determined*, it can hardly be *defined* except by erotic feeling and the behavior that manifests it. An orientation to nothing in particular is not an orientation. To speak of someone as having a homosexual or a heterosexual orientation makes sense just in so far as the psychic, emotional, and physical events that are actually occurring in his or her life have a consistent focus in other persons of the same or the opposite sex, as the case may be.

Accordingly, it is on the behaviors which manifest sexual orientation that the bishops base their judgment. Among these manifestations, which are many and various, "genital acts" are definitive. When such acts occur between persons of the same sex, the bishops judge them wrong, and their judgment would not be mitigated by the fact that the persons were both constitutionally homosexual. On the contrary, at the end of their statement the "homophile condition and its expression in sexual activity" are weighed together, as a continuous whole, and found wanting. The way of abstinence is therefore the only one that can be commended unreservedly to gay men and lesbians.[13] The bishops acknowledge that this is a hard saying; they affirm God's equal love for the homophile and the heterophile; but neither in the distinction between orientation and act nor in the corresponding argument from nature-as-heredity do they see any reason for altering the traditional position.

Because they rule out nature (sense two) as the standard for assessing the moral worth of homosexual conduct, it is all the more interesting to find that the English bishops not only affirm the traditional position but affirm it for the traditional reasons. They hold, as Christian tradition has always done, that homosexual conduct goes against nature. Is there a contradiction? No, because the nature that gay sex is said to violate is nature in the third sense, not the second; nature-as-essential-character, not nature-as-heredity. Homosexual conduct may or may not be in accord with a given individual's genetic makeup (nature, sense two); in any event it is not in accord with the proper, essential character of sexual intercourse (nature, sense three).[14]

The episcopate of the Church of England thus stands squarely and deliberately within the tradition of moral theology that has most deeply influenced secular custom and law as well as Christian teaching and practice. As their statement notes, if there is any individual who deserves the credit, or the blame, for setting this tradition on its course, it is St. Paul, who so notoriously says at the beginning of Romans that homosexual behavior, as we would now call it, is contrary to nature. What the bishops go on to present is basically an extended argument to the effect that St. Paul was correct. Their statement does not assume that Romans 1 is the last word on what makes homosexuality wrong; nor on the other hand does it assume that St. Paul and the other biblical writers were so entirely bound to their own times and places as to make their thinking irrelevant to the situation today. Rather, the bishops adopt the same general approach that the tradition they are following has taken: they present what they take to be the nature of human sexuality, and ask whether "the phenomenon of homosexual love" fits with it. In the end, their answer is that it does not. But as I have already said, it is an answer to the right question. In the rest of this essay I propose to ask it again. In what way, if any, does homosexual conduct go against the nature of things, contradicting the best available understanding of the relevant facts—facts in which consists the glory of God?

∞

I have heard the whole problem of homosexuality dismissed by saying that "the plumbing is all wrong." There is an obvious way in which that quip is true, yet it meets the issue no more adequately than it would now meet the issue of usury to announce the equally obvious truth that money is metal and metal is barren. The anatomy of organs and the physiology of sexual response are relevant to moral theology only because "the plumbing" plays a part in the lives not just of mammals but of persons. Understanding the nature (sense three) of sex means understanding it not simply as a biological mechanism but as a human activity. The question is not just what it looks like and how it works, but what it does and what it is for. In short, what good is sex?

There is no single answer; that seems to be agreed on all sides. Most of the quandaries in sexual ethics, including those surrounding homosexuality, arise precisely because sex is good in more ways than one. In the first place, obviously, it is pleasant. But pleasure alone is no criterion of moral worth if there are other, more important goods at stake—as, in this case, there certainly are. What then does sex do, above and beyond providing pleasure? One thing it often does (not always) is begin the process that leads to the birth of a child. St. Clement of Alexandria, writing in the third century, declared flatly that "to have sex for any other purpose than to have children is to violate nature,"[15] and since then many others have insisted that the whole nature of sex, its sole purpose and function, is defined by procreation, just as the function of money was once defined by exchange.

Now there is no denying that sex perpetuates the human race. But there is no denying, either, that sex for humans is not simply what fission is for amoebas. Nor has the church denied it. St. Clement's is an extreme position; by and large Christian teaching has recognized that the nature of sexual intercourse includes more than his rule allows. Sex brings into being a kind of human good that is neither mere self-gratification nor offspring, a good that concerns the couple who are involved, not as individual organisms that can experience pleasure, and not as members of a biological species that can propagate itself, but as persons, human in the fullest sense as members of an interpersonal community.

One key, perhaps the most helpful, to understanding the nature of sex in this personalist or intersubjective aspect is the observation that sexuality is a language. Far from being just plumbing, bodily organs and physical responses are like alphabet letters or phonemes in having the capacity to be carriers of meaning. It is a capacity that can be actualized in an enormous variety of behaviors, and like the words of a verbal language these behaviors have a grammar, a set of cultural conventions that tell how expressive elements are best put together in meaningful ways. Learning the language of sex, like learning other languages, is a matter of practice; it takes time and patience and usually involves mistakes. Once they have been learned, the same vocabulary and syntax can convey a range of very different meanings. Having sex, like having a conversation, can be "an adventure in discovery, an act of vengeance, a cold manipulation, an experiment in pleasure, a flirtation, an act of cowardice, an expression of sympathy, an act of theater, a passing fancy, an act of trust, a thoughtless relief, a defiance, a bored obligation, a willful expression of difference, a cozy evening at home, a fiery crash in the night, a rescue, and a way of belonging."[16]

Sex, in a word, is meaningful. It communicates. *What* it communicates depends in some measure on the intention of the persons involved, but regardless of what they intend it is inevitably themselves that they convey and express, each to the other and at the same time to herself or himself. Sexual intercourse is being exposed, made naked to another person, spiritually as well as physically. That person becomes more intensely and intimately present, more entirely here and now, than he or she is or can be otherwise, and this presence is reciprocal. Hence the theme of so much love poetry—that lovers find and become in one another the persons they are and were always meant to be.

Because sex communicates not only personal meaning but also the persons who mean it, sexual language can be a language of friendship—the only name that English has for *philia*, a kind of love that was honored by the ancients as the sum and summit of human virtue. Friends, according to one of their proverbs, have all things in common; the better the things friends share, the more noble their friendship. Friends in the fullest sense may have common possessions, but more important they have common experiences, projects, memories, hopes, ideas, beliefs, habits, aspirations, and qualities of character. They have a common past, present, and future. They have *themselves* in common, so as to be "one soul in two bodies," as St. Augustine says of himself and a friend in a famous passage of his *Confessions*. The common good that makes friends a community includes themselves, who they are and are becoming.

Now if a friend is "another self," "the half of one's soul," and if it is in sexual intercourse that another self is most intensely present, most fully known in every sense of the word, then sex can be not only an expression but an effectual sign of friendship—a sacrament, which actualizes the common good it means. This is not to say that all friendship is sexual, even potentially, or that all sex is friendly. It is, however, to say that friendship is the answer to the question of what sex, as a human language, is good for. Making friends and making love, *philia* and *eros*, can coincide as a single common good—one soul and, in the biblical phrase, one flesh. It is a good that belongs intrinsically to the nature of sex. It is a good that cannot be reduced to pleasure. Is it also, then, a good that can be brought into being whether the two persons whose good it would be are persons of different genders or not? Can speaking the language that is homosexuality be both the cause and the effect of friendship, the movement of a community of two toward a common good that is present in their being moved by it?

Timothy Murphy, whom I quoted a moment ago, argues that in so far as sex is communication in embodied language, homosexual and heterosexual behavior have equal standing. They are different, certainly, but they differ as French does from German. Each makes it possible to mean some things that have no exact equivalent in the other, but no moral comparison is involved and none is possible. Just as French and German can both be misused, so heterosexual and homosexual behavior can both involve wrongdoing—manipulation and exploitation, brutality and rape. Yet these are no more intrinsic to the nature of one sexuality or the other than blasphemy, libel, and slander are intrinsic to any verbal language. Everything depends on what is said. It is true that homosexual intercourse cannot express and effect the good of fecundity, as the intercourse of man and woman can. The question, then—in my judgment, the question on which nearly the whole moral issue of homosexuality turns—is whether the absence of fecundity, the impossibility that intercourse will increase the number of human beings, is enough to invalidate everything else that homosexual intercourse might effect.

John Finnis, philosopher and professor of law at Oxford, would have it so. His views on the nature of sex agree with the position outlined here, to the extent that he holds sexual intercourse to be both the actualizing and the experiencing of a community, united toward a common good. But that good is double. It consists in "children and friendship, which are the parts of its wholeness as an intelligible common good." Absent the possibility of one of these parts, namely children, the whole collapses entirely, so that only self-gratification is left. Consequently, between homosexual intercourse and masturbation there is "no important distinction in essential worthlessness." What became of friendship? Finnis insists that unless friends are man and woman, the common good of their friendship cannot possibly be actualized and experienced sexually. Two friends, both men or both women, who try to express and further their friendship in sexual language are doomed to failure. They "cannot express more than is expressed if...a man pleasures himself."[17] Finnis thus acknowledges the interpersonal good of sex, but makes it wholly dependent on fecundity. He acknowledges sex as language, but denies that it can mean anything worthwhile unless it also means offspring. He acknowledges the friendship of sexual partners, but only when "real" marriage is at least possible. In effect, his position is St. Clement's, updated. For, as Martha Nussbaum observes in a response to Finnis's argument, what he is saying, without using the traditional language, is that gay sex is contrary to nature because it produces no children. As to the argument he makes for this position, Nussbaum points out that it rests on an unsupported assertion: the only sort of community a sexual relationship can create is a procreative community.[18]

One way to refute such an assertion is to produce examples to the contrary. Whether sexual relationships create communities that instantiate and intend common goods other than procreation is a question of fact, and questions of fact are answered empirically, by evidence and not by *a priori* reasoning. Nussbaum herself, a classical scholar, finds evidence that supports an affirmative answer in examples from ancient Greece. But then, it would be more surprising than not to find much evidence of the same kind in the history of the Christian West. The whole point of the traditional prohibition, on the part of church and state alike, has been to prevent homosexual relationships from occurring at all. It is only recently that the sexual communities formed by lesbians and gay men despite the prohibition have begun to be tolerated, though hardly supported or encouraged. But it is in these partnerships if anywhere that the evidence can be found which either confirms or, as I think, refutes the assertion that procreation is the only common good of which sex can be the sacrament. That is perhaps the most important reason for the church to listen to what gay Christians themselves have to say about their sexual relationships. "By their fruits you shall know them."

Meanwhile, the same point can be reached by another route. I have said that the question on which Nussbaum and Finnis are at odds—whether the nature of sexual intercourse is such that excluding procreation vitiates it—is the crucial question in the moral debate about homosexuality. But homosexuality is obviously not the only issue on which it bears. The same question has been discussed, in a different context, throughout the present century, and in 1958 it was the subject of as formal and official a pronouncement as the Anglican communion is capable of making: a resolution of the ninth Lambeth Conference, which states in no uncertain terms that procreation is neither the only purpose of sex nor the only common good it effectually signifies:

> Sexual intercourse is not by any means the only language of earthly love, but it is, in its full and right use, the most revealing....it is a giving and receiving in the unity of two free spirits which is in itself good....Therefore it is utterly wrong to say that...such intercourse ought not to be engaged in except with the willing intention of children.[19]

Of course the bishops who approved this statement had only heterosexual intercourse in mind. Their concern was family planning and in particular the permissibility of contraception. Nevertheless what they say is relevant to the topic at hand, both because it marks a significant break with traditional moral theology, and because of the reasons for which the break was made. Two previous Lambeth Conferences had pronounced judgment against "unnatural means for the avoidance of conception," maintaining the traditional position that such means go against nature by thwarting "the continuation of the race."[20] When they reversed these judgments in 1958, were the Lambeth fathers simply "shedding their traditional principles to suit the demands of modern paganism," as one irate Jesuit complained at the time?[21] The documents of the Conference suggest otherwise. To be sure, modern developments in biological science and medical technology had changed the context in which the morality of contraception had to be evaluated. But the new evaluation was arrived at on the basis of principles that are quite traditional. For its content and direction, the final Conference statement quoted above has clearly drawn on the longest and most closely reasoned of three position papers that had been prepared in advance, and the line of reasoning set out in this anonymous paper is thus worth examining briefly.

The paper is framed entirely in terms of traditional moral theology. It takes as its central question, "What is the end of coitus?" The usual answer, that procreation is the principal end, is rather simple and rather abstract; it "hardly does justice to the complexities of the act or the realities of experience." What the paper proposes as a more adequate answer has three components. First, sex has a personal as well as a biological dimension. Second, these two purposes, "relational" and "generative," are distinct, so that neither is simply an extension of the other. Third, attempting to rank the two in supposed order of importance or priority is misguided. The assumption that the generative end trumps the relational one is just that—an assumption, fair enough so long as the specifically human mystery of sex was not clearly recognized, but no longer tenable. On the negative side, theologically speaking, it is not true to the nature of sex to think of it as a mechanism for reproduction "to which, in consequence of the Fall, a certain remedial function is now annexed in marriage." For, on the positive side, "God himself has radically differentiated human coitus from that of the animals by constituting it to be the means by which the one-flesh *henosis* [union] is established and consolidated." Sex is by its very nature "an act of unique quality and significance involving to a greater degree than any other the whole person as a psychosomatic unity" and as such it is "expressive of an attitude to life and to God."[22] All this leads to the conclusions that would later receive episcopal endorsement at Lambeth. "Fulfilment of the relational end of coitus is possible independently of the other end," and this possibility is actualized, not in any single act, but in the whole pattern of interpersonal relationship of which sexual intercourse is a component.[23]

Such was the Lambeth Conference's warrant for departing from tradition. In one sense it was no departure. The 1958 statement appeals, in traditional fashion, to facts—to the nature of sex, its essential character, its intrinsic purposes. The only novelty is the tacit claim that the relevant facts were better understood. It had become possible to give a more differentiated answer to the traditional question, "What good is sex?" than tradition had given. About this answer, from which the Conference's decision follows, there are three observations to be made.

The first is that it is no sudden novelty but the result of a gradual development in Anglican moral theology that has been studied in detail.[24] The second observation is that it is not an idiosyncratically Anglican answer. Much the same shift in understanding, away from an exclusive focus on physical reproduction toward recognition of a further, distinct, specifically human and interpersonal purpose of sex, can be found as well in Protestant and Roman Catholic authors writing at the same time.[25] A third observation leads back to the main topic. The argument that influenced the Lambeth Conference's reconsideration of "coitus modified by contraception" has further implications. The same line of reasoning applies equally well to "other sexual actions for which a certain relational value may be claimed," as was recognized at the time.[26] It is most unlikely that Anglican prelates in 1958 thought of their resolution on family planning as pulling the linchpin out of the oldest and strongest argument against the practice of homosexuality. Yet it does precisely that.

The oldest and strongest argument is that the practice of homosexuality is contrary to nature. I have tried to show that the one relevant sense of "nature" is the third sense I distinguished earlier, and that consequently the traditional prohibition means that sexually active lesbians and gay men violate the essential character of human sexuality by using their bodies for purposes that are not intrinsic to sexual intercourse. Now if procreation is the only end of sex, above and beyond self-gratification, the prohibition stands. But if, in the light of the best available understanding of the relevant facts, there is a further, personalist or relational end, not inextricably linked with the possibility of procreation, then it is hard to see how homosexual intercourse is any more contrary to the nature of sexuality than the intercourse of heterosexual couples for whom conception is impossible by reason of age, contraceptives, impotence, injury, or sterility.

Otherwise stated, the point is that fruitfulness can be real without being visibly obvious. What appears barren to imagination can turn out, in the light of intelligence, to be generating real human good. Christian moral theology recognized the difference between picturable and intelligible fruitfulness long ago where economic activity is concerned, and has begun in this century to recognize it with respect to sexual activity. Sex can be productive without being reproductive. It can be fruitful, and often is, in that it multiplies human life. But it can also be fruitful, and often is, in that it magnifies human life; and if this fact is the same fact irrespective of sexual orientation, then as I have tried to argue, homosexual intercourse is not, in and of itself, the unnatural vice that tradition condemns.

That does not put an end to the matter. Far from it. This essay has been concerned with a single question: What makes same-sex physical intimacy, as such, wrong? The answer I have proposed—that nothing does—is important, not because it automatically answers all the other, more concrete and specific questions that the fact of homosexuality raises, but because it makes asking them a realistic possibility. As long as the old "unnatural" verdict is in force, these questions need not even be taken seriously. They can be ruled out in advance. But if that verdict is mistaken, if sexual intercourse between men or between women is not invariably wrong, be the circumstances as they may, then it makes sense to ask, In what circumstances is it right? Sexual intercourse between a man and a woman is not unnatural either, yet the church has had an awful lot to say about how heterosexual Christians ought to speak the language of their sexuality. Most of what it has said has taken the negative form of prohibitions and restrictions that directly or indirectly forbid heterosexual activity apart from matrimony. Yet the rules that make up the traditional Christian grammar of sexual conduct can also be seen as positive exhortations that convey abiding insight about the nature of sexual intimacy. What they mean, despite their negative form, is that sex is too important to be taken lightly, that the mutual vulnerability of sexual partners belongs in the context of promise and trust, that the entireness of sexual self-giving extends in time as monogamy and has as its counterpart the public covenant that the church blesses; in sum, that the personalist, relational good that belongs to the nature of sex flourishes and is fulfilled in a relationship defined by fidelity and commitment. How this traditional wisdom might apply to the sexual relations of lesbian and gay Christians is not one question but many. If the argument of this essay is sound, they are questions to which the church would do well to give serious thought.[27]

Such questions belong to moral theology, but also lead beyond it. Anglicans have never been of one mind as to the status of matrimony, but like baptism and the eucharist it is called "holy" in the Prayer Book, and it has for the most part been deemed to be not just a morally permissible mode of human conduct but at the same time a means of divine grace as well. Faithfulness, beyond making it possible for the interpersonal good of sex to flourish most fully and freely, is also what makes matrimony a sacrament that signifies "the mystery of the union between Christ and his church." Have same-sex relationships the same potential for sacramental meaning and power? This essay has suggested that they can, and do, signify a natural good. But finally it will be as signifying a supernatural mystery that they take their place in "the pattern of the glory."

NOTES

For helpful commentary on earlier versions of this essay
I am grateful to Gardiner Shattuck and my colleague Stephen Pope.

1. The Episcopal Church's statements and resolutions on homosexuality are collected in the first chapter of *Continuing the Dialogue: A Pastoral Study Document of the House of Bishops to the Church as the Church Considers Issues of Human Sexuality* (Cincinnati: Forward Movement Publications, 1995), 1-16.

2. John T. Noonan, "Development in Moral Doctrine," *Theological Studies* 54 (1993): 662.

3. Psalm 15:6, in the older Prayer Book version. Modern translators, mindful of the change that has occurred in the meaning of "usury," usually resort to paraphrase, as has been done in the current *Book of Common Prayer.*

4. Exodus 22:25; Deuteronomy 23:19; Luke 6:35. Deuteronomy in fact sets out a double standard: usury is allowed when the borrower is outside, but not when he is inside, the Israelite community. This distinction added complication to the moral theology of usury, but not in any way that affects the parallel I am drawing. See Benjamin Nelson, *The Idea of Usury,* second edition (Chicago: University of Chicago Press, 1969), 3-28.

5. For Calvin on usury, see Nelson, *The Idea of Usury,* 73-82; John T. Noonan, Jr., *The Scholastic Theory of Usury* (Cambridge, Mass.: Harvard University Press, 1957), 365-367.

6. See also W. H. Auden's discussion of *The Merchant of Venice* in "Brothers and Others," *The Dyer's Hand* (New York: Vintage Books, 1989), 218-237.

7. See Harmon L. Smith, "Decorum as Doctrine: Teachings on Human Sexuality," in Timothy F. Sedgwick and Philip Turner, eds., *The Crisis in Moral Teaching in the Episcopal Church* (Harrisburg, Penn.: Morehouse Publishing, 1992), 15-40, esp. 32.

8. For a historical account of arguments from nature (sense one), specifically the behavior of animals, see John Boswell, *Christianity, Social Tolerance, and Homosexuality: Gay People in Western Europe from the Beginning of the Christian Era to the Fourteenth Century* (Chicago: University of Chicago Press, 1980), 137-143, 303-313.

9. The scientific and philosophical questions that have to do with the genetic roots of human behavior are vastly more complicated than this. For an excellent journalistic account that bears directly on the issue here, see Dean Hamer and Peter Copeland, *The Science of Desire: The Search for the Gay Gene and the Biology of Behavior* (New York: Simon & Schuster, 1994).

10. See Smith, "Decorum as Doctrine," 28-30.

11. Andrew Sullivan, *Virtually Normal: An Argument about Homosexuality* (New York: Alfred A. Knopf, 1995), 33-45.

12. *Issues in Human Sexuality: A Statement by the House of Bishops of the General Synod of the Church of England* (Harrisburg, Penn.: Morehouse Publishing, 1991), 31, §4.2.

13. *Issues in Human Sexuality*, 34-35, §4.9-4.10 and especially 40, §5.2.

14. *Issues in Human Sexuality*, 35-36, §4.12-4.14; 41, §5.6.

15. *Paedagogus* 2.10.

16. Timothy F. Murphy, "Homosex/Ethics," in *Gay Ethics: Controversies in Outing, Civil Rights, and Sexual Science* (Haworth Press, 1994), 12.

17. John Finnis, "Disintegrity," in "Is Homosexual Conduct Wrong? A Philosophical Exchange," *The New Republic* 209 (15 November 1993): 12.

18. Martha Nussbaum, "Integrity," in "Is Homosexual Conduct Wrong? A Philosophical Exchange," *The New Republic* 209 (15 November 1993): 13.

19. The Lambeth Conference resolution is quoted in *Continuing the Dialogue*, 53.

20. The 1920 Lambeth Conference's Report on Marriage Problems, quoted in Alan M. G. Stephenson, *Anglicanism and the Lambeth Conferences* (London: SPCK, 1978), 149.

21. Stephenson, *Anglicanism and the Lambeth Conferences*, 149, 209.

22. "Notes on the Morality of Contraception considered with reference to the 'Ends' and 'Object' of *Coitus*," incorporated into Appendix 1 of *The Family in Contemporary Society: The Report of a Group convened at the Behest of the Archbishop of Canterbury* (LC 1958/6; London: SPCK, 1958), 140-141.

23. "Notes on the Morality of Contraception," 137-149. The quotations are from pages 139, 141, 145.

24. Harmon L. Smith, "Contraception and Natural Law: A Half-Century of Anglican Moral Reflection," in Paul Elmen, ed., *The Anglican Moral Choice* (Wilton, Conn.: Morehouse-Barlow, 1983), 181-200.

25. Paul Ramsey, a Methodist, speaks of "two goods, or intrinsic ends" of sex, the one relational or unitive, the other procreative, in *One Flesh* (Nottingham: Grove Books, 1965), 4. Bernard Lonergan, a Jesuit, distinguishes between a "horizontal finality" to offspring and a "vertical finality" to friendship in a 1943 essay on "Finality, Love, Marriage" republished in *Collection* (Toronto: University of Toronto Press, 1988), 17-52. Examples could be multiplied. See also Lisa Sowle Cahill, *Between the Sexes* (Philadelphia: Fortress Press, 1985), 148-152.

26. *The Family in Contemporary Society*, 130, in the introductory discussion of the position papers appended to the report.

27. Probably the best Anglican discussion of the possibilities is Jeffrey John, *Permanent, Faithful, Stable: Christian Same-Sex Partnerships* (London: Affirming Catholicism, 1993).

THE
BODY
OF
CHRIST

∞ *Owen C. Thomas*

The Story of
Two Communities

For a long time I have noted, both in my own work and that of others, that theology is usually done backwards. By this I mean that convictions in theology and moral theology are usually arrived at by deep and complex processes nurtured by experience and intuition, processes of which we are largely unaware, rather than by conscious rational reflection. Then these convictions are articulated and tested by means of theological reflection on scripture and tradition. Needless to say, this reflection in turn influences experience and intuition.

I can put this another way by noting the importance of the sociology of theology. That is, the social-cultural context (race, class, sex) in which theology is carried out is highly influential in the development of theological and moral convictions. I recall that colleagues and students whom I had come to know at the Episcopal Divinity School and who moved to quite different contexts developed rather different theological and moral convictions. For example, I remember one of the best students I ever had, who was a conservative Anglo-Catholic in theology but who after teaching many years in the philosophy and religion department of a large midwestern state university gradually became an agnostic Unitarian Universalist. He agrees that his context has been very influential in the development of his convictions.

I am not proposing the extreme position taken by some sociologists of knowledge which holds that rational reflection is merely an epiphenomenon or by-product of psycho-socio-cultural factors, but only that these factors are always influential and sometimes highly influential in the development of theological and moral convictions. They are not, however, determinative; otherwise, why spend your life studying and teaching theology?

Now in regard to the current debate in the Episcopal Church about sexuality and especially homosexuality, I have the impression from reading many of the books and essays that have been produced in the course of this struggle that most of the exegetical, historical, theological, moral, and pastoral issues have been discussed quite thoroughly. And I hazard the guess that nothing radically new and decisive can be expected from this quarter. (I hope I am entirely open to being persuaded otherwise.) Therefore I suggest that we need to discuss the so-called non-theological factors in the debate.

The Episcopal Church is comprised of a large number of very diverse communities of worship and discourse with long traditions of diverse experience and intuition. I suspect that our divisions over issues in sexuality are derived in large part from this diversity. Therefore, I propose that one way forward in the discussion is to address ourselves to this diversity of communal experience in order better to understand how we have come to differ and to learn from each other's experience and intuition. Here I want to recount the stories of the ways in which two communities of faith of which I have been a member have dealt with issues having to do with homosexuality. One is the Episcopal Theological (now Divinity) School, of which I have been a member as student and teacher for forty-four years, and the other is the Church of St. John the Evangelist on Bowdoin Street in Boston, of which I have been a member for seventeen years.

∞

The Episcopal Theological School was founded in 1867 by a group of laymen who agreed that it should have a lay board of trustees in order to avoid ecclesiastical interference, and that it should be near to and affiliated with Harvard University in order to offer the best academic instruction. In 1974 the school merged with the Philadelphia Divinity School, which had a similar background. Off and on throughout its history, the school has been in trouble with various parts of the Episcopal Church—for example, for introducing the historical critical approach to the Bible, for harboring a radical ethicist who was the founder of modern medical ethics and situation ethics, for admitting women for the M.Div. degree, for advocating the ordination of women, for employing two women whose ordinations were at the time deemed irregular (though they were regularized within the year), and for admitting openly homosexual students. For these reasons, there has been tension between the school and some other parts of the church. The school has always believed that it was the right kind of tension, however, because it derived from an attempt to deal with issues which were facing the church.

It is primarily this last issue of homosexuality which is dividing the church at present. It is well known that the church has ordained homosexual men from the beginning. (And if the late Yale historian John Boswell is correct, the church has blessed homosexual unions from the early centuries.) The same applies to the Episcopal Church. Probably all Episcopal seminaries have admitted and graduated homosexual people who have then been ordained in virtually all the dioceses of the church. Probably most of them have been sexually active. In the past when the issue of homosexuality came into the open, usually through some complaint or scandal, it was handled secretly. When one of my seminary classmates disappeared overnight with no explanation, it was rumored that he had been involved in some homosexual "incident," and I have heard of similar occurrences in other Episcopal seminaries. Secrecy was the name of the game. What is new in the last quarter of this century is the appearance at seminary doors of openly gay and lesbian people, often in committed relationships, and also the beginning of the end of secrecy.

About twenty-five years ago an openly gay man applied for admission to the Episcopal Theological School. His application was discussed in the admissions committee, of which I was a member, and it was decided that the question of his admission required broader consideration among the various constituencies of the school. Over a period of months consultations were held among faculty, trustees, students, graduates, and benefactors, along with some outside consultants, namely, psychiatrists and psychologists. Finally a unanimous decision was made by the faculty, trustees, and the school senate of faculty, students, and staff not to discriminate against people because of their sexual orientation. This included offering seminary housing for gay and lesbian couples. The same decision was made later in regard to faculty.

Over the years since then, a number of openly gay and lesbian people have been admitted, graduated, and ordained in several dioceses. The percentage of gay and lesbian members of the school has probably been somewhat higher in recent years than in society at large, because it is considered to be a relatively safe place for them to live openly. While there are presumably considerable numbers of gay and lesbian students at all the other Episcopal seminaries, their degree of openness varies with the policy of the seminary.

Over the past quarter century we straights and gays at EDS have come to know, appreciate, admire, and love one another, and work together in this particular area of the church's life and ministry. For example, I recall a long discussion in a small conference group of first-year students with a young gay man about his homosexuality—when he realized it, whether any choice was involved, what it was like to live in a largely homophobic society. I also remember another discussion in a conference group of second-year students with a young lesbian woman who "came out" to us and wanted to talk about coming out to her parents during the Christmas vacation that was approaching. (She is now the rector of a large urban parish.) Finally, I recall after chapel one morning a colleague coming out to me and explaining that he had informed his bishop before he was ordained in the 1950s. This is the kind of experience of trust, friendship, and interchange which has brought the school community and myself to where we are today, and it has enriched our lives greatly. We believe that we are modeling a kind of inclusive community life for the church at large.

This is not to say that there have not been tensions, cliquishness, backbiting, and so forth. Before coming to the school, many straight students have never known any gay or lesbian people, especially any who were open about their sexual orientation and feeling confident in being part of a critical mass. Their reactions were similar to those of many men when the number of women students came to equal and then surpass theirs in the 1980s.

It is the policy of EDS to gather a community of diverse people who reflect society at large and to challenge them to deal with real differences and otherness. The suspicion, fear, and hatred of those who are different is the fundamental disease tearing the world apart today, whether in Bosnia, the Middle East, Rwanda, or the inner cities of our nation. In relation to this issue, however, the model of community that the church has adopted in the past half century is a disastrous one for church and society. Based on interpersonal transparency and intimacy, and exalting feelings of belongingness, it is disastrous because it requires homogeneity and the exclusion of those who are different.[1] So the school is seeking a new model of community that rejoices in difference, including difference in sexual orientation. The search is difficult but greatly rewarding.

∞

In 1979 my wife and I began attending regularly the Mission Church of St. John the Evangelist on Bowdoin Street. Located on the "wrong" side of Beacon Hill in Boston, it is one of the great old Anglo-Catholic parishes on the eastern seaboard. The church was built in 1831 as a Congregational church under the leadership of my great-great-uncle, the Rev. Lyman Beecher, father of a wild clan that included the abolitionist preacher Henry Ward Beecher and the author Harriet Beecher Stowe. In 1870 the building was purchased by the Episcopal Church of the Advent, and the Society of St. John the Evangelist, the oldest Anglican men's religious order, was asked to supply the ordained ministry.

In 1882 the Church of the Advent moved to a new building on Brimmer Street, on the "right" side of Beacon Hill, and the Society, commonly known as the "Cowley Fathers" from their original house near Oxford, took over the building on Bowdoin Street as its mission church to the down-and-out, homeless, drunks, pimps, and prostitutes of nearby Scollay Square. The brothers of SSJE lived in the Mission House next door until

1939, when all but four or five moved to their new monastery on Memorial Drive in Cambridge. In the 1960s Scollay Square was replaced by the new Government Center, but the northeast side of Beacon Hill remained an area of cheap rooming houses for the destitute and the aged as well as an area where the homeless gathered. During the first half of this century St. John's was also renowned for its elaborate Anglo-Catholic liturgy and its fine liturgical music under the direction of Everett Titcomb.

In 1976, in reaction to the vote of the General Convention to ordain women to the priesthood and the episcopate, the vicar of St. John's, who was a member of SSJE, and his assistant announced that they were resigning and walked out in the middle of the eucharist. Both became Roman Catholics. After that St. John's was served by vicars of SSJE who were not brothers, and in the late 1970s the parish sponsored for ordination one of the first women priests in the diocese. In 1985 St. John's became an independent parish of the diocese, while maintaining a close and friendly relation with SSJE. It has also continued to be an important center for ministry to the homeless, the needy, and shut-ins in the area through programs such as its Jubilee Senior Action Center, Neighborhood Action, Doorbell Ministry, and Food Pantry, as well as a diocesan center for instruction in liturgy and liturgical music.

For the past century St. John's has also been known as a parish where gay and lesbian people are welcome, and many of them have been regular members of the parish and parish officials. At the turn of the century, two distinguished church architects, Ralph Adams Cram, who designed the reredos and collaborated on the stained glass, and Henry Vaughan, who designed the rood screen, were members.[2] Today the Boston chapter of Dignity, the organization of gay and lesbian Roman Catholics, holds its meetings and services at St. John's. It has long been a part of parish lore at St. John's that for many years the clergy have quietly given blessings to same-sex couples. It would be difficult to pin down the facts about this, but the very existence of this oral tradition indicates the attitude of the parish. As at EDS, the presence of relatively large numbers of openly gay and lesbian parishioners has caused tensions and arguments, and some parishioners, both gay and straight, have left. There have been similar reactions to the presence of street people. But as at the school, the goal has been to create a community which accepts and rejoices in real difference and diversity.

The 1980s were marked by both joy and sadness at St. John's. One of the high points in the life of the parish was the annual Wardens' Ball just before Lent. Gay and straight couples and individuals in formal dress or costume came to party, eat, drink, and dance. Straight men and women danced with gay men and lesbian women amidst general rejoicing. The binary was totally problematized, as they say in feminist theory.

The source of sadness was that some members of St. John's had contracted AIDS and were dying. The feeling in the parish was that while there was a lot of mourning focused on the gay membership of the parish, there was also a lot to celebrate in their lives with us. Why was it that we seemed only to bury our gay members and not bless their unions? In 1989 the co-rectors, the Rev. Jennifer Phillips and the Rev. Richard Valantasis, informed Bishop David Johnson that, at the request of some gay and lesbian couples at St. John's, they were going to begin blessing committed same-sex relationships, which they understood as falling under their pastoral prerogative and responsibility. In response Bishop Johnson issued a formal inhibition forbidding them to proceed with the blessings. The parish, upset by this, invited the three bishops of the diocese to St. John's for an evening of discussion.

So in the fall of 1989 Bishop Johnson, Suffragan Bishop Barbara Harris, and Assistant Bishop David Birney all came to St. John's for one of the most remarkable evenings I have ever experienced in the church. Lisa Gary, the senior warden, presided and members of the parish were invited to address themselves not only to the issue of same-sex blessings but also to what it meant to them to live and worship in a congregation that included many openly gay and lesbian individuals and couples. For two hours, individuals and couples, gay and straight, stood up and spoke with great eloquence about how much it meant to them to work, worship, and celebrate at St. John's. There were many expressions of deep Christian piety and heartfelt gratitude for St. John's because of its inclusiveness and openness, especially to gay and lesbian people but also to homeless and street people. The clergy did not speak, but at the end each of the bishops did, saying they had been moved and assuring the congregation that they had been heard.

Discussions between the co-rectors and Bishop Johnson continued, and finally he agreed that St. John's could go ahead with the blessing of same-sex couples, so long as the blessings did not take place in the context of the eucharist. (They were in fact conducted just before the eucharist.) A process of exploration, instruction, and discussion about blessings, same-sex covenants, and marriage had been going on for some time in the parish. The results of this process have been summarized in this description of parish policy by the Rev. Jennifer Phillips:

> Every household of the community—whether a person living alone, a couple, a person or persons raising children or caring for aging parents, groups of friends, or those making their home temporarily or permanently within a large institution—is called to order itself as a small church community in which God is made manifest, hospitality offered and baptismal vows lived out. Over time, the wider community in its relationship with a household can discern whether that household shows forth God and builds up the community or not....Where a household is

discerned to be filled with love, respect, kindness and prayer, where it reaches out in care to others, where wrongs are forgiven and labor shared, the community rightly desires to return thanks to God for it. And when a couple find in one another a source of joy and comfort, strength in adversity, the knowledge and love of God, then they properly desire to return thanks to God for their relationship and to ask God's continued blessing and the community's prayerful support.[3]

The first blessing, in the fall of 1990, was of two former Roman Catholic nuns who had been committed to each other for seventeen years. I was privileged to assist the rectors at this blessing. It was a time of some anxiety and fear, but also of great rejoicing at St. John's. Because of increased violence against gay and lesbian people in the Boston area as well as other parts of the country, there was serious concern that some person or group might try to interrupt the service or attack the couple. When in the middle of the service someone dropped a book in the back of the church, everyone jumped. Later, after having dinner at this couple's house, my wife happened to mention it to her daughter, who asked with some surprise, "Where do you ever meet lesbians?" My wife responded, "Oh, at church." The following year my wife and I served as sponsors at the blessing of another lesbian couple, and the next summer we served as sponsors for a straight couple.

One of the most recent blessings took place in August 1994, when the union of a theology professor at Boston College and his partner of many years was blessed at St. John's. (The professor is a lay associate of SSJE and for several years he and his partner have conducted retreats for gay couples sponsored by the Society.) Many of the brothers of SSJE attended the blessing, including the present Superior and his predecessor, who is now Bishop of Massachusetts. A large and joyous reception for the couple and the whole parish was held after the service at Emery House, the Society's retreat center in West Newbury, Massachusetts.

∞

This has been the story of how two communities of faith of which I have been privileged to be a member have dealt with the issue of homosexuality in the church. At the school we made a decision of faith on a complex and difficult issue, and as a result enriched our life with the presence of openly gay and lesbian people. At the parish we came to be aware of a deep pastoral need, worked with the bishop to find a way to meet this need, and as a result brought gay and lesbian people into a fuller participation in our life together as parish. I hardly need to say that this experience has been a very important factor in my present conviction that homosexual people should not be discriminated against in the church in any way, especially in regard to ordination or blessing. If those who differ with me on this issue had had the same experience as I have had in these two communities, I believe that they would be at least nearer to my view than they are now.

At the beginning I suggested that convictions in theology and moral theology arrived at by the processes of experience and intuition should be articulated and tested by means of theological reflection on scripture and tradition. This is what we as a church have been doing over the past decade in the large number of discussions, conferences, books, and articles on issues concerning homosexuality. I have been a participant in this process. My judgment, as I have said, is that the exegetical, historical, theological, and moral issues have been discussed thoroughly, and that sufficient grounds have been found for going either way on the issue of the ordination (and blessing) of homosexuals in committed relationships, although it is my conviction that the grounds are stronger for a policy of nondiscrimination. My experience, confirmed by theological reflection, has led me to the conviction that it is time for the Episcopal Church to affirm and regularize what is already happening in this regard.

Since I am aware that the experience of others, confirmed by their own theological reflection, has led them to the opposite conviction, I must add one point. When I refer to experience here, I firmly believe that Christian love and justice require that this experience include firsthand knowledge of and friendship with more than one or two gay or lesbian people and couples. The alternative is to rely on stereotypes, hearsay, gossip, and so forth. The reason for stressing this point is that we live in one of the most homophobic societies in the non-Islamic world, a society in which discrimination and violence against homosexual people is increasing, a society which is moving steadily in a politically and religiously conservative direction, and a society in which anti-homosexual feelings, beliefs, laws, and actions are on the increase. In such a society any "experience" of gay and lesbian people that is not informed by a wider personal knowledge and friendship is liable to be very negative.

My experience, then, including that of the two communities in which I have lived, has been decisive on these issues. Now those who are acquainted with my writing on the relation of experience and theology may wonder at this conclusion, since there I have argued that experience cannot be the main criterion in theological judgment. On the issues under discussion, however, my experience has not been the main criterion but rather a supplementary one. I put it this way in 1983:

> Christian religious experience can be used as a criterion in theology subordinate to scripture and tradition. It can function to confirm or question theological proposals grounded on these authorities. A common situation in theology is that of judging between alternative proposals. When the appeal to scripture and tradition is equally well grounded for

two proposals, then that proposal is to be favored which is more complementary with Christian experience, that is, which orders, makes sense of, gives meaning to, and thus interprets the experience more successfully than the other.[4]

This is a version of the position taken by my teacher Paul Tillich. He argues against the appeal to experience in theology, and concludes that experience is the medium through which the norms of scripture and tradition speak to us, but that experience itself is not the norm. According to Tillich, the productive power of experience is limited to the transformation of what is given to it. This should be neither simply a repetition of the tradition nor an entirely new production. Thus our experience affects how we understand and interpret scripture and tradition.[5] I see this as an accurate description of how I have come to my views on the issues confronting the church.

Some years ago the dean of the Episcopal Divinity School was challenged by a Greek Orthodox priest who claimed that after befriending the Orthodox in America, the Episcopal Church had betrayed them by ordaining women. The dean replied, "That reminds me of the Episcopalian who was asked if he believed in infant baptism. He responded, 'Believe it? I've *seen* it!' So, as regards the ordination of women, I can say, 'We have seen it, and we wish you could too.'" And so also, in regard to the ordination and blessing of gay and lesbian people, I can say, "We have seen it, and we want you to see it too."

NOTES

1. See Iris Marion Young, "The Ideal of Community and the Politics of Difference," in Linda J. Nicholson, ed., *Feminism/Postmodernism* (New York: Routledge, 1990).
2. For details see Douglas Shand-Tucci, *Boston Bohemia 1881-1900*, vol. 1 of *Ralph Adams Cram: Life and Architecture* (Amherst: University of Massachusetts Press, 1995).
3. Jennifer M. Phillips, "Same-Sex Unions," *The Witness* 77/12 (December 1994): 28.
4. From chapter 3, "Should experience be the main criterion of theology?" of Owen C. Thomas, *Theological Questions: Analysis and Argument* (Wilton, Conn.: Morehouse Publishing Co., 1983), 32. For a more extensive treatment see my essay "Theology and Experience," *Harvard Theological Review* 78/1-2 (1985): 179-201.
5. See Paul Tillich, *Systematic Theology*, vol. 1 (Chicago: University of Chicago Press, 1951-1963), 40-46.

∞ *Susan Harriss*

What I Know, I Can't Say

We didn't talk about it.

My home parish—the one I knew best as a young adult in the 1970s—welcomed gay people, particularly gay men, with a tacit promise of discretion. No one would ask, no one would tell; at least not in the congregation at large, not outside an inner circle of which even I, as a priest, was not a part.

We did talk about *sex*, or rather, told jokes about sex. We teased each other, laughed a lot, made faces. But we didn't talk about homosexuality. In the parish that gave me its very best, the one I called home for years, homosexuality was described obliquely, as if the subject were taboo. *Being* gay was fine: *talking* about it wasn't.

This is not to say that no one knew. We all knew, to the extent that we wanted to know, who was gay and who was not. I, for one, assumed I knew; if I erred, it would have been on the side of thinking someone was gay who was not. A lot of the men in this parish were gay. A third? Two-fifths? More than a few. I knew; they knew I knew; we didn't talk about it.

Well, perhaps that's not fair. We did talk about it, once, the rector and I. He welcomed me to his study, poured a liberal glass of scotch for me and an equally generous hand of bourbon for himself, and promised more (liquor) if I wanted it. "Well," he said, "it's not the most interesting thing about a person, now, is it?"—and proceeded to enlighten me as to which of my favorite English authors had been homosexual. W. H. Auden. Evelyn Waugh. I don't think he ever used the word *homosexual*, though, or *gay* or *queer* or any equivalent. If he did, I don't remember. I do remember that line, though: *it's not the most interesting thing about a person, is it?*

That was the name of the game. Here was a place, a church, where sexuality, though present and presumably active, would never dominate the discourse in any open way. There were to be no support groups, no politicking, no advocacy. If someone from around the diocese suggested that the parish was gay, I flinched. It wasn't gay, it was church. Just church.

And what a church it was! The sizable talents of these people were given over to eleven o'clock Sunday morning, gathering in their wake the assistance of the rest of us, who after all were having a great time. They made it seem that nothing was impossible. Music, flowers, vestments, even the interior decoration of the church became more and more ornate, more beautiful, more articulate. So did the worship itself, as this proudly low-church parish crept its way up the liturgical scale, adding more frequent eucharist, more chant, more music, even incense. More style.

And the rest of the congregation—old West Indian families who had seen the parish through hard times in former years; college professors and retired musicians; young families who swept up the newly-renovated apartments scavenged from the decaying SRO hotels; kids from the projects up the street—the rest of the congregation tolerated, pretended not to see. There were veiled complaints, but these were mainly about feeling excluded. Certain people seemed always to pass over to the rectory after coffee hour, were forever drinking sherry. But that sherry group was never exclusively gay; it was just an extra hospitality offered to newcomers. It also gave the single folks a chance to gather groups for brunch; church was becoming an all-day affair. Sometimes Flora Sampson, ancient in days but not by the look of her eyes, would sit at the grand piano in the parlor and play "Begin the Beguine"; in time, the curate would push her aside and strike up "Rubber Ducky, I Love You," and then get everyone to bawl out hymns as loudly as we dared. Some loved to stay, some felt obliged. Exclusive? Perhaps, but in the sense that someone would have been looking out for the "attractive" people—of whatever color, preference, or class.

They never allowed sexuality to become, in a phrase coined by Ann Douglas, the dominant category. Literacy, maybe. A certain look, the ability to hold a drink, a sadder-but-wiser feeling; maybe that's what we had in common. Even more than those qualities, though, we shared an intense longing for a church—an old-fashioned church with Bible study, afternoon tea, bold hymns, white gloves; a place to dress up for. It gave a certain direction to the week, held down its disparate longings like a paperweight, was our ballast in a storm. A thorough, thoughtful, everybody-looking-up-and-singing Sunday morning. We wanted it, we relished it, we showed up for it.

Meanwhile, to me, these people were uncannily, supernaturally generous. Having run from the Salvation Army (evangelical) to Union Theological Seminary (Marxist/Calvinist) to St. Clement's, Manhattan (indescribable mixture of experimental theater, new liturgy, and urban squalor), I really needed a place to settle down, calm down, and figure out what I was doing. "This is Susan Harriss," the rector said, introducing me at a staff meeting. "She may read for Orders, and then again she may not."

And so they taught me everything I could retain, which was certainly less than they knew. How to walk in procession; when to sit, kneel, and stand; how to sing morning prayer. How to serve, function as a deacon, celebrate the eucharist. How to chant without vibrato. Where to buy vestments, what to order at a restaurant when your stomach is off, what to wear. Granted, my acceptance of this may have been over-zealous. It may not have been necessary to dress from Brooks Brothers, for example, or to wear penny loafers; and it was probably going overboard to pull my hair back, tight, into a chignon every Sunday, or to wear only black shoes. I reasoned that I was just trying to fit in, to be as carefully groomed as they were. The nail brush in the sacristy washroom was not lost on me.

But it may also be that the quiet suppression of sexuality was having its effect on me as well. Was it untidiness we wanted to banish? Or was it something bigger? Was it womanliness that was unwelcome, all that hair all over the place (mine was exceptionally thick and wavy), all that clicking of high heels?

One summer my husband and I planned a trip to Ireland and Italy. A friend at church had recommended Ireland, but unlike him I knew I wouldn't be doing any church work there. And I listened to suggestions that I turn up in Rome in a clerical collar, but decided it would spoil my vacation. I was not going to spend my holiday advocating women's ordination: I had done enough of that already. Instead, the last day before we left I spent dressing up. I let the hairdresser trim my hair just past my shoulders, and then asked her to brush it full out. I went to Boyd's Chemist, known for their facial makeovers, and let the woman behind the counter work on my face. She darkened my eyes, lifted my cheekbones with carefully applied blush, deepened my lips with a browning red. I had my nails painted scarlet. And I went home looking like another person, giggling—and knowing I could never go into my church looking so, so rebellious, so Out There.

When I returned to work after the vacation, I put my hair back in the bun. But I hadn't forgotten what it felt like to relax, to look like somebody else. My husband, who had not been especially comfortable in that parish with me, was working somewhere else on Sundays. Also it seemed, in a way, that news of my married life was not of interest at church. When I told the clergy I was pregnant, one of them remarked, "Well, you're not the first, and you certainly won't be the last...." Homosexuality and its effects were not discussed: nor were heterosexuality and its occasional triumphs. We were having a baby. The congregation was overwhelmingly supportive and generous—the baby shower was huge—yet there was a touch of sadness in much of it. This might have been envy, it might have been that the question of children and family brought to mind some of the comforts they had left behind, the places where they felt excluded. Bemused, my husband compared my role there to Wendy's with the Lost Boys in *Peter Pan*—the one girl among the fun-loving, lonely boys.

She'll be waiting at the door
We won't be lonely any more...
We have a mother, at last we have a mother....

∽

Did it work to my advantage, not to talk so much about our lifestyles, who we were? Compared to other places where I had worked, it occasionally seemed stifling, unfair. At the same time, I was learning more than I had ever dreamed possible. And they were accepting of me. As a woman, a really new Episcopalian, and a graduate of a non-Episcopal seminary, I had three counts against me already, and yet they were taking me in. And the protective silence that surrounded their private lives also surrounded me. I did not have people pounding me at coffee hour about the morality of homosexual believers; but also I did not have people pounding me on the question of women's ordination. Somehow the protection was pervasive. We didn't talk about it.

Maybe others talked about it more, behind closed doors. I assume they did. But for me the silence was soothing, protective. It guarded me from questions about my own priesthood as well as theirs. We shared a certain marginality, the gay men and I. Though they were in priestly vestments, and I was in priestly vestments, and we were officiating correctly and in a way that was valid as far as we knew, we also knew there were others in the Episcopal Church who would not hold our ministry valid at all. In the eyes of some I would never—will never—be a priest in quite the same way as a man. In the eyes of some, a homosexual person, however faithful, will never be quite the priest a heterosexual male would be.

Some of it is for lack of opportunity: all those parishes looking for a priest "with a family." (How did I know that this didn't include me? I just knew.) Some of it had to do with nagging doubts about gender and sexuality, and who we really were. But we never asked ourselves, we never uttered the doubt, as to whether *we* felt truly priestly. In every circumstance we could control, we acted as if we were. We answered every doubt with Quality. In this I joined them, drowning the unasked questions in sheer effort and excellence. So long as the parish thrived, what could the doubters say? We did not ask.

Meanwhile the parish kept me involved in a non-stipendiary ministry while I worked at the diocese and looked for full-time parish ministry. My break came in 1984, when I was called as associate rector to a large parish across town. I had my friends' blessing—and recommendation; their word was welcome and respected. But I felt guilty, worried that my brother and mentor, the parish curate, was not having any luck moving to another parish himself. He could have worked rings around me, anywhere he went. He was untiring, with a breathtaking capacity for drawing in new people and seeing that they stayed. But he Wasn't Married. And later he grew ill.

And so, eventually the support groups did start. People were getting sick, including some of the clergy. The first of a long series of funerals began, and the intense energy which produced that eleven o'clock liturgy now produced a columbarium just behind the pulpit. When I returned in 1989 it was like coming home to a village that had turned all its young men out for a war. The gaps were unnerving. Again, no one talked about being gay. One simply talked about who was sick. It seemed irrelevant to wonder how it happened. It was too late for that.

We certainly did enjoy ourselves, though, in those early years. We would look at the filling pews, hear the tumultuous rise of all the singing, and say to one another, "This is too good to be true." Perhaps it *was* too good to be true—a place where it was safe to be, and not to talk about it; not to have one's being up for discussion and scrutiny; not to have one's sex life be the Most Interesting Thing. But it came at a price. Sexuality may not be the *most* interesting thing about a person, but it's right up there, isn't it? Isn't it an interesting, an enormously interesting, vivifying part of ourselves? And if we find a way to live that out, isn't it worth talking about, at least a little?

Looking back, I remember feeling that my own sexuality needed, somehow, to be checked at the door of the church as I went in. Talk about my life at home seemed not to be of interest; it sounded too much like whining. When the sexual life of women came up, it was often in jokes but rarely otherwise. No matter how much it pressed upon us, as it did when I was pregnant, or when choir members met and married, family talk was a conversation-stopper. Among ourselves, the women talked about it, let it go. Was it out of pity, because of a feeling that the gay men were being shut out in so many places that it was only fair to let them have their way here? Or was it out of gratitude, because we enjoyed them so much, because any party worth attending was being thrown by them, and they were counting us in? Whatever the reason, there was a kind of embarrassment. Though the subject was quiet, its effects were not. It was a funny thing to be a woman there—a kind of oddity. One felt ill at ease, on edge at times, without knowing why.

∞

It's 1995, and I'm remembering. I'm in a yoga class, tentatively poking at that boundary between mind and body, wondering where I've been all these years. Didn't I know that when I was praying I was in this body, and didn't I expect it to count? I'm supposed to be watching my breathing, but I let my thoughts run back along the years, revisiting the chancel of my old home. I remember sitting up straight, pulling my hair back, holding my breath, trying not to be so...so untidy, so unkempt, so bodily. So we didn't talk about sex. Did that mean that all sex was bad? No one ever said that, but no one ever said that it was good, either. Just as there was no talk of persecution, or oppression, or gay rights, neither was there any talk of joy, of satisfaction, of relief in the company of the beloved.

We didn't talk about it. I can't help wondering how that affected me, how it affected us all. I don't think we meant to say that sex was bad, but the silence may well have had that effect. Not just homosexuality, but sexuality—period. It was just too important that it—our sexuality—not show on Sunday morning. It was as if we all saw the priesthood as somehow excluding our sexual lives, and we forced ourselves into the mold, cutting off certain kinds of expression as if to lie on a Procrustean bed.

Now, in the yoga class, so many years later, I am stretching, hard, not just in body but in soul, trying to find the ways the soul and body work together. To my surprise a sudden compassion wells up for that time, for those men, for us all. We certainly tried to get it right. We tried to get it right, but we were afraid. I was afraid.

Afraid of what, I wonder? At the time, I was probably afraid to find out what I thought: afraid that I would turn out on the conservative side, after all. I don't worry about that now. But at the time I wouldn't have been likely to start the discussion, or even to help it along. Neither did anyone else. Perhaps we were afraid that only one question would dominate: should homosexuals, should women, be ordained? But that's not the best question, is it? A better one, the one I wish we had pursued, is this: What does it feel like to be praying, to be celebrating the eucharist, *in this body*? Is this body good? Has the church been telling us *no*?

We might have raised those questions, but we chose not to. Instead, we lost ourselves in the work—the joyous, precious work—of building up that parish. The work of preaching, of welcoming, of teaching, of gathering people together. The work was everything, the church was everything. What fault to us if we let what might have been an absorbing interest float beneath our pages like a footnote? What fault to us if the footnote gradually overtook the page? If we had talked about it, if we had shared our misgivings with each other—even among the clergy—perhaps we would have found a kind of healing together that wasn't possible otherwise. Perhaps that healing would have helped other people too. We can't know that now.

They taught me everything I knew. But, learning more, I've started wondering about the secrecy and its unwitting partnership with shame. It troubles me some, and yet I'm so very grateful for the time, for those years, for a group of people with the wit and sophistication to live gracefully, with dignity. I am grateful for their quiet insistence on the truth that the church is theirs, is mine, as much as anyone's on earth. And maybe freedom, in the end, means not *having* to talk about it.

∞ *David L. Norgard*

Lesbian and Gay Christians and the Gay-Friendly Church

*Is there any among you who, if your child
asks for bread, will give a stone?
(Luke 11:11)*

As a priest who is known to be both gay and gay-friendly, it has been one of the great privileges of my ministry to hear the stories of other gay or lesbian Episcopalians about their experiences of church. At the same time, however, this privilege has often been a deeply disconcerting aspect of my ministry, due to the litany of tragedy many of these stories constitute. To cite just a few examples: Two women were long regarded as pillars of their parish, but when they found genuine love and happiness in each other they were totally ostracized by their fellow parishioners and eventually told that it would be best if they found another church. A teenager who had shown great promise for future ministry nearly ruined his life with a suicide attempt after his rector told him his life would amount only to sorrow and shame if he "turned out gay." An organist who had served her parish faithfully and effectively for nearly two decades was suddenly dismissed when the rector discovered her to be a friend of lesbians. A talented priest was denied serious consideration by one search committee after another due to her unwillingness to regard her partner as anything less than her immediate family. They are all sad circumstances but they are remarkable only because they are exemplary of a bias that is still pervasive within the Episcopal Church. To its own detriment, the Episcopal Church has failed time and again to treat its lesbian daughters and gay sons charitably.

Nonetheless, bad news is not the only news for lesbian and gay Christians these days. There is cause for prayers of thanks as well as cries for deliverance. There are congregations who have begun to see the lesbian and gay people in their midst not as demons to be exorcised but as the valuable members of the body they are. Even more, there are congregations which have gone a step further and begun to see lesbian and gay people outside their doors not as potential threats to their long-standing moral order but rather as potential guests and members of God's coming new order. While debate continues in various ecclesiastical and academic arenas over sexual ethics and biblical interpretation, some churches have done what is truly remarkable and begun to proclaim good news by word and deed to those who were not expecting it from them.

∞

Much of the conversation over the role and place of homosexual people in the church has focused on rather narrow (although important) questions of biblical interpretation, theological ethics, and ecclesiastical discipline. In legislative and judicial bodies at the diocesan and national levels of the Episcopal Church, debate has continued for years over the legalities of certain ministries with and by lesbian and gay Christians. Yet those churches which have presented the gospel to lesbian and gay seekers in such manner as to receive a positive response generally have moved beyond the confines of intellectual debate, and have actually begun to proclaim and demonstrate the good news of God's love. They have welcomed the lesbian or gay person to worship. They have offered pastoral care and spiritual guidance. They have taken a stand for justice for the sexual minority. And thus, homosexual seekers and Christians have felt welcome in these churches, but not mainly because of some articulation of a logically valid, gay-positive ethical framework or gay-inclusive theological anthropology. First and foremost, they have responded warmly to these Christian faith communities because they experience them as Christian. They sense that their dignity as persons is respected by these churches. They detect a complicity with God's conspiracy of love for them.

In the gay-friendly church, the life-affirming, hope-filled traditions of Christianity have been taken as models and precedents for how it should relate to peoples who are today experiencing death and alienation. And, given this actualization, to the degree that these traditions are put in practice by those who hold them dear, homosexual persons are able to find in these stories deep inspiration and encouragement. They are able to understand and appreciate them as good news that applies to them. Lesbian women and gay men are able to see themselves as people for whom God does show keen concern, while all in the congregation see that God's kingdom includes a wider variety of peoples than they once assumed. By daring to pursue reconciliation, in essence, gay, lesbian, and straight Christians alike are not only hoping in but living out a vision of a humanity that is comprised of many peoples but who live to the fullest as one, in the sight of God.

This has been no small feat, for it has required nothing short of an emotional and spiritual reorientation by these congregations, from homophobic to gay-friendly. It has meant undergoing a thorough self-examination. Where hospitality has been found lacking or prejudice found operating, diligent attention has had to be given to reform. These congregations have remodeled their environment, in effect, so that they might function as comfortable and nurturing spiritual homes to people they may have not previously thought to invite inside.

The pattern of this emotional and spiritual rehabilitation program may be compared to a home remodeling project. In most circumstances, it has started with a careful inspection to discover negative attitudes, which are usually hidden by veneers of politeness and caution. This is followed by repair and/or removal of these perspectives, so that both foundation and framework are solid enough to permit expansion. Then, after any dry-rot of prejudice has been replaced with strong timbers of good will, the builders of this better home have proceeded with improvements that make room for a larger, more diverse household. The entrance is enlarged, the welcome sign is placed more prominently, the common areas expanded, and additional rooms made ready for new members of the household. The result is a house that will hold all who seek its safety and comfort.

First among the attitudes that need repair is one typically expressed by the comment, "They are welcome here, but why do we need to talk about it?" Those who pose this question already find the church a comfortable place. Often, they really cannot see any need for change. Yet on a deeper level, they fear what might take shape if questions are raised that lead them into unknown territory. They may welcome some of the results a reform process might be expected to have, such as increased attendance. Yet, once such a process has begun, they fear that they may not be able to limit it only to those results of which they approve. Consequently, they prefer no explicit conversation about change, even if the predicted outcome might reasonably be considered a positive one.

To overcome this reticence, a church that wants to become gay-friendly must identify the deterioration of good will that comes from not being forthright. They need to determine that such deterioration is far more damaging in the long term than any short-term loss of placid discourse. Then, having established the principle of open communication, including discussion of sexuality, they will proceed to discern who, in fact, is currently welcome and whom they want to invite into their fellowship.

This discernment brings the church to a point where it must confront a presumption about the effectiveness of its own message of hospitality. It is quite common for churches to make a general statement that "All are welcome here" and to presume that there is no need to deliver specific invitations to any individual or group. On the contrary, though, a message to everyone tends to be received by next to no one. General invitations are generally ineffective, according to many writers in the field of evangelism, and this is especially true among people who have had no prior understanding of being welcome.

To demonstrate the counterproductive quality of this presumption, reversal exercises have proven useful in some places. Church leaders have asked straight members to imagine themselves visiting a predominantly gay church and receiving no reassurance that it was proper for them to be there. They were further asked to identify for themselves what it felt like to be with a community where there was no explicit mention of their type of person. As expected, feelings of isolation were identified, along with the insecurity and frustration that normally attend a sense of not belonging. The result of these exercises has been a recognition of how persons who are different from the majority can feel less than welcome in a community unless they are specifically recognized and affirmed.

At this juncture, congregations desiring to be gay-friendly may confront those who have been disinclined to address the subject at all but eventually find it unavoidable lest "some in the congregation be made to feel uncomfortable." Launching what is basically a rear-guard action, these reluctant speakers may make a declaration such as, "This church can welcome gay people if it wants, but it had better be careful not to alienate those who are already here."

The threat implicit in this declaration will be met in the gay-friendly church by a clear communication of its bottom-line commitment to inclusion. Without any ambivalence, it will attempt to reach and nurture everyone possible, but at the same time recognize its defining characteristics and thus its limits. It will acknowledge the truth that no church, however broad its appeal, can be all things to all people. Identifying as an inclusive church implies just that: including those who want both to include others and to be included. Such a corporate identity precludes setting a high priority on attracting, or keeping, members who themselves would prefer to exclude whole classes of people. Thus, in extreme cases, inclusive churches have to help certain members choose between maintaining their membership in the community and maintaining their bias.

Dealing decisively with the question of inclusiveness will often raise the final objection posed to leaders of churches aspiring to be gay-friendly. Ironically, it will be raised by people who are generally supportive of the objective of inclusiveness. At some point in the process of becoming a congregation genuinely welcoming of gay men and lesbians, some well-intentioned soul will express the fear that "Saint Swithun's might become a 'gay church' if it is not careful." To these people such a change, whether only in the perceived identity of the church or in its actual membership, would be unfortunate because its main effect would be to deter non-gay people from belonging and participating.

Responding to this fear requires special sensitivity, because its expression exposes anti-gay prejudice at its root level. On the surface, the implication is that a "gay church" is inherently less than what a good church should be. Fundamentally, however, the issue is one of power—the power of defining. Consequently, the churches that have successfully resolved this fear are those which faced directly the questions of who holds the decisive power of definition and how that power will be exercised. To that end, "what if" exercises have proven particularly useful. For example, one congregation considered how their evangelistic outreach might be affected by positive, specific reference to lesbian and gay people in their welcome brochure. Vestry members reasoned that some recipients of the brochure would likely be disturbed but, just as likely, others would be moved to joy by the unexpected reference. While it was assumed that the results would probably be mixed, the overall effect was judged to be positive, inasmuch as the parish was attempting to reach people who would respond to the invitation of an inclusive church. Thus, as a result of reviewing a possible scenario realistically, the darkness of the unknown began to fade and, with it, the fear. Church members began to see that the practical implications of being gay-friendly were not entirely dismal but rather also had their fortunate aspects.

Once they have removed the barriers of these negative attitudes, churches that are fully committed to welcoming gay men and lesbian women into their midst will demonstrate genuine care and concern for their spiritual welfare. Surprisingly to some, perhaps, this has not required any radically innovative program. On the contrary, gay and lesbian people have shown their appreciation for what non-gay people also value in a healthy parish or mission: authentic worship, sensitive pastoral care, enriching Christian education, community service and advocacy.

Gay and lesbian persons come to church primarily because they have a strong desire to be inspired and edified. For the most part, openly gay persons in particular do not attend because of social pressure or family obligation. They genuinely want what only a corporate worship experience can provide—a sense of the presence of God through an experience of community caught up in mystery. Yet beyond that, they need to know that their participation is welcome in any of the roles found in Episcopal worship, assuming a call and proper training. As was the case with women, they do not want to be limited as a class only to certain orders or functions. With respect to the ministry of the clergy, the question of lesbian and gay participation is a larger one than any single congregation may answer on its own.

Any congregation is, however, able at least to make its position known through preaching and other areas of parish life.

With regard to pastoral care, most gay and lesbian people cherish an approach by clergy and lay pastors that respects their dignity as human beings. Just as much as straight people, lesbian women and gay men value being visited when sick, counseled when troubled, befriended when lonely. Conversely, they want to share in the pastoral ministry of their chosen congregation—again, without special limitation. For example, some may want to teach Sunday school without needing to defend themselves against the stereotype of being dangerous to children. They want to give and receive, touch and be touched by the faith community to which they belong.

In recent years, even congregations that are not consciously gay-friendly have attained a higher level of awareness of gay men and lesbians as being ordinary people. Members of many congregations have come to see us as human beings bearing the image of God and thus qualified to be treated with respect. Yet considerable work remains to be done with respect to same-sex couples, for they are consistently relegated to second-class status in our church. The holiness of their relationships is debated and the genuineness of their love ignored.

The educational program of a healthy church is also appreciated by gay and lesbian members. No less than straight learners, gay and lesbian Christians seek knowledge of holy scriptures and sacred traditions, church history and Episcopal liturgy. And again, not only do they want to learn, they also want to teach. They want to share insights that derive from their unique relationship with the church and with God. They enjoy contributing to the dialogue out of which comes new insight and inspiration for all.

Making all this a reality necessitates a significant change of mindset, since those already in the church tend to assume that they have knowledge, whereas outsiders and newcomers do not. With this mindset, the church becomes the magnanimous purveyor of privileged information. Fully incorporating lesbian women and gay men into congregational life, then, involves a revision of the collective understanding of church, seeing it not only as a source of knowledge but also as a body of seekers pursuing truth together.

Finally, welcoming congregations have begun to do what they have done from time to time for other communities contending against unfair bias: they have stood by their side and offered support to the extent possible. They have realized that the Christian mandate to strive for justice applies to the struggles of sexual minorities, such as gay men and lesbian women, just as much as it does to any other. And so, rising to the political challenges of the day, these churches have taken unambiguous stands against anti-gay discrimination in business and government as well as in the church.

This step in the developing friendships among the lesbian, gay, and Christian communities has been the most difficult for some. Because it inevitably involves taking a public stand, it leads into the widespread and often frustrating conversation many congregations have over the proper relationship between church life and civil politics. These conversations, however, usually assume the perspective of the unaffected bystander. It has therefore helped to frame the question of involvement instead from the perspective of those who might or might not be helped. For them, the question is, "What does it mean for the church to be a herald of good news if not also a champion of it?"

∞

These are some of the experiences, and the consequent insights, of churches that have sought to welcome and include lesbian and gay people fully into their corporate life. They are invigorating, inspiring communities that have taken risks for love and justice. Sadly, however, they remain exceptional congregations within the larger church. They are like oases in a desert, rare places of refreshment and renewal surrounded by an often still inhospitable environment.

It is impossible to ignore the fact that, through the very offices of this Christian church, lesbian women and gay men are still condemned for loving whom we love, denigrated for having faith in who we are, chastised for striving for what we might become. Just beyond the limits of our hard-won safe havens, we continue to be dismissed and denied, humiliated and inhibited, prosecuted and even excommunicated. Thus, looking at the expanse of our whole church, the oases notwithstanding, the landscape still appears bleak to many a lesbian or gay individual. From this perspective, then, the question that wells up from the heart is simple but all-important: Is there really any hope?—hope for a place in the household of faith known as the Episcopal Church?

In pondering the question over the course of my own ministry, I have been moved toward an answer by two passages from scripture associated in our lectionary with the resurrection, the narrative that for me is central to Christian faith. The first passage is the vision of the valley of dry bones in Ezekiel. As the story is told, Ezekiel is taken to a forsaken valley where he views the physical remains of a people long dead. He is then told by God to prophesy to them and, wondrously, they come to life again. In its original context, the story served as an allegory about how the then-exiled people of Israel would yet be returned by God to their promised land. Despite years of despair and alienation, the reader is given reason to hope that the life of the community will ultimately prevail over the death that has been exile.

Paired in the liturgy with Ezekiel's vision is John's story about Jesus' raising of Lazarus. Here the reader hears Jesus say, in effect, "Come out now and live, for I am resurrection and life." Resurrected life, we are given to understand, lies not only at the end of time, when Jesus will return in glory, but also in the present moment in which Jesus acts as friend.

Taken together, these narratives witness to a God who leads those who love him out of exile, even the exile of death. Moreover, the call to freedom of life in its fullest is for *now*, not just for some distant point in the future. In the light of this hope, it is fitting for lesbian and gay Christians to apply Jesus' imperative to "come out" to their own situation in relation to the church. Coming out, as accepting our own God-given sexual identity as well as our baptismal identity, becomes itself an act and expression of faith.

Still, once having appropriated these hopeful stories for our own individual and collective lives, we become painfully aware that there is more to what they are saying. The struggle does not end. Today, we who respond to the call to come out may very well sense God's love and acceptance, but often we do not sense the same from God's people. While God says, "Come!", anti-gay alliances jealously guard the ecclesiastical kingdom against the entry of those they deem unworthy. Instead of encouragement to live, we are treated to admonitions to hide, to be quiet, to stop being ourselves—in essence, to die.

Even in the light of the hope that shines from our sacred scriptures, then, the question lingers like a shadow that will not disappear: For us who are gay or lesbian, is Christian faith finally an impossibility? Or, more precisely, is the Christian vision of new life—as it is manifested in the corporate life of the church—ultimately inaccessible? Is the church that preaches a message of resurrection really for us a place of exile?

Perhaps we lesbian and gay Christians are fools, after all, as we run to a captor in liberator's clothing, tragically seeking our life among those who seek our death. To those crying out for justice now, to those reaching out for reconciliation now, to those praying for a peaceful life now, half-gestures of half-welcome feel quite far removed from any approach we could recognize as respectful or charitable. It seems we are left in a dilemma. Do we curse the darkness, or reject the light?

Yet, as I have pondered the struggles of my friends, I have discovered that there is consolation and strength in the very place we would least expect it or desire to look for it. We garner the strength to choose life in the very face of our life's foes, for that is where we find the indomitable Lord of Love. Indeed, we discover that the power of his presence is greatest in those moments of greatest vulnerability. As Jesus would say of himself later in John's gospel:

No one has greater love than this, to lay down one's life for one's friends....I have said these things to you so that my joy may be in you, and that your joy may be complete....In the world you face persecution. But take courage; I have conquered the world! (John 15:13, 11; 16:33)

Given that enlightenment and encouragement, when we reflect on the wrenching moments of our lives when we either had to love boldly or surrender totally, have we not found that the dilemma is false? Have we not found that since all love is of God, the choice for love and justice is always and altogether the way of life? Today, then, it is our beloved yet sometimes heartbreaking church that faces the challenge of discernment. When it reaches out its hand to a gay man dying of AIDS, it must steel itself to let go only if it cannot sense the hand of healing in that touch. When a lesbian couple who have been rejected everywhere else seek camaraderie in the assembly of the faithful, then it must ask them to leave only if it does not discern in their mutual affection a living symbol of uncompromising love. When church members take their stand with a community that has often stood alone, then they must walk away only if by such company they have not been exhilarated with a life-giving Spirit. When their ears hear and their eyes see the witness of gay Christians whose faith their church has scorned, then they must renounce that faith only if they do not discern in the witnesses' courage that of the One who gave his life for his friends.

And thus I am convinced that the time has come when the church will have to cease its self-defeating practice of consoling those who hate, and to start embracing those whose only conspiracy has been to love. It will have to let go of ancient goods made uncouth by the clearer understanding the Spirit gives us now.

I am convinced that faith demands the witness of every lesbian woman, every gay man, every straight soul possessing the courage to befriend. Time has come when Christians must lead the way to that place where every life is deemed dear. The time has come to hold fast to a discipline of celebrating life and love. The time has come to stop giving our sons and daughters stones when it is the bread of life they seek.

∞ *David Crawley*

A Parish Transformed

I have always had a propensity, inherited I believe from my mother, for telling stories. For a long time I felt the need to apologize for this tendency with some such self-deprecating phrase as, "I know anecdotage precedes dotage." But lately storytelling has become not just respectable but sanctified. Indeed, I understand that I now can describe my approach as "phenomenological." The best or at least the easiest way for me to discuss pastoral ministry among gay and lesbian people is to tell you a story.

In 1985 I applied to become incumbent of St. Paul's, an old parish in the West End of Vancouver, British Columbia. The West End is a peninsula jutting into the sea. Between the magnificent Stanley Park on the western tip of the peninsula and the bustle of downtown Vancouver to the east, there is a jumble of large and small apartment buildings in which some forty thousand people live, of whom about ten thousand are gay or lesbian and another ten thousand are elderly. The density of the population, the gentle if damp climate, the location in the city, the naturally defined boundaries, the beauty of the setting, the individuality of the residents and their energy combine to create a vibrant, lively, bewildering, enervating, exhausting, frightening, enchanting community.

St. Paul's, founded in 1889, has a distinguished past. Once the "carriage trade" church, it has produced a bishop and four archbishops. In 1985 the lovely little wooden church, overshadowed by its high-rise neighbors, was home to a faithful but dwindling and very elderly congregation. A 1983 newspaper article had described it in these words:

> At the corner of Pendrell and Jervis in the West End, St. Paul's Anglican Church huddles against a backdrop of high rise apartments. St. Paul's has been a spiritual lighthouse in the West End since 1898. Today, there is a secular tide running so swiftly around it that Rev. Harold McSherry says his parish is fighting for survival....
>
> The 85 year old church feels more like a museum than a house of hope and charity. During the weekdays the lights are low. The heat is turned down. A scent of musty decay pervades everything. On most week nights it is "locked up tighter than a castle," McSherry says....

McSherry says the elderly members of his congregation need to be re-assured that there are still social values in the community. "I think it is my duty to try and comfort them." The 63 year old Anglican priest says St. Paul's is fighting "a holding operation, biding its time for a better day."

The parish profile accurately described the parish as deeply mired in the di-lemma of many downtown neighborhood parishes, where to remain un-changed would mean disappearance, and to change would alienate the faithful:

> We must change or in a decade we will be a fairly well endowed mu-seum. We must reach into the community where, among others, we must involve the gay and lesbian community which feels overt hostility from us, young married couples who do not know of our existence, single mothers to whom we offer nothing and young couples living together of whose life style we disapprove.

The parish knew what had to be done but not how to do it.

A churchwarden *emeritus* drove me to my interview with the selection committee. Short, wiry, quick moving, in his youth he had been a deckhand on a seagoing tug and a lumberjack. After military service in World War II he became a log scaler, a job he still did in his early seventies, jumping from floating log to log with an agility that belied his years. A churchman of a kind familiar to many, committed and faithful, he would nevertheless have snorted in disgust if anyone had called him devout. He had watched in despair as his beloved parish church had declined. Not knowing what else to do, he had waged a savage rearguard action, questioning every deci-sion, guarding every penny, resisting every change. During the interview his main concern seemed to be ascertaining my views on whether the parish should spend the capital of its relatively small endowment.

Near the end of that somewhat odd interview, during which the chair-man seemed to think he had both to ask and to answer the questions, I was asked if I had any questions. I was pretty sure that one member of the com-mittee, a churchwarden, had written the key sections of the profile, and so I asked if the profile was "owned" by the whole committee. When they as-sured me it was, I said that I knew how to do what needed doing but that if we were to accomplish it they would have to support me. They said that they would and, with two exceptions, they did.

My first service in St. Paul's was on Easter. As we droned through an odd combination of matins and the eucharist I became aware of an almost total absence of energy in the place. My heart began to sink and I thought, "Crawley, what have you done?"

I was inducted on the following Tuesday. There was a noticeable lack of other clergy, but sitting unobtrusively near the back was a man wearing a clerical collar. As an immigrant from another diocese I knew almost none of the local Anglican clergy and assumed him to be a neighbor. He introduced himself as the minister of the Metropolitan Community Church. It clicked in my memory that the MCC ministers principally in the gay and lesbian community and I remarked that I would like to chat with him about the West End.

Late the next afternoon the wardens and I were meeting in my office, drawing up the agenda for a church committee meeting to be held that evening. The parish secretary had left, so when the phone rang I answered it. A young man told me that the Metropolitan Community Church, which met in a small rented room, was seeking a hall for their annual spring dance. Could they rent space at St. Paul's? I discussed his request with the wardens, and to my surprise they agreed we should recommend to the church committee that we rent the MCC our parish hall. The committee, again to my surprise, agreed. Among the members of the committee was a woman in her mid-eighties with a distinct air of being a gracious lady. I noticed that the other older women waited to see how she voted before raising their own hands in favor.

The next morning I telephoned the MCC minister to say the hall was theirs. He replied, "We never expected you to say 'yes.' We were phoning every church." By Sunday the word had gone out in the community that St. Paul's was gay-positive, and there were several new faces in church.

I was frightened by the prospect of encountering the gay and lesbian community. I had, from time to time over the years, known gay men, and indeed had two close friends who were gay. But I had no familiarity with the subculture and, like most people, I fear the unknown. I thought I would not be accepted as a person or as a priest. Remembering my conversation with the minister of the Metropolitan Community Church, I phoned him and asked if he would have lunch with me and tell me about the gay community.

During that lunch in an outrageously funky restaurant my fear began to vanish, to be replaced by a sense of compassion. I could not believe the degree of gratitude evoked by my simple act of asking him about himself, his community, and his church. I began to sense the immense fear of rejection that is ingrained in so many gay men and lesbians. I realized that my own fear of being unacceptable to them was nothing compared to their fear of being unacceptable to me. They hungered for someone to say by word and act, "You too are an infinitely valuable child of God."

On another occasion the power of a simple act was brought home to me when, for no particular reason, I added the phrase "and those whom you love" to the blessing at the end of the eucharist. A man came up to my wife with tears in his eyes. "Did you hear what David said? He blessed *those whom we love.*" He had heard that commonly used, casually added phrase as an acceptance of his sexual orientation.

Although the abrupt switch in the gay and lesbian community's perception of us was a major step, St. Paul's had a long way to go.

After my induction I received a letter from an earlier incumbent who described how the rapid changes in the area during the post-war years had made him feel smothered everywhere but in the church. I realized that I felt the opposite—smothered in the church but alive in the community. A parable of the parish and my role in it came to my mind. There was a large cave with many people living in it. There were many entrances through which light and air entered and those who lived in the cave came and went. One day one of the cave-dwellers noticed a strange furry creature lurking about outside. Fearful, they decided to block up all the entrances except one tiny opening high on the wall. Gradually the air became poorer and poorer and they grew more and more lethargic until one by one they began to die. Realizing that something must be done or they would all perish, they decided to hire an outsider to carry in air in a sack. But the outsider told the cave-dwellers that air could not be carried in a sack and that they would have to open up all the entrances and let the air and light flow in. This frightened them, but the outsider told them not to worry—he was not afraid of the strange furry creatures, and he would protect the cave-dwellers until they got used to them.

With great courage the little community of the faithful at St. Paul's set about opening itself to the wider community. This opening and a blossoming sense of mission began to attract many who were not gay or lesbian—single parents, young adults living together or married, recovering alcoholics, street people, entertainers, university teachers, newly retired people moving into the area, and a constant throng of those with lives in disarray who had moved to the West End for a fresh start.

I began to be aware of a strange phenomenon. It seemed that every time the parish needed someone with a particular gift, a suitable person would appear. For example, I wanted to liven up a very anemic 9:15 a.m. "modern rite" eucharist and thought we needed some music. One day a middle-aged man walked in, explained he was a lapsed Anglican, a schoolteacher on sick leave, and asked if he could help us. He said he could play the organ, so I asked him to play for our 9:15 a.m. service and suggested he might look at some modern musical settings.

The next Sunday he introduced us to a lovely new setting of the eucharistic texts. When I asked him where it came from, he replied, "Oh, I just wrote it." A church organist since the age of sixteen, he had led choirs in very large churches and had performed on recital tours, playing Bach in Germany and the low countries. He was the finest church musician I have ever worked with—enormously talented, liturgically sensitive, theologically aware, and pastorally concerned. His emotional turmoil and guilt about his sexual orientation had driven him out of the church. Not long after he arrived he came to me with tears in his eyes and said, "Thank you for giving me back my church."

It was the time when the public was growing increasingly aware of the onslaught of AIDS, and inevitably St. Paul's was drawn into a ministry with HIV and AIDS sufferers and their loved ones. We hired a young English priest (now rector of the parish) who had been involved in such work in London. At first he worked on a half-time basis, principally in the nearby general hospital that was the major center for treatment of AIDS patients in the province; then he expanded the ministry into the community on a full-time basis. In spite of the presence of other churches in the West End, St. Paul's soon became "the parish church" to which the unchurched turned in times of crisis. The little community of the faithful began to rejoice in its blossoming sense of the contemporary mission of the church.

About that time a newspaper article mentioned that St. Paul's welcomed gay people. There was indignation in the parish, for as one person said, "We don't welcome gay people or straight people. We welcome people." A very bright young woman summed it up when she said, "Our friends in suburban churches sit around discussing the church's mission. Here we know what our mission is. We are fulfilling it when we stand at the door welcoming all."

After I had been at St. Paul's for some time, my wife Joan and I were invited to a dinner party at the home of a couple at whose recent marriage I had officiated. There were four couples present, three straight and one gay. The six straight diners all had been divorced and had remarried within the last year. The gay couple, who had been together for almost twenty-five years, spent most of the meal telling the rest of us how to build a lasting relationship. Yet in spite of that episode, and other experiences of stable, long-lasting same-sex unions, I began to have doubts about what we were doing—or, more precisely, what I was doing. To state it in traditional terms, I began to wonder if by condoning same-sex relationships I was encouraging those for whom I was pastorally responsible to continue in a state of sin. Or, in somewhat different terms, was I reinforcing them in a state of brokenness rather than helping them toward wholeness?

I read most of the easily available discussions of the subject and found that the conclusions tended to depend on the predisposition of the writer. I was hesitant to place the same weight on John Wesley's fourth leg, experience, as I did on the three "Anglican" legs of scripture, tradition, and reason. But in the end I decided we are so informed and shaped by our experience of God, the world, and ourselves that it could not be ignored. Our experience was drawing both Joan and me to conclude that life as a gay man demands such sacrifice and involves such pain that, except very rarely, no one would choose it unless compelled to by his nature. I was less certain about lesbians, for although it was apparent that, for many in our community, orientation was not a choice, others had turned to same-sex relations because of brutal treatment by men or as a political statement about oppression by a male-dominated society.

If we were right in our view that, for most gay men and lesbians, sexual orientation is not a matter of choice, did society and the church have the right to deny them love and intimacy? I remembered a gay friend saying to me, "David, we are not different. We both just want someone to love us." After a time of soul-searching I came to the conclusion that as a priest I must exercise love and compassion according to my best insights, and that if I was wrong in what I was doing I would have to answer for it on Judgment Day. I could not ignore the pain I was meeting in so many people—people such as the young man, a French Canadian Roman Catholic, who came to ask me if I would conduct a memorial service for his partner, who had died of an AIDS-related disease. He told me that his partner, an Anglican from a good church family, had telephoned his home in eastern Canada the week of his death. His father and brothers refused to let his mother, an invalid, speak to him. The last words he heard from his family as his father hung up the phone were his mother's as she screamed, "Let me speak to my baby!" I could not imagine that such cruelty could be acceptable to God. What part had the church played in creating it? And how would we answer for it?

We averaged twenty AIDS funerals or memorial services a year, most of them for people who lived in the parish area but who were not formally connected to the church. One day the crusty churchwarden *emeritus* who had driven me to my interview came to me and said, "It's not right that all these funerals are taking place with no one from the congregation present. I have instructed your secretary to notify me when one is taking place, and I will be there to represent the church."

In 1990, after five years in St. Paul's, I was, to everyone's considerable surprise, elected bishop of Kootenay. As the parish began the process of seeking a replacement, the warden *emeritus* accosted me with these words: "Rector, there are a lot of single men around here now. I make no comment about their lifestyle. Not my business. But do you think we could put in the parish profile that anyone who can't accept these fellows better not apply?" I commented that I thought most clergy knew what St. Paul's was like. "Well, you never know," he said. "Someone who doesn't know could apply, and in the interview might say something to insult the young fellows on the committee."

A week or two later I had just finished conducting an AIDS memorial service. The warden *emeritus* had been in his usual back seat. He speared my breastbone with a rigid forefinger and said, "You see, that's what we are here for, to look after these boys." I realized that as the parish thought it was ministering to the gay and lesbian community, what was really happening was a process of mutual ministry. A community of the faithful cannot decide it will minister to this or that group. All it can do is try to live out the radical equality that is at the core of both baptism and eucharist, and welcome all who wish to share that life. St. Paul's had not so much found a mission as it had regained its soul.

After I left the parish the wonderful woman who had cast such an influential vote at my first church committee meeting confided that a beloved nephew of hers was gay. A short time ago I received a letter from her. She told me of the "great news" that after twenty-eight years of relationship her nephew and his partner had sold their respective homes and moved in together. A priest had blessed their new home and them, but they had so wished they could have been blessed in church. "Oh, David," she wrote, "Do you think it will ever happen?"

I could not answer her question. But I think it points the way in which we should be moving. I have come to believe that the real gay and lesbian issue for the church is not ordination but the affirmation of same-sex relationships. To try to decide about the ordination of gay men and lesbians who are, or hope to be, in committed relationships before we have decided whether the church can affirm such relationships at all is to try to answer the secondary question without first answering the primary one. The issue of the affirmation of same-sex relationships touches personally a much greater number of faithful church members than does the question of ordination. I believe and hope it to be, for many in the church, a less explosive and less divisive issue, and as such the place where debate ought to be focused. Such a focus may not lead us through the further issues, but it should lead us into them in a more useful, and more loving, fashion.

Questions for Discussion

The Passionate Debate

∞ William Countryman suggests using the model of "spiritual discernment" in discussing divisive issues in the church. How do you think such a model might have changed the way the church handled recent debates, such as the ordination of women and the revision of the Prayer Book? How might using the model of spiritual discernment shape the way we discuss sexuality?

∞ Bonnie Shullenberger argues that "America has become a culture in which ideological absolutism has infected almost every form of discourse, and conversation across ideological positions has grown increasingly troubled." Do you agree? In what ways has this been your experience of discussions of complex issues in the church?

∞ In what ways do you agree or disagree with Shullenberger's theologian friend who remarked, "The problem in the church is not homosexuality. It's promiscuity"? How would you describe the theological basis for your position?

∞ Concerning human sexuality and the institution of marriage Timothy Sedgwick states that what we actually do—our "practice"—shapes our experience and forms our understanding as much as our understanding shapes our experience and leads to changes in what we do. Do you agree? In what ways have you seen this process of revisioning occur in your lifetime?

∞ How would you answer Sedgwick's question: How far should particular congregations, and the church at large, respect and support differences in the consciences of their members?

Sexuality and the Soul

∞ How does Thomas Breidenthal answer the question, "Why is our sexuality a spiritual concern?" How would you?

∞ Breidenthal concludes, "Marriages with built-in escape hatches are not likely to be engaged in the work of sanctification." Why? Do you agree?

∞ What do you think Rowan Williams means by "the body's grace"?

∞ Williams states: "The life of the Christian community has as its rationale—if not invariably its practical reality—the task of teaching us to so order our relations that human beings may see themselves as desired, as the occasion of joy." What do you think he means? How does your community help you to "order" and understand your sexual relations?

∞ Discuss Williams's assertion that "sexual 'perversion' is sexual activity without risk."

∞ As a spiritual director, Martin Smith believes that in order for the church to discern what the Spirit is saying concerning homosexuality it needs to pay attention to the religious experience of lesbians and gay men themselves. Do you agree? How and where might the church learn to listen to such experience? What are some of the barriers to paying "prolonged and patient attention"?

∞ Smith states: "If we are still at an extremely early stage in the process of attending to this primary level of experience, then where homosexuality is concerned our existing theology and ethics can only be provisional." In what ways would you agree or disagree?

∞ Peter Hawkins's essay could be seen as part of the "gradually accumulating evidence" of the religious experience of gay men in the church today to which Smith refers. How did reading his account of his experience affect you?

The Christian Household

∞ Cynthia Crysdale seeks to hold two dimensions of marriage together: marriage as a salvific mystery, a "journey of encounter and redemption," and marriage as a social institution. How have human expectations concerning those two dimensions changed over the centuries? What expectations about marriage do you see reflected in the culture and in the church today?

∽ How would you respond to Crysdale's "challenging question" concerning marriage as a model for same-sex unions?

∽ James Price talks about the conflicts that arise when "mutually exclusive stories" clash. What different stories about sexuality are being told in the church—your own congregation or the church at large? Is conflict between these stories inevitable? How could they be reconciled?

∽ What does Price mean by the "doing" promoted by Jesus' story (see pp. 114-115)? What examples can you add to those he gives?

∽ How would you respond to Sheryl Kujawa's question, "What part should the church play in relation to the healthy sexual development of young people?"

∽ With your own congregation in mind, discuss Kujawa's suggestions for ways the church can begin to address the challenge of helping youth "navigate the difficult journey from adolescence to adulthood."

Scripture and Tradition

∽ What taboos are being toppled in the story from Acts 10-15, according to Marilyn McCord Adams? What cultural and religious taboos have you seen toppled in your lifetime? What happened afterward? What taboos are you afraid will topple in the next ten years?

∽ Adams proposes that "we find many and various ways to create taboo-free zones within the church where human sexuality can be openly and prayerfully explored." What would you imagine those "zones" would look like? Where would they be? How would they be created? What would you find appealing in them? Frightening? Challenging?

∽ Barbara Hall asserts that "in Paul's notion of the new creation...there is clear warrant for taking a new look at old positions." Discuss how what Paul might have meant—and not meant—by his notion of a "new creation" might inform the church's discussion of sexuality.

∽ Hall imagines that Paul would urge the church today, "Do not give the issue more importance and more power than it has. Find ways to live *as if* there were not a debate on homosexuality." How would that change the discussion?

∞ Charles Hefling agrees with the bishops of the Church of England that the important thing about sexual orientation is not its causes but what it orients a person *toward*. How is it, then, that he reaches quite a different conclusion from the bishops? Do you agree with his reasoning?

∞ At the end of his essay Hefling suggests that, even if he is right, there are many further questions to be considered. What questions do you think need to be raised next?

The Body of Christ

∞ Owen Thomas discusses the relationship of theology and experience when attempting to judge between conflicting beliefs or perspectives, and he describes how his experience of two communities has altered his own theological views. In what ways has your experience of your church community informed your theology of sexuality?

∞ Thomas believes that theology-shaping experience must be based on first-hand knowledge, not on stereotypes or hearsay. Do you agree? What stereotypes do you see shaping the church's theology today?

∞ Susan Harriss describes a parish church in which sexuality was never discussed. How does your church community deal with issues of sexuality and homosexuality? Where are such issues talked about in the larger community in which you live?

∞ What were some of the barriers to hospitality described in David Norgard's essay? Do people experience these or other barriers in your congregation? If so, how have the barriers affected the congregation? What does your congregation do to welcome gay and lesbian people?

∞ David Crawley states: "A community of the faithful cannot decide it will minister to this or that group. All it can do it try to live out the radical equality that is at the core of both baptism and eucharist, and welcome all who wish to share that life." Do you agree? How does your congregation attempt to decide to whom it will minister? What would it mean to welcome all who came to worship with you? How would your parish be changed?

Overview and Summary

∞ In his introduction to this collection Charles Hefling judges that the authors are not all "singing the same tune" yet they are "in harmony." Do you agree? How would you characterize this harmony?

∞ What are the most significant *differences* among the contributors?

∞ Both Adams and Countryman draw on the story of Gentile inclusion told in the book of Acts. How similar are the conclusions they reach? What role do they and other contributors see scripture playing in the church's discussion of sexuality? What role has scripture played as you have developed your own views?

∞ How would you compare Crysdale's and Sedgwick's handling of changes in the institution of marriage? In what ways do you think changes in social institutions in general affect the church's life and worship?

∞ The experience of particular parish communities is described in each of the four essays in the final section of the book. In what ways do these experiences complement each other? How are they different? How are they similar to and different from your own?

Cowley Publications is a ministry of the Society of St. John the Evangelist, a religious community for men in the Episcopal Church. Emerging from the Society's tradition of prayer, theological reflection, and diversity of mission, the press is centered in the rich heritage of the Anglican Communion.

Cowley Publications seeks to provide books, audio cassettes, and other resources for the ongoing theological exploration and spiritual development of the Episcopal Church and others in the body of Christ. To this end, it is dedicated to developing a new generation of theological writers, encouraging them to produce timely, creative, and stimulating publications of excellence, and making these publications available widely, reaching both clergy and lay persons.